NIGHT OF THE
INTRUDERS

Other books by the same author:

FINAL FLIGHTS
Dramatic wartime incidents revealed
by aviation archaeology

EIGHTH AIR FORCE BOMBER STORIES
Eye-witness accounts from American airmen and
British civilians of the perils of war
(co-authored with Russell Zorn)

Patrick Stephens Limited, an imprint of Haynes Publishing, has published
authoritative, quality books for enthusiasts for more than 25 years. During that
time the company has established a reputation as one of the world's leading
publishers of books on aviation, maritime, military, model-making, motor
cycling, motoring, motor racing, railway and railway modelling subjects.
Readers or authors with suggestions for books they would like to see published
are invited to write to: The Editorial Director, Patrick Stephens Limited,
Sparkford, Nr Yeovil, Somerset, BA22 7JJ.

NIGHT OF THE
INTRUDERS

**First-hand accounts chronicling the slaughter
of homeward bound USAAF Mission 311**

IAN McLACHLAN

Patrick Stephens Limited

First published in 1994

British Library cataloguing-in-publication data:
A catalogue record for this book is available
from the British Library.

ISBN: 1 85260 450 6

Library of Congress catalog card no. 93 80185

All pictures belong to the author except where stated.

Patrick Stephens Limited is an imprint of Haynes Publishing, Sparkford, Nr Yeovil, Somerset, BA22 7JJ.

Typeset by G&M, Raunds, Northamptonshire
Printed in Great Britain by
Butler & Tanner Ltd of London and Frome

Contents

Dedication

*For my Mother and Father and countless
others of their special generation who
stood against tyranny.*

*Detail from a map found in the buried wreckage of a 448BG Liberator shot down
during the "Night of the Intruders".*

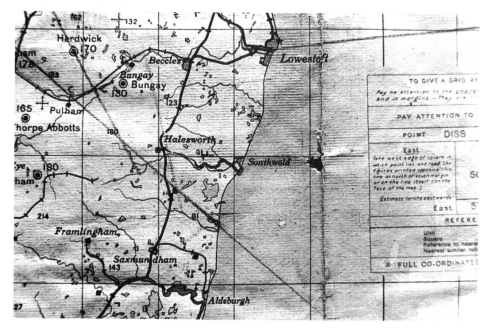

Author's Introduction

IN 1968, THE discovery of maps in the wreckage of a World War II bomber, long buried beneath East Anglian marshland, proved to be the starting point for this book. The navigator, whose pencilled lines led to Seething, never did reach his destination. Neither did a tragic number of other USAAF pilots and crews that night.

Mission 311, on 22 April 1944, went badly wrong. With invasion of Europe threatened, the Allies launched an audacious assault on Germany's largest marshalling yard, at Hamm, nerve-centre of the Reich's railway system. Any raid would face fierce opposition from enemy fighters and flak. But this one was even more dangerous. Because of adverse weather reports, the American airmen, usually deployed as daytime bombers, did not depart for Hamm until late afternoon. The 824 B-17s and B-24s — with more than 8,000 aircrew — had to contend with the additional hazards of darkness. Nearly 1,000 American and British fighters accompanied the bombers, but they could do little to alleviate risks such as disorientation, mid-air collisions, getting lost, or being savaged by night fighters.

The fighting over Europe was ferocious. Then, as the survivors limped home, Luftwaffe intruders mingled with them, under cover of darkness. The battle-worn Americans were attacked by the enemy as they sought the sanctuary of their own airfields — and in the resulting carnage and confusion, Allied coastal and airfield defences were firing on friend and foe alike. Agonized, local inhabitants could only look on as aircraft, consumed in flames, seared across the night sky to destruction on farmland and marshes. Others, too low for baling out and too damaged to climb, struggled to land before fire severed vital controls or detonated ruptured fuel tanks.

That night the Americans suffered their highest ever losses to German intruders. I hope that this book, which tells the full story for the first time, will serve as a memorial to the men who died, and a tribute to the courage of all those involved.

Ian McLachlan
Suffolk, 1994

Acknowledgements

I INTENDED THIS book to be my first, but changing circumstances saw *Final Flights* and *Eighth Air Force Bomber Stories* appear, hopefully providing a platform of credibility before the challenge of Mission 311. While not a constant activity, my research started nearly 30 years ago and has threaded through my life ever since. I would like to thank Jenny and Julie for the contributions they made, and admire my partner Susan Rose, for not only typing this lengthy manuscript, but taking on an author still smitten with the writing bug.

Throughout the years of preparation, one feature clearly emerged — the courage of that "special generation" now in the twilight of their lives. Ordinary people, they faced the horrors of war and surmounted them to win a peace for us all. Mission 311 was a small part of that conflict, but exacted a heavy toll. It is important that the generations inheriting that peace will value and protect it, in a world where tyranny still exists. To those who played a part in resisting the Nazis during World War II, I offer my respect and admiration. Specifically, I would like to thank the following veterans, East Anglians, fellow enthusiasts, organizations, friends and family:

A E Abendroth, S Adams, R and B Adamson, G S Alexander, K C Allstaedt, John W Archer, H E Armstrong, A E Anker, E Arnold, C Atkins, Mr J Auman, Thomas E Bass — A Fort Nut, M J Bailey, Susan Sneed Bailey, J M Balason, Jake & Maddie Balls, G Barker, R P Bateson, *Beccles & Bungay Journal*, N Beckett, C R Bell, Henry G Bennett, Sheldon F Berlow, Bert A Betts, B Bines, Mrs G A Bickers, Cliff Bishop, Stan Bishop, Dr H Bläsi, Allan G Blue, Rosemarie Boje-Pike, Steve Blake, Vernal L Boline, Martin W Bowman, C Bowyer, Dr V J Boyle, J D Bradshaw, W K M Braithwaite, Homer L Briggs, Mabel Brooks, D Brown, I L Brown, H Brühl, Ron and Don Buxton, R Cain, Donald L Caldwell, *Cambridge Evening News*, Mrs J Carey, Jeff Carless, Glenn D Carlson, F Carman, Lt Col L K Carson, W Cartwright, S R Chaplin, Tony Chardella, Amanda Chester, N Cocker, D N Collier, K Collinson, Robert J Collis, Harlan L Cook, Mrs J Cowley, G Cross, William L Cullen, R M Cunningham, Philip G Day, Lt Col Merritt E

Derr, Lt Col A P De Jong, Deutsche Aerospace, Wolfgang Dierich, Arthur F Dirks, Abel L Dolim, John J Driscoll, Major Kenneth L Driscoll, C T Dungar, P Dunham, S Dunham, George P DuPont, Colin Durrant, B G Dye, J Dye, *Eastern Daily Press*, *Eastern Evening News*, *East Anglian Daily Times*, Hans Ebert, Lee B Eddington, W A Edwards, C R Elliott, Dan Engle, Stewart P Evans, J H Everson, Pat Everson, J P Flanagan, R Forbes-Morgan, John C Ford, R E Forward, Ursula & Ted Foster, Roger A Freeman, Royal D Frey, F C Frost, J G Frost, Garry L Fry, Dr Carl Fyler, Adolf Galland, I Garstka, Gene Gaskins, Mick Gibson, M L Giddings, Maj Gen Edward B Giller, W Girbig, B Gladden, George Glevanik, Harry D Gobrecht, H C F Goff, E Goldsmith, Stuart Goldsmith, C K Gollagher, C Gotts, S Gotts, P G J Gray, Lt Col Charles W Grace, V Grimble, *Gt Yarmouth Mercury*, B J Guymer, R M Hague, A Hall, Cliff Hall, Col Frank N Halm, K Hammel, A Hammer, A Hanagarth, Teague G Harris, Sid E Harvey, J B Haycraft, Charles F Hayes, Ian Hawkins, A W Heiden, R Herbst, John A Hey, S High, R M A Hirst, Lily Housden, A Huber, G Hukins, Imperial War Museum, Glenn B Infield, Brig Gen James H Isbell, Phil Jarrett, Tony Jeckells, G B Jermy, E S Keeler, John A Kennedy, Lt Gen W E Kepner, G Keppler, James N Kidder, F Kozaczka, Dan C Knight, D Knight, E Knie, J Kronschnabel, N Krüger, D G Land, E Lea, Mr & Mrs Leamon, Col F H LeFebre, James K Leonard, V Lewis, W Lindermeyer, E T Little, Lt Col R M Littlefield, D Loades, I Loades, Jesse D Long, *Lowestoft Journal*, John L Luft, E Lux, J Mace, Edward F MacLean, B Mastin, R Malster, M Martin, Vic Maslen, Glenn R Matson, Harry L Matthew, Paul R Maxwell, Mrs R Messenger, Abram A Millar, Kent D Miller, John Mills, Walt Mitchell, William G Mitchell, Eric Mombeek, Danny Morris, Mr & Mrs Morrish, Louis D Morrison, J Mortinson, Les & Vi Murton, Mr & Mrs A Musto, Robert B Mynn, Vere A McCarty, Charles J McClain, Ralph McClure, Ernie McDowall, David McGuire, William P McGovern, Alan McLachlan, Bethan & Rowan McLachlan, James K Newhouse, Dr W D Noack, Tony North, Gilbert M O'Brien, Joe O'Hara T Olausson, R Oldman, Margaret Oldrin, Don Olds, Merle C Olmsted, M Osborn, M C Pannell, George W Parks, Simon W Parry, Lt Col Thomas B Parry, D Pascoe, M Payne, Herman A Peacher, Robert G Peel, James A Pegher, Clair A Penners, *Peterborough Evening Telegraph*, C W Peterson, Loy F Peterson, W A Phillips, Mike Pike, R L Pinson, H L Pittam, Russ & Babs Pleasance, C B Pluck, M J Podd, J Poetter, R Pointer, Irwin L Pomerantz, Alfred Price, Ron W M A Putz, P-47 Thunderbolt Pilots' Association, Mrs L R Pye, H Radkat, P Ramm, C J Ramsbottom, P Ransom, F Rayns, P A W Rausch, C E Rawston, A F Rely, George A Reynolds, G Reynolds, Mrs E Richmond, Bill Robertie, Samuel C Robeson, Col George L Robinson, Ormond E Rolfe, Klaus Romanek, Marvin J Rosvold, A Rowe, Ken Rusby, Kenn C Rust, Gene E Ryan, John W Ryan, Miss W F Sadd, V H Saville, Harold E Schildknecht, Dr W Scheiter, Earl F Schmidt, Dr Helmut Schnatz, Mervin M Shank, W E Sharrock, Francis

X Sheehan, H Siederer, Peter Simmonds, Alvin D Skaggs, Ivan Skipper, Keith Skipper, Harry E Slater, Dorothy B Slaymaker, Jonathan Smith, J S Smith, Frank S Sneed, K J Sorace, A C Spencer, R Spooner, Keith J Spink, Wendell R Stanton, L Stevens, Raymond E Strate, Russell A Strong, D J Stubley, Earl J Stutts, Dr L Suschko, C R Temple, H Thein, O Theisen, Art Thorsen, P & N Thrower, C M Thurgar, M Tipple, Col George E Tormoen, K H Trimble, Paul J Trudeau, Carl J Valentine, J Vasco, C Vincent, Curt M Vogel, G Waag, David Wade, Clinton E Wallace, Lt Col Delmar H Wangsvick, Geoff Ward, Mrs M B Ward, Richard H Watters, Bill Weaver, John L Weber, Lt Col Walter P Weigle, K Weinert, Allan J Welters, *Whitley Bay News Guardian*, G Willimott, Bert Wilson, Mervyn Wilson, A Wöffen, Col V R Woodward, John Woolnough, Mrs R Wooltorton, George Wortham, M Wysocki, Earl L Zimmerman, Ray and Russ Zorn.

American Ex Prisoners of War Inc, Albert F Simpson Historical Research Centre, 100BG MAM, 390BG MAM, Eighth Air Force Historical Society, Second Air Division Association, General Archives Division Washington DC, 2nd Air Division Memorial Library, Radio Norfolk, Public Records Office, Lincolnshire Aircraft Recovery Group, 19(F) Squadron RAF, Bundesarchiv, Gemeinshaft der Jagdflieger.

Finally, thanks to my editor Flora Myer and others within Patrick Stephens Ltd and Haynes Publishing, for encouraging *Intruders* and, hopefully, making it as successful as my other titles.

CHAPTER ONE

Cee Gee II

ANXIOUSLY SCANNING THE lower darkness, Staff Sergeant Ralph W McClure felt lonely and exposed. Trained as a B-24 tail-gunner for daylight operations, "Mac" had little experience of night-flying — and none in combat conditions. His crew's Stateside training included limited nocturnal hours in clear, friendly skies with towns twinkling below like inverted stars. Mac cursed the planners responsible for what he felt was a foolish April Mission — even if it was the 22nd and not the 1st. His ship *Cee Gee II* sat amidst a "whole darned mess of airplanes" descending in late dusk over the sullen, stygian swell of the North Sea. The proximity of other 453BG Liberators, comforting in daylight, now threatened the nightmare of collision, which was barely alleviated as position, passing, recognition and formation lights transformed fading silhouettes into diamantes of red, white, green and blue paste set in a sky of indigo velvet. Fearfully, Mac recognized that reducing one risk heightened another — the display of lights might alert prowling intruders. His senses tautened with each darkening second. Into his mind came the advice from an RAF Lancaster gunner whose battle-damaged craft had sought refuge on Mac's base at Old Buckenham: "Look low, especially between 10 o'clock and 2 o'clock —

Cee Gee II. *A painting by Mike Bailey commissioned for the author. Named after the pilot's daughter, Carole Geane.* (M J Bailey)

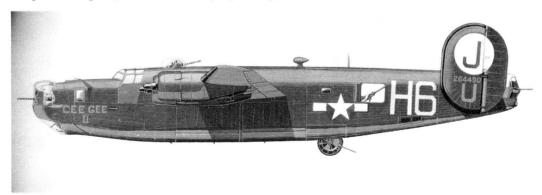

Staff Sergeant Ralph W McClure (left) *relaxes with Technical Sergeant William C Grady on board* Cee Gee II. *Only one of the two gunners survived the "Night of the Intruders".* (Don Olds)

segment your search area — shoot first, you may scare him off. Remember, you're first on his list!" Mac shivered. He pulled his makeshift scarf — a towel — more closely, but his shivering was not entirely due to the blast of cold air thrashing his back from the open waist-windows. The tambour doors of his turret had remained open on every mission since February when a spent shrapnel-fragment penetrated the aluminium skin near his head and dropped harmlessly beside him. Open doors doubled the thickness of aluminium on either side and promoted some sense of security. His decision to fly with this physical discomfort would prove providential — fate had much in store for the crew of *Cee Gee II*. The Pilot, Lieutenant James S Munsey had named their first B-24 after his young daughter, a bouncy toddler, Carol Geane, nicknamed Cee Gee. (The youngster's namesake had been lost with another crew, hence the replacement being christened *Cee Gee II*.) Munsey led his crew on most missions but his coolness and leadership made him an ideal choice for breaking in new crews. Only two days before he skilfully landed *Queenie* after flak smashed the rudder controls, decapitated the tail-gunner and panicked her neophyte crew. Munsey kept to himself his opinion of this mission to the marshalling yards in Hamm, but Mac would have subscribed to the 735th Squadron diarist's view, "It was a 'snafu' affair from start to finish. Somehow, the lead airplane got off course in the target area taking everyone across the Ruhr Valley. Flak was terrific . . . the time lost on this brilliant manoeuvre was immeasurably important, the difference between arriving at bases in daylight or darkness . . ."

Darkness. Mac cursed it — then, momentarily, he thought he saw something. A shadow? Maybe, maybe not. A second's hesitation. Yes — 8 o'clock low — there WAS something. The RAF gunner's warning

Hit during the attack, Technical Sergeant John F McKinney was found on the fuselage floor too badly injured to bale out. As Cee Gee II *raced for the coast, McClure tried to help.* (Don Olds)

leapt to mind like a neon. *Scare him off.* Calling the left-waist gunner, Technical Sergeant John F McKinney, Mac fired at least two short bursts towards their real-or-imagined assailant, the opening rounds for "Night of the Intruders". An instant later, their enemy's substance was devastatingly confirmed as cannon shells raked *Cee Gee II* from tail-turret to port wing. Mac's open turret doors spared his life. For now. A tremendous explosion blasted him backwards completely out of the turret on to the fuselage cat-walk. In reality, it must have been only moments but it seemed an age before his senses struggled back from the depths of unconsciousness to the noise, glare and nightmare of reality. Lying still, he felt blood oozing down his face. Gingerly touching his skull he discovered there was no torn leather helmet or gaping wound, and remembered from college sports how minor head injuries often bled profusely. He took stock. McKinney's prone figure was in the centre fuselage just forward of the waist windows. Hurrying to the inert gunner, Mac could not tell if his friend was unconscious or dead. In the glare, Mac saw no visible wound. What glare? Suddenly Mac realized why he could see such detail — the fuselage was floodlit by a massive fire just behind number two engine. *Cee Gee II* was trailing her torment in a long, fiery banner as burning fuel burst into the bomber's slipstream. How long would it be before flames seared through the port wing or her gas tanks exploded? Baling out into the icy North Sea meant certain death. Discipline forbad such thoughts. Mac's job now was to factually report injuries and damage, but the intercom had been shot out. The tail-gunner's slight build and familiarity with the route helped him scuttle across the bomb bay to the flight deck. Airplane-speak meant shouting to overcome the thunder of four Pratt & Whitney engines still pulling resolutely for home. Mac yelled at Munsey, quickly explaining how McKinney was either wounded or dead and they had, "a hell of a lot of fire on the left wing".

In the nose, bombardier Second Lieutenant Arthur W Orlowski had heard Mac call the bandit in to McKinney and noted their altitude as 8,000 feet with about 15 miles to run for the English coast. Orlowski both heard and felt the attack — one pass, firing constantly. Number two gas tank was set alight and the hydraulic system knocked out. In addition to McKinney's wounds, the radio operator, Technical Sergeant William G Grady was blinded with debris or shrapnel. The news from McClure confirmed their desperate situation and Munsey hollered at Mac to go back and bale out. Hesitating, Mac argued, "you might need something, I think I'll stay awhile". Still wrestling the controls, Munsey turned partially sideways in his seat and bawled at the gunner — "Get the hell back there and get your butt out of this goddamned airplane because I'm gonna fly this son-of-a-bitch to the ground. That's an ORDER!" At this juncture, the normally reticent co-pilot, Robert O Crall, turned to his pilot and calmly announced, "Well, I'm staying — I'm a lieutenant too, you know". Part Seminole Indian, Munsey was a hard, no nonsense commander who would not brook insubordination but he was not foolhardy either. Recognizing Crall's courage, and conceding he might need help, Munsey called the navigator, Second Lieutenant Leon Helfand, for a direct heading to Old Buckenham. Together, the two pilots chose to keep the burning bomber airborne as long as humanly possible. This gave time to help the wounded prepare for a bale out, hopefully over England. Determined, disciplined and loyal, the crew of *Cee Gee II* flew for their lives . . .

CHAPTER TWO

Mission 311
— a Summary

MISSION 311 ON 22 April 1944 is remembered in Eighth Air Force history more for what happened afterwards — the highest USAAF combat casualties over England — than for events over the Continent. However, any narrative should encompass the attack overall, and we begin by reviewing the then secret Report of Operations. This was compiled in June 1944 by Headquarters Eighth Air Force, and summarizes the mission's purpose, planning and problems.

The attack's comparative lateness in the day is explained by a weather forecast indicating, "that visual bombing operations against targets in Western Germany, where less than five-tenths low cloud was expected, would be after 1900 hours DBST" (Double British Summer Time). With the invasion of Europe pending, it was essential to take every opportunity to smash the enemy's communications and transport infrastructure. The marshalling yards and railway repair facilities in Hamm were classified "highly strategic" and Intelligence reports described them as "the largest in Germany with a capacity of 10,000 wagons per day dealing with rail traffic between the industrial Ruhr and northern Germany". The complex was one of Germany's busiest rail-yards. Regarded as a nerve-centre of the Reich's railway system, it was an imposing target measuring over three miles long and 630 yards at its widest point.

This was the USAAF's first major assault on Hamm. Launched against the facilities were 824 B-17s and B-24s — over 8,000 bomber aircrew. Their tribulations were unemotionally condensed by the compiler of the report, Colonel Walter E Todd of Headquarters Eighth Air Force. Under Planning, he commented: "Predicted strong winds from the northwest and concentrated anti-aircraft defences in the area dictated downwind bombing runs. Further considerations in the routing were the very heavy defences of the Ruhr area situated to the west of the target. As a consequence, the bombers were routed from England to the Dutch coast, north of the Rotterdam and Amsterdam defences, then almost directly to the Hamm area and, withdrawing, to the east and then south of the Ruhr defences and across northern France. The bombers were to fly as three forces, the first departing Lowestoft at 1750 hours, the second at 1802 hours and the third at 1821 hours". The first force comprised four B-17

Combat Wings of 12 Bombardment Groups from the Third Air Division. Then followed five more B-17 Combat Wings, 16 Groups, from the First Air Division and, finally, four Combat Wings made by 11 Groups of Second Air Division Liberators. Each force was allocated specific objectives within the marshalling yard. The first wave of B-17s would deal with the yard's northern entrance, main stations and transhipment sheds, with the next B-17 assault planned to strike engine repair sheds and the northern chokepoint and sidings. Liberators would then pummel the southern entrance, chokepoint and sidings.

Providing protection for the bombers were nearly 1,000 American and British fighters — Mustangs, Lightnings, Thunderbolts and Spitfires. These were assigned for both close escort and to maintain the policy of offensive sweeps introduced only a few weeks earlier but already proving decisive in the battle for air supremacy. A sweep saw free-ranging fighters foraging for combat, and the intention on 22 April 1944 was to comprehensively cover designated areas, "in northwest Germany, southwest Germany, northern France and Belgium with the intent of destroying enemy aircraft in the air and on the ground. It was planned generally that these fighters would reach areas of German airfields . . . at a time when the enemy aircraft would be taking off and assembling . . . Groups were warned against strafing heavily defended airfields on which only a few aircraft were parked. In addition to the Groups assigned to sweeps, all escort Groups were to be permitted to deploy at the leader's discretion provided that at least one squadron remain with the bombers at all times . . ." For most fighter Groups the intended strategy worked — spectacularly so for Mustangs of the famous 4th from Debden. But the report reveals problems for the bombers.

"The flight to the target by the first and second forces as well as the last two Combat Wings of the third force essentially followed the briefed route and the time control points were generally adhered to. Due to an error in judgement of distance on the part of its pilotage-navigator, the lead Combat Wing of the last formation turned south before the Initial Point was reached (from the IP, bombers began their unwavering run to release) and was followed by the second Combat Wing. Upon reaching what was believed by the lead navigator to be the Initial Point the bombers were over the Ruhr Valley and were subjected to strong anti-aircraft fire. Approximately half of the lead Combat Wing then turned left to approach Hamm from the southwest; the other half of this Combat Wing made a 360° turn to the right and subsequently approached the target as briefed. The second Combat Wing broke away from the lead Combat Wing upon entering the Ruhr Valley and entered the target area from the west". This navigational error lost four Liberators to flak, saw many more damaged and diluted fighter protection by separating the bomber formations.

In USAAF parlance, conditions were CAVU — Clear And Visibility Unlimited — as the 95th BG led the attack directed by their Operations Officer, Lieutenant Colonel Harry G Mumford, on board the lead ship

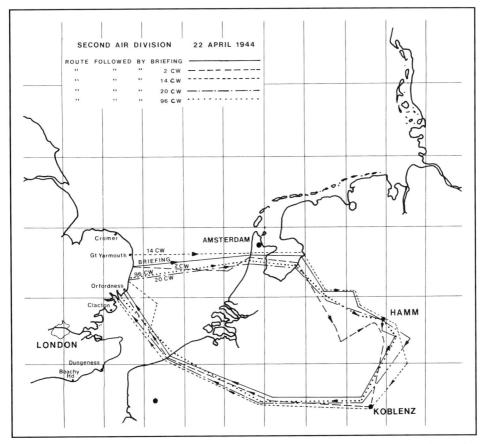

SECOND AIR DIVISION   22 APRIL 1944

ROUTE FOLLOWED BY BRIEFING ————————
   "   "   "   2 CW — — — — — — — —
   "   "   "   14 CW - - - - - - - - - - -
   "   "   "   20 CW —·—·—·—·—·—·—·—
   "   "   "   96 CW ·····' ·'······· · ·

"Due to an error in judgement of distance the lead Combat Wing of the last formation (Second Air Division) turned south before the Initial Point was reached . . ." The briefed course shown was essentially the same for all three Air Divisions. (I Loades)

flown by Captain J H Hubbs and crew. At the IP, a red signal flare was fired and bomb doors whirred open. It was exactly 1846 hours. Flak, "meagre accurate following", crumped close to the bombers causing damage but no injuries. Three minutes later, Flight Officer John S Bromberg triggered the Group's release at 23,000 feet and 209 x 500 lb bombs tumbled into the evening's slanting sunlight. On board *Full House* one reluctant specimen hung up because a tired armourer had fitted the shackle in backwards, and Second Lieutenant Deluca took it back to Horham. Stronger than predicted winds increased ground speed and the 95th 'B' Group found itself in danger of passing beneath the high 390th Group at release so it bombed Soest, a "target of opportunity" some 14 miles southeast of Hamm and en route to the RP (Rally Point). The unforecast wind velocity disrupted several Groups, resulting in numerous short bombing runs. Another weakness in planning emerged when it became apparent that the interval between forces was too brief. Smoke from preceding attacks obscured the aiming points for succeeding forces.

Compounding this, the course deviation by elements from the first two B-24 Combat Wings found them converging on the target simultaneously with the third and fourth Liberator Combat Wings. This forced the 445BG and part of the 453BG to select as a last resort target the marshalling yards in Koblenz. Smoke obscured Hamm for some bombardiers in the 466BG and one squadron from each Group also kept their bombs for Koblenz. In all, 631 bombers released 1,581 tons of bombs on Hamm marshalling yards, 18 bombers released 53 tons over the city and the 48 aircraft raiding Koblenz dropped 102 tons. Other "targets of opportunity" included Konigswinter, Swevecelle, Niederfeld and a selection of airfields. Colonel Todd's secret assessment summarized successes and failures, whereas the Allied popular press headlined the raid as "Super Blitz Hits Hamm at Sunset". Enemy radio broadcasts described how "German fighter formations attacked strong American bomber forces with strong fighter escort over Hamm . . . the aerial combats between German and US fighters were particularly bitter".

Commenting on fighter activities, Colonel Todd continued, "Fighter support at the target consisted of only one P-47 group . . . there was a slight gap in the cover . . . Approximately 15 FW190s took advantage of a momentary absence of friendly support to make several damaging passes at the lead force during the bombing run". Todd's superiors were informed of further enemy fighter attacks and heavy flak which cost 15 bombers over Europe. Thirteen fighters also "failed to return" but, on the credit side of his balance sheet, he noted claims by bombers for 20 enemy aircraft destroyed and, more plausibly, by fighters for 37 of their opponents shot down plus six eliminated by strafing. Noted also were further categories of "probably destroyed" and "damaged". The effectiveness of fighter sweeps was illustrated by a series of claims — "24 locomotives destroyed, 15 locomotives damaged, 1 searchlight and crew destroyed, 6 factories damaged, 2 railway stations damaged, 2 barges destroyed, 31 barges damaged, 1 canal tanker destroyed, 2 canal tankers damaged, 1 train destroyed, 14 trains damaged, 2 tugs, 1 bridge, 2 houses damaged, 3 oil tanks destroyed, 1 oil tank damaged, 1 flak tower destroyed, 3 high tension towers, 1 river steamer, 1 radar tower, placer mining machinery, 1 oil derrick damaged, 1 switchman killed".

Complying with orders, fighter protection was afforded to the bombers during their withdrawal from enemy territory, and a decrease in the velocity of westerly winds enabled the Third and First Air Divisions to reach their bases early. Some Liberators also made up lost time, but most of the Second Air Division were still over the North Sea at the official blackout time of 2138 hours. Taking advantage of the situation, Luftwaffe tacticians despatched a small force of Me410 intruders from Kampfgeschwader 51 to attack Liberators on their landing approaches to airbases in the Norwich region. It was correctly deduced that detection of the intruder force would prove difficult with so many bombers still airborne. Allied controllers feared such operations because radar returns from the bombers swamped their ability to single out the enemy. In a brief, final paragraph to his report,

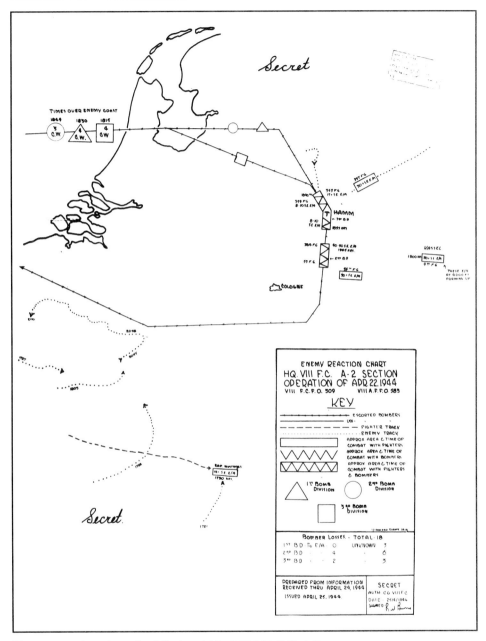

Enemy reaction chart for Mission 311. (USAF Official)

Colonel Todd admitted, "The late hour of this operation allowed the enemy to employ intruder tactics with considerable success".

This book will retrace and amplify his report, especially those incidents now established in East Anglian folklore as "the night Jerry followed the Yanks home".

•CHAPTER THREE•

Bombers:
First Casualties

IT WAS 1620 hours when Lieutenant Roland C Schellenberg lifted his B-17G carefully away from Chelveston. Just ahead, climbing into the afternoon sun was the 305BG lead ship, WF-G, *Dailey's Mail* flown by Flight Officer Coburn and crew. In alphabetical sequence, Schellenberg's ship was coincidentally WF-H, with the assigned task of deputy lead. At intervals of less than two minutes, 21 Fortresses strained skywards from Station 105, each B-17 evily pregnant with 12 x 500 lb bombs. The stressed chorus of 84 Wright Cyclone engines became an unusual evensong over Northamptonshire. Easing away from the spring dressed countryside, at some 400 feet per minute, the Group gradually melded as Schellenberg slipped into position astern and on the starboard point of a triangle from *Dailey's Mail* with Lieutenant W W McAllister closing in left to form the first vic. Aided by flares fired from the lead aircraft,

". . . and the group created a wedge-shaped formation, safely spaced yet compact for maximum fire power and ease of escort."

other ships moved carefully into their slots and the group created a wedge-shaped formation, safely spaced yet compact for maximum fire power and ease of escort. The wedge would be magnified as the 305th merged with the 379th 'A' and 'B' Groups at 10,000 feet over Molesworth to form the 41st "A" Combat Wing. Matters went smoothly as the enlarged formation cohered and kept to planned times over England. By 1806 hours, the phalanx had finalized into the First Air Task Force — 285 Flying Fortresses droning majestically seawards over the fishing and naval port of Lowestoft, the most easterly point of England, some 17,000 feet below.

Pilots usually squinted into the morning sun as formations climbed towards the enemy coast but, this evening, cockpits were shadowed and the sun's rays danced and flashed from the perspex on top and rear turrets. Perched on the tail-gunner's seat in *Dailey's Mail*, Second Lieutenant R L Holt had to monitor the formation, but there was little to report as they continued climbing towards Holland. Most pilots shared the burden of formation flying, and Holt had no way of knowing who was piloting the deputy lead — but Schellenberg's co-pilot, Second Lieutenant Lee B Eddington could draw on the experience of 24 missions so formation flying was a mastered art. The Group's intention was to cross-in at 1835 hours, 22,000 feet over Egmond aan Zee. However, 10 minutes from the Dutch coast, the deputy lead suddenly slid from its slot. Seconds later, smoke began streaming from the cockpit. Things on board had gone horrifically wrong.

Schellenberg had just noted their altitude as 20,000 feet when there was a tremendous flash from the flight-deck behind him. Swinging round, all he saw was a burgeoning core of flame centred below the upper turret. In the midst of this conflagration, like a man burning in hell, stood the flight engineer, Technical Sergeant Vincent J Fay. Horrendously burnt, Fay was flailing his arms in a desperate struggle to beat out the fire on his body. Within seconds, exploding ammunition and signal flares had filled the flight-deck full of dense, choking smoke. Swiftly giving control to Eddington, Schellenberg unsnapped his seat harness, thumped the quick release box on his parachute and rushed to aid the flight engineer. Without his oxygen mask, Schellenberg met the acrid, stifling odour of burning flares. Raising himself from his seat, he was unable to see clearly and slipped, falling heavily into the tunnel catwalk leading to the nose compartment. Hauling himself upright, the pilot discovered flames had already surged forwards and the navigator, Second Lieutenant John D Brandino, was struggling unsuccessfully with a CO_2 extinguisher. Grabbing this, Schellenberg triggered it into action and smothered the nearest flames. Their only hope lay in defeating the fire. Realizing his pilot had been off oxygen and inhaling smoke for long enough already, Lee Eddington responded as Schellenberg moved to tackle flames seated nearer the upper turret. The co-pilot had coped with the controls and avoided colliding, but smoke now completely obscured his vision and his face was painfully scorched. His reaction was simple but drastic. Sliding open the cockpit side window, he thrust his face out into the freezing fury of a 150 mph slipstream and pushed the B-17 into a steep, diving turn away from the formation.

Twisting seawards, the falling Fortress attracted compassionate attention from other crews but there was little they could do. First Lieutenant Clarence E Darnell of the 379BG authorized Technical Sergeant Tome W Wilkens to break radio silence at 1830 hours and report two parachutes from the seemingly doomed B-17. A returning spare aircraft of the 92BG radioed that the Fortress had exploded, and counted four parachutes. Air-sea rescue took a radio transmission fix on the reporting B-17 50 miles west of Egmond aan Zee. Two 356FG Thunderbolts on spotter patrol for such a contingency were vectored to the scene and saw an airman in the water in his Mae West. More practical help was en route in the form of an RAF 277 squadron Walrus amphibian flown by Flight Lieutenant N D Mackertich and crew, with Flight Sergeants King and Allen providing a Spitfire escort. When the

Blinded by smoke, Second Lieutenant Lee Eddington put his head out of the cockpit window.
(L Eddington)

trio reached the scene, the man had disappeared — but what had happened to the others?

Gripping the controls, Lee Eddington held the dive as slipstream shrieked through the fuselage and the increasing howl from the engines warned of the aircraft's anguish. The maximum permissible diving speed for a B-17G was 270 mph — beyond that they risked structural failure — and they were already registering 250 mph. The blast of air cleared smoke, flattened flames and sent loose articles swirling crazily throughout the aircraft. Before anyone could retrieve it, Schellenberg's parachute was sucked from his seat. Tumbling forwards, it vanished through the open nose-hatch, also apparently torn away in the dive. At 6,000 feet, Eddington eased back on the control column and levelled them on a course for England. The flames had diminished and a combined effort from the crew extinguished the remainder before Schellenberg called for a crew-check and damage assessment. Only then was it realized that three men were missing. Brandino and the bombardier, Second Lieutenant Curtis C Poe, had evidently baled out from the nose hatch while the unfortunate Fay had either parachuted or fallen from the bomb-bay because the doors had been sprung. None of the remaining crew had seen anyone leave, although their departure was understandable. Despite the damage, Schellenberg circled the area while Staff Sergeant Donald Davis transmitted their plight to air-sea rescue. Once confirmation had been received, he and Eddington headed homewards. Attempts to salvo the bomb-load proved fruitless because the automatic release system had been burnt out, so Davis clambered into the bomb-bay and used a screwdriver to prise open the shackles, jettisoning bombs individually. There were still six 500 lb bombs and one smoke-marker on board when they reached the English coast but Schellenberg elected to land with them. The 446BG base at Bungay was nearest and he ordered the crew to crash positions as they began their approach. Eddington pushed the landing gear switch to "down" and a satisfying whirr resulted in three reassuring greens — a visual check — all seemed well. As their airspeed decreased towards 120 mph, Schellenberg called for flaps and controlled an anxious descent. Gently, gently, the damaged bomber eased earthwards. Moments later, the airframe rumbled as tyres touched tarmac and settled. Mission 311 was over for the remaining crew.

Brandino, Fay and Poe were never found. Nor was the fire's cause explained, but one malfunction experienced at this time with the B-17G was the fraying of oxygen lines and electrical circuits fed into the top-turret. Operational problems arose when wiring insulation, worn through by turret rotation, would short-circuit and ignite leaking oxygen. The resulting blaze was fierce and frequently destroyed the aircraft. USAAF cumulative loss listing records Schellenberg's ship, 42-39818, as being salvaged on 24 April. Material losses were redeemable, men were not.

•CHAPTER FOUR•

Target Area Troubles — Third Air Division

THE THIRD AIR Division, vanguard of the attack, crossed the Dutch coast near Egmond aan Zee at 1818 hours. Leading the force was the 13th 'A' Combat Wing composed of the 95th 'A' Group followed by the main 390BG and a 95th 'B' Composite Group. USAAF operational procedure often put squadrons from different Groups in a composite Group which took its title from the parentage of the leading squadron. On this occasion, the 95 'B' Group was led by six Fortresses from the unit's 336 Squadron followed by squadrons from the 100BG and 390BG. The high elements of the Wing skimmed through thin patches of cirrus at 24,000 feet. Defiling an otherwise graceful scene came bursts of flak, ugly and disturbing but doing little damage. The Fortresses, avoiding the heavier AA defences in Amsterdam, nudged their course southwards crossing the Zuider Zee and south western Holland. Making ground speed faster than briefed, they almost overshot the next dog-leg points on their route and, reaching the IP, Lieutenant Colonel Mumford told the 390BG and 95 'B' Groups to 'S' left and right because there was insufficient interval between the three Groups. The 390BG managed

Piloted by Captain J H Hubbs, Silver Slipper led the 95BG, Third Air Division and the Eighth Air Force on Mission 311. (Cliff Hall)

to maintain its planned position during the bomb run, but the 95 'B' Group could not slow down in time and risked disrupting the 390BG's approach by being too close below them. Jinking course to starboard, the 'B' Group opted for a run on Soest as a target of opportunity. Their aiming point was the "centre of city" but a hasty, 30 second run saw many of the 100 lb M47A2 incendiary bombs scattered across open land and residential areas on the southeastern side of the target. Little damage was done to their intended objective, Soest's marshalling yards, and their manoeuvre had broken the bomber stream leaving behind the protection of its escorting 353FG and 359FG Thunderbolts. Compounding the bomber's predicament, the P-47s were on limits of endurance and awaiting relief by P38s from the 20FG. German fighter controllers noted their opportunity and the RAF Wireless Intelligence Service, eavesdropping on enemy transmissions, heard fighters being vectored to attack.

First Lieutenant H R Rivenbark, already unhappy with their "Piss Poor" bombing, spotted the enemy fighters "not less than 50" Focke-Wulf 190s flying parallel to the bombers. Overhauling the B-17s, the enemy fighters gained altitude and positioned themselves up-sun. Tensely, the Fortress crews waited for the inevitable — upper turrets swivelled to face the assault, chin and nose guns canted towards the enemy, symbolic lances in a deadly, aerial joust. One thousand yards away, young knights of the Luftwaffe listened for their leader's signal. To some gunners the enemy formation simulated their own, but the resemblance ceased as the attack began and the fighters split firstly into two Groups then, closing fast from 11 o'clock high, they divided into elements of three in two waves. From the ranks of threatened Fortresses an enfilade of fire seared towards the enemy. At 500 yards, the sparkle of firing cannon flashed spitefully as fighters chose targets, but veteran bomber crews sensed that their adversaries were inexperienced. Subtle

The Interrogation Form filed by First Lieutenant H R Rivenbark comments on the "Observed Results of Bombing" as "Piss Poor".

Wild Children *of the 390BG participated in the attack flown by C D Nesbitt and crew. She returned safely to Parham at 2131 hours.* (390BGMAM)

skills, respected and feared, were lacking. Only the leaders demonstrated deadly competence. For some, the skirmish was brief; others it cast into eternity.

Concentrating on B-17s in the purple-heart corner, low squadron of the low Group, the FW190s punched into the 390BG ship flown by Lieutenant Harold E Reich and crew. Culled from the herd, Reich's B-17 dropped from formation, its agony a harsh nucleus of flame. At the same instant, a 100BG Fortress, *Dobie*, piloted by Lieutenant Frank Harte, also fell away. Up to eight parachutes were counted from the two B-17s; others were also in trouble. On board *I'll Be Around*, of the 390th, Second Lieutenant Earl F Schmidt watched the fighters hurtling towards him. His 24th mission would be memorable, if he survived. Ducking instinctively, Earl thanked the tenacity of his crew chief, Athanasius "Pop" Cummings. Three missions earlier, shrapnel or a shell casing had crazed their bullet proof windshield and Supply said no more were available. Even though they were only a "junior" lead crew, Pop took their welfare seriously: they were "his" crew. Storming off to Supply, Pop had staged a scene and left one of his groundcrew arguing with the Supply sergeant for release of a replacement laminated glass "bullet-proof" screen. Prising open a rear window, he broke into the storage area and took the last available heavy glass screen by "moonlight requisition".

Pop's prowess proved providential as a 20 mm cannon shell hit the glass and detonated in front of Schmidt's face. The explosion smashed a fist-sized hole into the cockpit and Earl was slammed into his seat as if clubbed with a baseball bat. Strapped in, he wore a British parachute harness for his chest pack and one shell fragment sliced through six of the eight doubled thicknesses of webbing where the straps overlapped on his shoulder. An inch to the right and its only resistance would have been clothing and flesh. Another fragment of glass punched his nose and broke his polaroids. Blood streaked from a cluster of small cuts. Earl would find for several months after this that morning ablutions included picking minute slivers of glass from his face. Most of the pulverised glass acted like sand-blast on the control pedestal. The pilot, Lieutenant Roger J Sterr suffered a burn-like welt on his left leg from finely powdered glass penetrating his flight suit. Their number two engine began burning, but actioning the extinguishers killed this deadliest of enemies before it caught hold. *I'll Be Around* would be just that for some time yet, and things were evened up when their ball-turret gunner, Charlie Baker, claimed the destruction of an FW190. Experienced enemy pilots rolled belly-up as they dived beneath the B-17s but some of these pilots remained upright, risking increased exposure to bullets hitting the cockpit. Whether Charlie Baker really destroyed an FW190 is uncertain because the confusion of combat could cause duplicate claims. Historians now know that figures were exaggerated, especially where several gunners genuinely felt the credit was theirs. More certainty can be attached to the likelihood of these fighters coming from I and II Gruppen of Jagdgeschwader One who scrambled from Stormede and Bad Lippspringe to engage the "Viermots" — four motors. That *he* was inexperienced would be admitted by Obfhr Herbert Neuner who, just 20 years old, was on only his second mission. Flying a Focke-Wulf 190A-7, *Black 16*, the young pilot had less than one month's experience of the type, but youthful exuberance overcame fear and his aggressive, head-on dive into the enemy formation was exhilarating. Hurtling through the 95th 'B' Group, Neuner did not make any claims and indeed felt grateful at finding himself unscathed after flying through the formidable Fortress formation. Seeing an FW190, apparently damaged, Neuner flew alongside then, suddenly, *Black 16* was hit, possibly by his own side's flak. Neuner's concern for his comrade abruptly converted into a struggle to land safely. Wrestling the controls, he struggled towards the nearest airfield at Dortmund. The damaged BMW801 engine vibrated vigorously until it literally fell out and *Black 16* tumbled on to a house some two kilometres west of Dortmund. Neuner, extracted from the burning debris suffering serious head injuries, concussion and burns, was hospitalized until July.

Each side had incurred casualties, but clarification of losses proved difficult with both the 100BG and 390BG confused regarding the fate of their aircraft. The 100BG reported, "our aircraft number '783 was apparently hit by enemy aircraft in the attack at 1905 hours, near 5100N-0800E. It fell out of formation and eight 'chutes were reported. It appears likely that these 'chutes came from one of the two 390th aircraft that were shot out of formation at this place. Our aircraft is believed to be the one that continued to fly in a position below and at 3 o'clock at our formation. At 1928 hours 5027N-0700E, its crew was observed to be jettisoning some of their equipment. It fell further and further behind and was last seen at 2007 hours, 5044N-0413E".

Frank Harte's Fortress did not head for the coast but plummeted to destruction near Obershelden, north of Siegen. The attacking fighters savaged the B-17, setting it alight and wounding four crewmen. Grievous injuries were suffered by the right waist gunner, Staff Sergeant Thomas C McDonald who collapsed, bleeding profusely from wounds in his lower back. His opposite number, Staff Sergeant Edward T Coley, thought McDonald was dead and, although himself wounded, Coley rapidly escaped from the waist door. Seconds later, the ball turret gunner, Staff Sergeant Felix W McIntosh found McDonald crawling up the steeply inclined fuselage in a bid for life. Assisting McDonald into his parachute, McIntosh helped him jump, but German civilians later told the captured co-pilot, Second Lieutenant John J. Coppinger, that they had found one flier dead. McDonald either bled to death during the descent or never opened his parachute. Coppinger himself had been urged out by his pilot as Harte held the steeply diving Fortress steady for his crew to jump. His bravery saved seven lives but he and the navigator, Second Lieutenant Carl F Conley, were presumably the two bodies found in the wreckage by Luftwaffe investigators.

The 390BG records relate, "About 1904 hours, near Iserlohn, aircraft '130 flying number 6 position, low squadron, 95 'B' Composite Group was knocked out of formation after attack by enemy aircraft. One engine, number three or number two, was afire. Aircraft fell behind formation and began to lose altitude. According to one crew, red flares were shot from the aircraft. Two P-47s provided fighter support for aircraft '130 which was last seen, on the deck, near Ostend at 2041 hours".

The B-17 seen near Ostend did not belong to the 100BG either — the remains of Reich's Fortress were burning near Alsbach, a few miles from Koblenz. Moments after the pilot alerted his crew, their B-17 was hit by at least one fighter. Tense and cramped inside the sphere of his ball-turret, Staff Sergeant Peter M Filippone waited for the chance he knew from their 19 previous missions would come as the enemy dived through the bomber formation. *Now!* In a few, hectic seconds he fired at four fighters. Smoke belched from one but the gunner's jubilation was brief — a 20 mm cannon shell burst into the fuselage over his turret. The explosion spattered the waist gunners with shrapnel and shredded the vital control cables for rudder and elevator control. Filippone's interphone went dead and he could see smoke streaming from their number three engine as the Fortress dropped into a dive. Over the din, he sensed rather than heard someone thumping on his turret and released the door hatch to find out what was happening. As his hatch fell open, he saw more smoke swirling through the fuselage and the top-turret gunner, Technical Sergeant Horace Huron looming anxiously over him. Huron hollered at Filippone to bale out. It took only seconds to disconnect his heated suit and clip on his parachute but by that time he was alone. Afraid the ship would explode, Filippone hurried to escape as the bomber's dive steepened. Thickening smoke and anxiety prevented him from checking if the tail gunner, Staff Sergeant John M Zediak, had gone and, reaching the waist exit, he threw himself clear and pulled his ripcord.

Dangling in his parachute, Reich's radio operator, Technical Sergeant Carl E Marsini counted at least seven others, but he may have missed some. Reich never escaped. His body was found in the wreckage. The tail gunner, Staff Sergeant John M Zediak did escape but landed heavily amidst some rocks and died of severe head injuries — the remaining crew members were captured.

I'll Be Around, presumably the second 390BG aircraft referred to, regained formation and her anxious crew waited for the enemy to return. After climbing and regrouping, Jagdgeschwader 1 repeated their tactics, only this time there were noticeably fewer fighters. Between 10 and 15 FW190s again selected the 95 'B' Group. As Sergeant J C Bognor, left-waist gunner on Lieutenant R B Parke's 390BG crew commented, "The Fighters hit us twice, hard. The other waist gunner (Sergeant J A Basciano) was wounded in the first attack. The radio operator took him to the radio room for first-aid, and from then on, I manned both waist guns". That the enemy came close was evidenced by damage to their ship, 42-32026, some of which was caused by the propeller blades of an enemy fighter. JG1's records show that Unteroffizier Heinz Weber crashed "near Hilbeck" after ramming a B-17 although Weber had apparently destroyed one B-17 attacking from astern and collided with the rudder of a second as he disengaged. Both Fortresses were claimed but Parke landed at Parham over two hours later.

The lack of spacing between combat wings, unpredicted wind strength and the deviation to Soest cost the 13th 'A' Wing its casualties and resulted in the 13th 'B' Wing leading the Third Air Division home. However, the 13th 'B' Wing would have target area troubles of its own. Led by the redoubtable 100BG's main Group, the Wing had a mixed high Group from the 388BG/452BG and, in what one participant remembers as "coffin corner" — the low Group — came the 385BG from Great Ashfield. The Wing's difficulties were minor until 1842 hours when they turned south towards the IP and the 100BG lead navigator was unable to identify it. Already unhappy over the lead Group's loose formation the 385BG and 388BG were further frustrated by this error. Eight minutes elapsed before the 100BG eventually saw the target itself and took an arbitrary IP at 51-43N/07-25E, several miles south of their briefed course. Unchanged, the wedge formation was too compact to release bombs for fear of hitting other aircraft so SOP (Standard Operational Procedure) instructed Wings to bomb in train — lead, high, low. This entailed the high and low Groups fanning out some five miles prior to the IP and going line astern for a turn over the IP. With the 100BG missing the briefed IP and taking an arbitrary turn, the following Groups became confused as the low 385BG waited for the high 388BG to turn and "uncover", but there was no reaction from the high Group. Acting unilaterally, the 385BG eventually turned towards

Left *"Acting unilaterally, the 385BG eventually turned towards the target as second group to bomb."* Contrails from escorting fighters curve protectively overhead.

Right *Looking right, Harlan saw* The Golden Goose *close alongside, her forward guns already engaged.*

the target as second group to bomb, although they were now several miles off course with insufficient time for an effective bombing run. The 388BG were also unhappy with the 100BG and felt the lead Group had flown too slowly for following Groups to hold a cohesive Wing formation easily. In addition, excessive groundspeed and two turns without enough interval added to the difficulties. Compounding their irritation, the 385BG's decision to bomb second resulted in the 388BG 'B' Group being too close to the 385BG and unable to bomb.

Adding to the self-inflicted woes of the 13th 'B' Wing approaching Hamm, FW 190s of JG1 broke through the P-47 fighter escort to hurtle head on into the low squadron of the 385BG. Flying number six position was B-17G 42-38200 piloted by First Lieutenant Cleatis

Crew of the unchristened Miss Cheyenne. *Rear: L-R; Cleatis Cornwell, Pilot; Harlan L Cook, Co-pilot; Ray H Hitzel, Navigator. Kneeling: Robert G Peel, Tail Gunner; Delbert F Dimig, Togglier; Irving M Janzen, Gunner; Wheeler V Urban, Radio; John A Kennedy, Top-Turret; George J Bartell, Gunner.* (H L Cook)

Cornwell and crew. They were on their 11th mission in a new ship only recently assigned. Today the crew's on-going debate about her name would be violently terminated by the opposition. Harlan L Cook, the co-pilot, had wanted *Miss Cheyenne* because he and his wife had been school sweethearts in Cheyenne, Wyoming. His schooldays now seemed distant dreams in the nightmare reality of a rapidly-unfolding attack with their element of Fortresses obviously chosen as target. Looking right, Harlan saw *The Golden Goose* close alongside, her forward guns already engaged. Above the pounding of Cyclone engines, Harlan heard and felt the harsh, staccato rasp from his top-turret's twin machine guns as Technical Sergeant John A Kennedy challenged an in-coming FW190. Nailed to the bombing run, the Fortress shook with indignation at the intended assault. Moments later they were hit and hit hard. Even through his oxygen mask, Harlan inhaled the acrid aroma of cordite. More hits. The world was a crazy rush of happenings. Close in front of his eyes flickered a series of large, white flashes. Cannon shells exploding? An FW190 skimmed by. A hunter's breath behind hurtled a P-47. Both vanished. The defiance of their guns continued shaking every sinew of the Boeing's structure. The togglier, Staff Sergeant Delbert R Dimig hollered excitedly that he had shot off the wing of an enemy fighter. Their jubilation was stifled by compassion when the pilot's parachute was seen burning like a dried flower. Vengefully, flak rocked the B-17 but the mortal blow they took came from an FW190. Their linkage with life shot away, the control wheels slackened uselessly in the pilot's hands. Glancing over his shoulder, Harlan saw a huge, gaping hole behind their number three engine and sheets of flame bannered from ruptured fuel cells. Events hastened remorselessly. John Kennedy continued firing — he saw the wing shear off the FW190; he felt cannon shells slamming into the B-17; large holes splashed suddenly across each wing. Other hits hacked pieces off the stabilizer and the left landing gear sagged wearily from its housing. Cornwell ordered Dimig to salvo the bombs and Harlan hit the extinguishers and feathering buttons. It was bedlam on board as the crew fought for their existence. Dimig came on the intercom, the bomb-release system had been shot out, all the bombs had hung up. Kennedy said he would try the emergency release in the bomb-bay and dropped from his turret to the flight deck. An instant later, the perspex of his turret shattered in a storm of machine gun bullets. Ducking into the bomb-bay, Kennedy confronted the awesome spectacle of fused bombs wreathed in flames drawn inboard from a fire near their number two engine. He tugged the emergency release handle hard. Nothing happened. Getting a firm grip on the aircraft's structure, Kennedy did the only thing he could think of and kicked open the doors. They parted. The bombs vanished. Kennedy clung on, feeling the Fortress shudder as her remaining guns responded to a renewed attack. Climbing back to his wrecked turret, he found the guns functioned and promptly stitched a series of holes along the fuselage of a fighter passing almost at touching distance.

Their valiant struggle was witnessed by Staff Sergeant Chuck Flynn, tail gunner of *The Golden Goose* who heard the fighters called in from 12 o'clock and poised for a shot. The FW190 flashing past gave him no chance — there was a P-47 in hot pursuit. Flynn recalls, "As they flashed by, the FW190 whipped into a picture book Immelmann turn — half loop and roll upright — firing as he nosed down . . . no way the P-47 could follow. I could see the cannon shells ripping in . . . it all happened in seconds or less . . ." Flynn saw the FW190 closing on the tail gunner of the neighbouring B-17. Facing this onslaught was Staff Sergeant Robert G Peel whose tall frame made it impossible to wear a flak-suit and parachute while manning his guns. Instead he positioned purloined flak suits around himself as best he could and at least one cannon shell exploded among these. A large hole was blown in the port side, the left tail gun was smashed and the detonation threw Peel into overhead controls for the rudder, knocking him senseless. How long he was unconscious is unknown but, coming round, he called Cornwell saying he was hit. No reply. Bleeding badly, he shuffled himself backwards up a fuselage too damaged and too tight for him to easily turn round. Reaching his parachute, he snapped it on and jettisoned the emergency hatch before peering into the void. To a dazed and fearful flier, it looked a long, long, long way down. Bob changed his mind. Looking along the fuselage for comfort he saw only the waist gunners waiting near the door. The Fortress seemed straight and level, the starboard wing was burning but Bob, his judgement impaired by injuries and anoxia, cherished hopes of reaching home. He felt drunk, almost carefree. Home was not really *that* far — time for another scrap with the Hun. Now the Fortress was nosing steeply earthwards as Bob crawled to his guns again and sprayed bullets at enemy fighters, real or imaginary. By some fluke, he and the ball-turret gunner, Sergeant Francis S Diemer may have hit one but then Diemer heard Cornwell give the command to bale out. Peel heard nothing.

John Kennedy also heard the order to bale out and the clatter from the alarm. Clipping on his parachute, he leapt from the bomb-bay, counted "a slow 10" and tugged the rip-cord — "it seemed like forever for the 'chute to open". Floating down, he saw a B-17, perhaps his own, explode in mid-air. Then he noticed another parachutist, Francis Diemer, had also escaped. In the uncannily peaceful aftermath of battle, the two descending airmen exchanged views on who had escaped and who had not. Several thousand feet higher, Chuck Flynn also wondered. It would be nearly 50 years before he found out. As the stricken Fortress fell back, he repeatedly urged, "Bail out you guys, BAIL OUT!" Streaked with flames, the Fortress drifted back, then a figure fell clear, his parachute opened. One . . . then another . . . two . . . "BAIL OUT YOU GUYS, BAIL OUT!" . . . three . . . four . . . Racked with explosions, the bomber fell from view. Others saw a section of wing tear, away then the Fortress exploded leaving an ugly grey-black octopus of smoke in the sky with tentacles of blazing debris.

Harlan Cook tumbled and spun — head down, feet up. Enough of this, he pulled his ripcord and greeted the blossoming parachute with a prayer to see his Julia again. Back there in the cockpit, Cornwell had gesticulated with his thumb down and Harlan needed no further urging. Pulling the chest pack from beneath his seat, he hooked it on his harness and crawled to the open escape hatch. Sitting a moment with his feet buffeted by the slipstream, he observed the dangerously near arc from the number two propeller, he re-checked his harness, then leapt away from the cacophony of engines, explosions and the shrieking, dying bomber, into tranquility. Now, from his parachute, he seemed stationary, the ground looming slowly up to greet him. Tiny figures were running to his estimated landing place. He tried guiding himself but this was his first jump and his inexperienced efforts made no difference. Clearing a river, then a fence, he thumped heavily on his back in the centre of a hard road, completely winded. A small crowd gathered, hands prodded, harsh voices shouting, "pistole, pistole" but he did not carry his .45. Discovering this, his captors offered a cigarette, a friendly gesture politely declined by the non-smoking co-pilot who would at least be able to trade his rations in Stalag Luft III.

Bob Peel had fought to the last. Heroism was disclaimed because he was not fully aware of his actions and his unsteady scattering of bullets probably hit nothing, but it looked like heroism as the gunner continued firing from within his dying aircraft. Then the Fortress exploded. A full day later, Bob Peel awoke to see a man in brown uniform offering him a cigarette while a Catholic sister stooped caringly at his bedside. "Is this England?" he asked. "Nein, Deutschland", she answered. It seemed her boss had taken direct care of the injured airman. How his parachute opened he never knew but it must have been tethered to an angel for it floated the unconscious flier almost into the courtyard of the small,

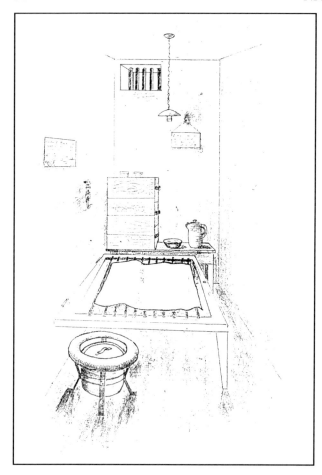

Left *During his first evening in captivity, Harlan L Cook sketched this view of his magnificent surroundings . . . but at least he was alive.* (H L Cook)

Below right *Sergeant Robert Pulsipher cleaning 42-97358 XM-D* Ordnance Express *with 100 octane fuel. This famous 94BG B-17 had participated in Mission 311, and completed 118 missions by VE Day.* (Cliff Hall)

private order Meiningen Hospital on the edge of Werl. Their excellent emergency treatment and subsequent ministering saved his life, and years later, Bob returned to thank them for the extra time they gave him. He died of cancer in 1991. Amazingly, all 10 airmen parachuted from the wreck of what was to have been *Miss Cheyenne*, and fortune favoured 10 more 385BG fliers when flak hit the B-17 flown by Second Lieutenant John C McDevitt as it approached the target. The number three engine was feathered and smoking as it turned out of formation but still under control. A vulnerable straggler, McDevitt's Fortress was reportedly pounced on by fighters but all the crew safely parachuted before one wing came off and the B-17 disintegrated.

With their planned approach disrupted, the 385BG sighted on Hamm but the reduced bombing run left lead bombardier, First Lieutenant W A Beveridge unable to synchronize his Norden bombsight. Synchronization usually began several miles before the IP and entailed entering into the sight's electro-mechanical computer system a combination of ballistical characteristics for the bomb-type carried plus allowances for air speed, altitude and drift. Lacking time, Beveridge approximated the cross-hairs for his sight on a smoke-enshrouded target and his release signalled release from the remaining 385BG aircraft whose results were later assessed as only "poor to fair".

Despite trying to 'S' behind the 385BG, the 388BG 'B' Group still found themselves too close and, facing similar synchronization difficulties, they chose a riskier solution in opting for a second run on the target. Calling in fighter support, the 388BG set course to circle Munster and return. As First Lieutenant Wayne A Barnett, lead bombardier, reported, "A second run was necessary to obtain satisfactory results. We crossed the target area and made a second IP just south of Munster . . . the second run was entirely satisfactory. I had approximately one and one-half minutes of steady sighting time and was troubled only by the smoke of previous bombing obscuring my aiming point. I dropped my bombs from an indicated altitude of 24,000 feet, tangent 0.66, drift 7° left and magnetic heading of 139°. The main body of our pattern is obscured in the smoke . . . however the few bursts that can be distinguished indicated excellent bombing results". Their proficiency would have been further enhanced had not a rack malfunction on 42-30195 caused seven bombs to fall out when doors were opened at the IP. Three other aircraft mistook this for a release signal and similarly bombed the town's suburbs but the second-run gamble paid off. Their only casualty was Sergeant C J Potenga, slightly wounded by flak. They never rejoined the 13th 'B' Combat Wing and a parting gesture saw coastal guns hit 42-97130 of the 452BG. Two crewman were wounded, First Lieutenant Jack O Elliot, the pilot, and top-turret gunner, Technical Sergeant Elmer Smeltzly. Feathering their number one engine, the crew came safely home.

Fortune also favoured the main 452BG which led the 45th Combat Wing, next over the target. Initially, the 45 CBW faced some assembly problems mainly caused by the 4th Combat Wing also forming up

nearby. En route, altitude variations in wind velocity caused the high 96BG to overshoot and the low 388BG to lag. Near the IP, the 452BG turned too soon forcing the following two Groups to maintain bombing interval by snaking. Effective use of countermeasures including "carpet" and "chaff" frustrated flak's radar directed fire control systems. "Carpet" consisted of jamming transmitters in leading aircraft to block the Wurzburg radar frequency, while "chaff" was simply strips of aluminium foil showered in the atmosphere to create myriad synthetic aircraft on German radar screens. These devices reduced the flak to "moderate and inaccurate" and the 96BG Group Bombardier Captain John L Latham recorded how bombs were "walked across the target area leaving the whole area a mass of flames and smoke". Bombs carried by the 45 CBW were a mixture of 500 lb GP and 100 lb incendiaries. These were intended to rip open buildings before showering incendiaries into the exposed structures.

By turning early, the 45th Wing created considerable propwash — an invisible wake of air-turbulence — across the path intended for the approaching 4th Wing who were obliged to route south of their briefed course. Furthermore, the 4th Wing were less experienced at using "carpet" and faced increasingly vehement flak. Leading this last Third Air Division Wing was the 447BG 'A' Group. The 94BG from Bury St Edmunds took the high slot and the unenviable low position was assigned to the 447BG 'B' Group, a composite force of 12 aircraft from Rattlesden and nine ships from nearby Gt Ashfield. Selecting a new heading, the Wing saw Hamm settled in the reflective hue of an evening haze. The town was clearly visible although smoke boiled angrily skywards from damage inflicted on the marshalling yard. Hoping to hinder the enemy, German defences had activated smokepots but these proved ineffective and more bombs battered the target.

Peering through the nose-perspex of the 94BG B-17, *Ordnance*

42-102380 QE-Y was flown through the flak over Hamm by Lieutenant Wendt and crew. (Cliff Hall)

Express, Lieutenant Abel L Dolim was navigating on his first mission. As they cleared the target, a German-born gunner pointed out the farmhouse in which he was raised. Abe always remembered the strange impression this left. Down there were ordinary people upon whom it would be his duty to try and inflict war at least another 25 times. Down there, too, were people whose cancerous Nazi creed sought to infect mankind and whose railway network was used to further this evil ambition.

At the other end of the scale, flying his 25th mission, was Lieutenant Vernon J Boyle, also from the 94BG in their B-17, *Puddin*. Reaching Rougham later that evening he could not resist the "lucky bastard" custom of firing red and green flares despite the risk from intruders. His luck held. Fate was less kind to the 94BG ship, *Gloria*. Slapped hard by flak, she fell from formation with two engines out and fire burning in the nose and bomb-bay. Three crewmen baled out but the pilot Lieutenant Frank Bartos regained control and brought home his bomber to fight another day.

Trailing the 94BG, the 447BG composite Group faced increasingly accurate flak — 75% of the Fortresses sustained damage as shrapnel

The 94BG B-17 Puddin *carried Lieutenant Vernon J Boyle for six hours 30 minutes before turning safely to Rougham and completing his tour.*
(Cliff Hall)

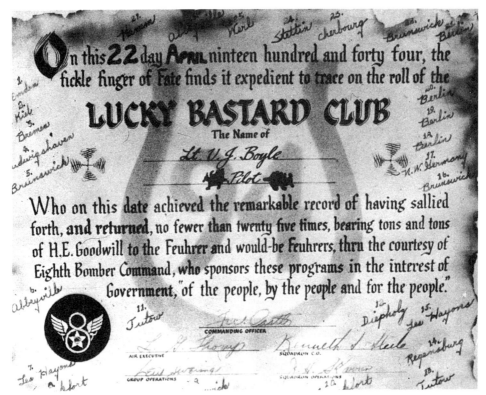

Lucky Bastard *certificate awarded to Vernon J Boyle on 22 April 1944.* (Dr V J Boyle)

showered off fuselage skinning, like ball bearings shaken in a garbage-can. It would be miraculous if they emerged without loss, yet the formation seemed impervious to the malicious black bursts. Then, moments after release, at least one round hit home and 42-31724 flown by First Lieutenant Thomas W Gilleran keeled over. Vaporizing gasoline streamed from torn tanks in the starboard wing, then it ignited, flashing into a burning shroud. Wreathed in flames, the Fortress peeled gradually, almost gracefully, away into an ever-steepening dive with tiny figures tumbling free. When it exploded there was one miracle, the survival of all 10 airmen. Thirsted now, the flak was ready for the First Air Division.

•CHAPTER FIVE•

Flak for the First

TO THE CREW of *Satan's Lady* it looked like hell above Hamm as their reliable B-17 ushered the 306BG towards a flak-ridden target. They had the uneasy distinction of leading the 40th CBW and the First Air Division. Not only that, but their pilot, Captain Loy F Peterson was

Right *Flak greeted First Air Division Fortresses over Hamm.*

Below *The veteran 306BG* Satan's Lady *headed the First Air Division's assault.* (Loy F Peterson)

Above *Nose art to taunt, torment or titillate —* Satan's Lady *completed over 75 missions.* (Loy F Peterson)

Left *Colonel George L Robinson, 306BG, was no "armchair commander".* (Loy F Peterson)

today in the co-pilot's seat with his commanding officer as pilot. Colonel George L Robinson was no armchair commander. This was his 19th mission and he knew enough about flak to realize there was little you could do on a bombing run, "you just tightened up the straps on your flak suit and bored on through". Loy Peterson had worked out a personal evasive manoeuvre after release and would make a level, left turn, count eight seconds and make a diving turn intended to confuse the gunner's calculations. It had kept him alive so far, but the flak batteries protecting Hamm had their own theories and were apparently overcoming some of the effects from "chaff" and "carpet". Their bursts now accurately tracked the lead Group. They damaged 15 of the 18 ships including, possibly, the release circuit on *Satan's Lady* because it failed when operated and bombardier, First Lieutenant M A Phillips lost important seconds in salvoeing via a back-up system. This delay meant the 306BG's bombs fell beyond their intended section of the target although Phillips estimated they hit the eastern edge of the marshalling yards at 1910 hours.

One minute later, the defenders demonstrated their own aiming efficiency and bracketed the 306BG with accurate bursts, one of which hit the veteran B-17F *She Hasta*. Thrown from formation, *She Hasta* spiralled earthwards, her pilots fighting for control. Co-pilot, Second Lieutenant William G Mitchell recalls, "we received hits over the target in both of the two port side engines. Curtis (First Lieutenant John W Curtis, pilot) was flying at the time. I managed to feather the outboard engine — number one — but could not feather number two due to loss of oil pressure; we had lost the oil cooler on that engine. We dropped out of the formation but were able to maintain flying speed at about 12,000 feet altitude. The number two engine continued to windmill, and soon heated so that it was burning. We decided to continue, and soon the heat 'froze' the engine so that rotation stopped. However, after the engine cooled, it again began to rotate. This continued until heat froze it again. This cycle continued most of the way back to England.

"We had other hard choices to make in addition to whether to stay with the plane. First was what route to take. The closest distance would have been to turn back west immediately. However, Cullen (Second Lieutenant William L Cullen, navigator) pointed out that this would take us over heavy flak areas. He advised a route to the south toward Frankfurt, then west. We took that, though it meant longer before we could hope to get home. Another choice was power settings. To maintain altitude, we were running both good engines at maximum RPM and inches of mercury. The B-17 manual stated this could only be done for a period not to exceed 15 minutes. However, we felt to go lower was a worse chance, so we continued at full throttle. Even so, we could only slow-fly at 110-115 mph. I flew most of the way out while Curtis maintained communication and tried to reassure the crew, etc. After about a half hour, we were joined by two P-47s of the fighter escort. They asked about our problems, then elected to stick with us to guard against German fighters. They dropped flaps and flew formation with us, one on each side. You can bet we were grateful! However, our troubles weren't over. As we passed over the coast of Belgium, we received another burst of flak, which was very well aimed. We lost another engine, but what was almost worse, one of the P-47s was hit, and we believe went down. We never knew his fate".

Between them, the two B-17 pilots could only just keep airborne with full right rudder and the trim wheel adjusted to its maximum setting.

Officers on board She Hasta. *L-R: John W Curtis, Pilot; William L Cullen, Navigator; Paul R Carsten, Bombardier; William G Mitchell, Co-Pilot.* (G Wortham)

The B-17 shuddered, shook and rattled its way homewards with the number one engine emitting sparks and trailing smoke. Just after leaving the enemy coast, the smoking motor "really fired up" but they risked side-slipping to blow out the flames. Nearing England, Technical Sergeant C E Lane called for assistance on the "Darky" emergency frequency. This drew a response and homing directions towards RAF Manston on the tip of the Kentish coast. Mitchell continues, "The other P-47 stayed with us all the way to the emergency field. He said he wanted to see us safely in! After losing the third engine, we immediately gave the order to toss out anything which could be spared. We threw out the flak suits, guns, ammunition, even personal effects. Of course, we were in what was really a powered glide, but luckily we had enough altitude and the distance wasn't too great to make it across.

"We made a straight in approach. I was still flying the plane, Curtis carrying out the other cockpit duties. Just as we were about a mile from the edge of the field, the fourth and last engine cut out. We glided the rest of the way in dead stick. We were of course firing red-red flares and were met by fire trucks, as well as an ambulance. Luckily, no one was hit. When we got out and looked at that last engine, we found it was hanging on by only three mounting bolts. The prop which had windmilled was still on the engine, but could be moved backwards and forwards almost a foot. I don't know what kept it on the plane. We were all given heavy shots of medicinal booze, and spent the night at that base. I called my wife, who was a nurse at Winchester, and told her I was back safe, but just barely. We were picked up by another plane from our own base next day, but I was later told that 454B never flew again. It probably was scrapped right there".

Mitchell's suspicions about the fate of *She Hasta* are confirmed by 306BG records. The Operational Record Book for Manston provides a further flavour of events on 22 April 1944. "Many crashes and forced landings today, detailed hereunder — Manston is indeed rapidly becoming a Prangers' Paradise. At 1150 a Marauder from 574 Squadron (391BG, USAAF), Matching, landed downwind with starboard engine shot up, crew were uninjured. 1221, a Marauder from Chipping Ongar landed downwind on one engine overshooting the runway, fortunately without further damage, crew again OK. Shortly afterwards, a Spitfire with a burst tyre landed in a hurry . . . Next on the list were two Albacores, both landing with burst tyres. We next afforded sanctuary to two Thunderbolts, one of which is badly shot up and minus left brake, the other having part of a wing missing, the result of hitting a train on enemy territory, both pilots OK. Manston is next kept busy by the erratic arrival of five Fortresses in various stages of disrepair. The first landed with two u/s engines, the second, two engines u/s and flak damage, the third damaged by flak landed with one engine on fire, while the fourth, also damaged by flak, had two engines u/s and no flaps, the fifth and final Fort was extensively damaged by flak. All crews happily uninjured. The last emergency landing for today was a Liberator which landed without flaps and with two engines u/s. An intensely hectic day with damaged aircraft coming to rest in the most unaccountable and awkward positions about the airfield. Indeed, had it not been for the prompt and skilled action by the various personnel of the crash parties and the servicing wing, we may have been mistaken for a rather large and dispersed salvage dump".

Some of the aircraft destined for that dump were still airborne and, while the leading 306BG were the unwelcoming recipients of so much flak, the 92BG were comparatively unmolested. They reported "an excellent concentration of bombs on the southern portion of the marshalling yard . . . the entire yard and city of Hamm was one mass of smoke and flame". The final Group from the 40th CBW was a 306BG/92BG composite which stoked the havoc wreaked by their predecessors but were unable to observe results because of dense smoke. Following closely, the next two combat wings encountered similar sighting difficulties. Such was the capacity of Groups involved that both wings were almost entirely made from 41st Combat Bombardment Wing aircraft. Slight bending of organizational command occurred by borrowing 305BG aircraft from the 40th CBW to form the high Group of the 41st 'A' CBW. The lead and low Groups were from the 379BG, Kimbolton, which was large enough to launch 44 Fortresses. Flak continued to challenge and damage many aircraft, but the leading 379BG 'A' Group straddled its bombs across the target into the northeast choke point and sorting sidings. Some of the freight wagons must have contained explosives because the bombs triggered a series of blasts culminating in an enormous explosion pulsating shockwaves skywards. A malfunctioning bomb-rack in the lead aircraft frustrated the low 379BG 'B' Group. Failing to release over Hamm, this unit kept its bombs for a further 20 minutes, then deviated from its homeward course to hit Konigswinter as a target of opportunity. Damage in this town was expected to be severe because it was "a compact residential area". The 305BG B-17s borrowed from the 40th CBW achieved only "fair" results on Hamm when they released at 1912 hours. Unfortunately, they also obscured the target for the 41st 'B' CBW which was already on its run-in. Leading this wing was the 303BG 'A' Group whose crews looked in awe at the grey-black smoke column convulsing some 10,000 feet over the target. To Colonel Kermit D Stevens in the lead ship, "The whole place seemed to be on fire by the time we got there". Nonetheless, at 1913 hours they added another 216 x 500 lb AN-M64 bombs from 22,000 feet but with "poor results".

Determined to improve the Wing's accuracy, the 384BG low Group rode a steady, seven minute run to release, "a dense concentration of bombs" covering the southwest end of the marshalling yards. Pushing the dagger still deeper, the high 303/384BG composite Group pounded the same section, ripping across the main railway lines to Duisburg and Duisburg-Ruhrort. In only three minutes, the 41st 'B' CBW had dropped 650 x 500 lb bombs brewing the target into an increasing torment of fire. In retaliation, flak struck the 303BG's *Nero* at 1916 hours as the high Group made for their rally point. (Illustrating the confusion that can bedevil researchers, this 359th Bombardment Squadron B-17 was flown by Second Lieutenant John R Seddon and crew from the 358th squadron. Furthermore, she was given the wrong serial number, 42-31213, when reported missing in the 303BG's, Narrative of Operations. Her correct identity was 42-39807 but even the circumstances of her demise remain unclear.) First Lieutenant James H Melton, flying number six position immediately astern, saw Seddon having problems with his number three engine: "The engine would almost quit, and then start up again with the power surging on and off intermittently". Seddon seemed unable to feather the propeller and *Nero* slid back through the ranks, either a victim of flak or mechanical failure. When last seen, Seddon seemed in control but *Nero's* hardstand at Molesworth remained empty that evening. Limping homewards, she reached the small town of Inglemunster in Belgium at 2100 hours. Another engine then failed and caught fire, sealing her fate. The bale-out alarm rang the end of her crew's 11th mission, but they all safely parachuted.

Less fortunate was Second Lieutenant Roy A Larson and crew on 42-39785, *Thru Hel'en Hiwater*, also from the 303BG. Five minutes from Hamm, anti-aircraft fire scored a direct hit flinging the Fortress into a spin with its number one engine ablaze and no hope of recovery. From nearly four miles high, the B-17 twisted earthwards in an anguish others could only witness. Some parachutes were counted but *Hel'en* took Larson, Second Lieutenant Milton Feinman, his bombardier, and Staff Sergeant Thomas J Campbell, the top turret gunner to their deaths near Werl. Flak also created two more candidates for the Manston dump when accurate coastal fire chased the 384th BG homewards. Second

Taken only three days earlier, the crew of Thru Hel'en Hiwater *board transport to Interrogation. On 22 April 1944, her hardstand remained empty.* (USAF Official)

Lieutenant William G Mackichan slipped his *Silver Queen* on to the recently-constructed emergency runway, as did First Lieutenant Walter L Harvey flying 42-97320. Neither crew suffered serious injury, but they were undoubtedly disgruntled by their Wing Leader's decision to fly at only 140 mph on the return journey. The 384BG crews felt this slower-than-necessary speed cost them considerable battle damage.

The 94th CBW was the penultimate First Air Division Wing over Hamm. Its three Groups — the 457BG, 401BG and 351BG — found their bombing accuracy challenged by defensive smoke pots and, even more so, from smoke created by the bombing. Sighting a clear spot in the northern part of Hamm itself, the 457BG released with "excellent" results. Emerging from the target, they incurred only minor flak damage, but their lead ship with the Commanding Officer, Lieutenant Colonel James R Luper, on board was forced to crash-land on return to Glatton. Once again, the vicissitudes of wind strength contributed to a change in bombing order and the 351BG high Group attacked next, followed by the 401BG. Both Groups shared a lull in defensive fire, perhaps caused by the need to cool the barrels of anti-aircraft guns whose crews were preparing for the 1st Combat Bombardment Wing, the ultimate force of Fortresses that evening.

Heralding the 1st CBW was the 91BG from Bassingbourn. Their record would ultimately include the distinction of suffering the highest losses for any Eighth Air Force bombardment Group. Behind the 91BG 'A' Group came the 381BG, followed by a 91/381BG composite Group. Sitting literally in the nose of this force was First Lieutenant John W Ryan, the Wing Lead Navigator who appreciated flak more than most because his career had encompassed two years' gunnery experience with US coastal defences. Ryan recalls, "I understood the gunners' situation, his capabilities and his limitations — in other words, I could navigate and think like a gunner". However, through no fault of his own, matters went drastically awry for him on this mission. He continues with his role and experiences on 22 April 1944: "As to my duties as Wing Lead Navigator, certain navigators and bombardiers were selected to fly in the lead ship along with most of the basic crew that flew the aircraft. Sometimes a staff member, Wing, Division or Group, went along as Command Pilot for the mission. Each of these lead people was an 'old head' or most qualified type in his field. I was a specialist in pin-point pilotage or visual navigation and was able to identify specific targets in the target area. Those of us who flew lead missions received special target training from Intelligence people — photos of the target area, special flak info and charts etc. It was our job to fly the best route under the conditions we found en route — avoid flak, fly evasive action, identify the target, direct the aircraft to a point where the bomb-aimer could get his Nordern bombsight cross-hairs on the Aiming Point, direct the evasive action away from the target and the Group home. An extra DR nav — Dead Reckoning navigator, usually a fairly new crew member or the regular navigator — went along to keep the navigation log, leaving the lead man free to move about, make observations, consult mission briefing materials, help the bomb-aimer in target identification etc. We who flew lead slots had a great deal greater knowledge of targeting, flak tactics, et al. Our tours lasted a bit longer because we did not fly every sortie. Each squadron had at least one navigator and bombardier moving toward Wing Lead position. I was to replace one, Bruce Moore, who was the number one Wing Lead Navigator when I joined the 401st Squadron. Bruce and I flew a couple of missions together before I was selected to train up to replace him. I enjoyed the job because of the greater feeling of being a vital cog in things and the greater freedom from normal duty. We flew fairly often on practise missions for the purpose of refining various air-techniques — turns for evasive action, Group assembly, practise bombing, special navigation techniques such as the use of the 'Gee' box . . . "

Ryan knew that enemy fire was often directed against the lead aircraft but felt there were factors which gave advantage to the fliers. The infamous 88 mm gun's rate of fire was about 20 rounds per minute but it had to cool for five minutes after every 25 rounds. It also took about 10 seconds for a shell to reach 25,000 feet and the aircraft would be moving at over 150 knots, so skilled use of the predictor was essential to calculate the future position of the target which might, of course, turn, dive or climb. Additionally, the projectile's course could vary slightly owing to wind velocity. John Ryan continues, "The ground fire control people had to put up a burst or two — usually one round each from a battery of four guns — to get a ranging burst into the air in the vicinity (hopefully) of the target aircraft. Knowing where the ranging batteries were was part of the lead navigator's responsibility and so was flying an irregular 's' pattern through such areas thus making targeting very much a chance of out-guessing the navigator on the part of the gunner and vice-versa. We had flown one of the first daylight raids on Berlin . . .

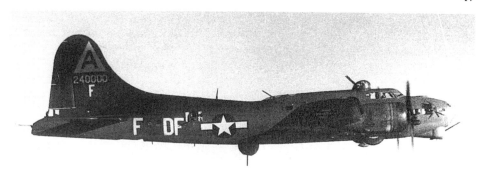

Just Nothing of the 91BG fell victim to flak because evasive action was not taken in time. (George W Parks)

and flew through flak for over 40 miles utilizing evasive action and watching massive barrages burst where the trackers predicted we would be based on their tracking information but where we weren't due to our evasive action — irregular turns of 10°, 15° and 20° designed to keep us close to track but never exactly repeating a manoeuvre. I had used the technique on several missions with great success. Flak is just another weapon with many limitations".

Captain Harvey G Hesse and crew, 324BS, 91BG, pose beneath Just Nothing. (USAF Official)

That evening, John Ryan was in the nose compartment of an early-model B-17G christened *Just Nothing*. This referred to the custom of denoting a ship by the last three digits of its serial number. More personally, an earlier crew had adorned *Just Nothing* with a saucy, Vargas girl nose-art based on a pin-up in the December 1943 issue of *Esquire*. Ryan remembers, "on 22 April the aircraft was assigned the lead position for the Wing and was manned by a composite crew. Major Charles Lee flew as Command Pilot, occupying the co-pilot seat, while Captain Harvey G Hesse flew in his usual position as pilot in his own aircraft. I flew as Wing Lead Navigator with Captain Provost Marshall as bombardier. We were to hit the marshalling yard about an hour before sunset . . . and make a beautiful run on the target, straddling the rail yard with our bombs. At 'bombs away' we were to execute a 15° turn to the left to begin our post-release evasive action for flak, but when I looked at the compass a few seconds after the bombs went I realized that we were still in level flight, so I called for the turn. We will never know what happened in the cockpit, but there was some confusion, and the aircraft continued on course.

"About 10 seconds after 'bombs away' the bombardier and I both noted a flak burst a few hundred yards ahead, followed by a second and a third, each splitting the distance. We were flying right on to them. We weren't really surprised when the fourth one hit us. We'd been able to see the red flashes when they burst, they were that close. The hit was directly between the engines on the right wing. The burst was deafening and the aircraft immediately filled with dense, black smoke. We heard Charlie Lee call into the intercom, 'Hey, there's a fire in this aircraft somewhere'. Perhaps two or three seconds later, 'Jesus Christ! Get the hell out of this airplane!'

"In the nose compartment, now nearly black with smoke, I could see my assistant navigator, First Lieutenant Jay H Suldan, groping for his chest pack under the navigation table. I saw that the bombardier was buckling his 'chute on as he moved away from his position at the bombsight. Since I was wearing a back-pack, I was free to go and so was the first to get to the escape hatch in the bottom of the aircraft just aft of the nose compartment. I jerked on the emergency handle several times, skinning my knuckles a bit in the process, before I realized that the release cable that ran to the pins in the hatch hinges was frozen solid in the channel along the airframe ahead of the hatch. (We used to use a spare steel helmet as a urinal and would set it on the floor aft of the navigation table where it would freeze. Then as we descended to warmer air it would thaw and we could dump it out, or if it did not thaw we would knock the block of frozen stuff out on the ramp when we landed. Those aircraft were not fitted with many conveniences.) Since the hatch would not release, I proceeded to open it with the normal handle — that meant swinging the door open against the slip-stream, as the hinges were on the leading edge. I wriggled out through the hatch into the rushing wind and dropped clear. That was the last I saw of *Just Nothing*.

"I tumbled for some seconds before I straightened out to stabilize my fall and see where I was headed. I was a lot more interested in the ground below than in anything above me and was only vaguely aware of the formation of aircraft that were rapidly disappearing. I could see that I was falling toward the centre of a large lake, the Mohne Stausee, and pulled the rip-cord at about 10,000 feet by my rough guess. (We had bombed at 22,000 feet altitude.) As I had hoped, I drifted with the wind on across the lake and landed in a wood perhaps a mile from the shore. The trees were very tall. As I plummeted into them the 'chute spilled and I dropped quite a distance straight down through the branches, making a very hard landing. I heard a loud snap! and I didn't have to be told that I had broken my right leg. I wasn't going anywhere, so I got rid of my gun and sheath knife and a few odds and ends that I found in my pockets that didn't appear to be useful any more. I was captured a half hour later by a farmer on 'home guard' duty while lying quietly there in the woods as twilight fell. My capture was not a very military-like event. The female members of the family that owned the farm got a small wagon and helped me to the farmhouse where we all drank a few toasts to the end of the war with wine that was brought up from the cellar. The proper military authorities had been called and a couple of soldiers were sent to bring in the 'terror flieger'. They had to get in on the party, and by the time they took me in it was far into the night and no-one was feeling any pain.

"At a hospital where I was taken to treat the broken leg I learned that an airman had been found dangling from his 'chute in a large tree, dead from a massive head injury, apparently suffered when he swung into the bole of the tree, striking his head on the stub of a broken limb. The nurse who told me of this thought the man's name was Williams".

Technical Sergeant Charles E Williams was the top-turret gunner on *Just Nothing*. Ryan continues, "A year later I met Charlie Lee who told me he had left his seat and climbed down into the cat-walk leading to the nose hatch when the aircraft exploded. He subsequently found himself floating with his 'chute open and one leg dangling loose. He landed without further incident, was immediately captured and learned he had a broken hip. He was still in a cast a year later. He said that Captain Hesse was still on the flight deck, possibly still in his seat, when the aircraft blew. Had Captain Hesse taken the correct turn after 'bombs away' we would have been on a heading of at least 20° left and thus hundreds of yards from the shell bursts which we flew into . . . a simple oversight that cost him his life".

Just Nothing fell near the town of Belecke and was the final Fortress victim for those defending Hamm. The concluding blows from the First Air Division were delivered by the 381BG and the 91BG 'B' Group with results "believed to be good". Now approaching Hamm came Liberators of the Second Air Division.

•CHAPTER SIX•

Divided Division

AT 1130 THE agitated chatter of teleprinters presaged later events. Field Order number 269 was received by Combat Wings of the Second Air Division from their HQ at Ketteringham Hall. Alerted for its arrival, Watch Officers and Duty Clerks saw the first lines of print stuttering coded references, then promising that fighter support details would follow. Noting the departure times for their sister divisions, the Field Order summoned four Combat Bombardment Wings — the 2nd, 14th, 20th and 96th — to attack Hamm. Speeding with noisy authority, the print head danced out secondary and last resort targets codes, Group positions, numbers of squadrons and aircraft required. It rattled through routes and timings with Buncher and Splasher details — both were forms of transmitter used for assembly by bombers homing on their signals and following prescribed procedures for forming up.

Under the heading of "Bombing" the teleprinter provided altitudes and the code word "Black Jack" for visual bombing in squadron order. If PFF conditions prevailed, bombing would be by CBW on the receipt of code-word "Madhatter". Intervalometer settings were given as "Minimum" — the intervalometer on each aircraft signalled the release system and could set time delays between the release of bombs or be used on minimum to salvo the bombload. Zero hour would be 1730 DBST. This enabled groups to plan individual details based on a common reference time. For the 2nd, 14th and 20th CBWs, bomb loads were to be 36 x 100 lb GP (General Purpose) bombs fused 1/10-1/100 of a second on impact plus one M17 IB fused to burst at 6,000 feet. For the 96th CBW, five squadrons would carry maximum loading of 500 lb GP bombs. Busily continuing, the incoming signal assigned PFF aircraft supplied to other CBWs by the 389BG, and fighter reference points. Then it stated, "This operation is a comparative test between effectiveness of 100 lb GP and 500 lb GP on this type of target . . ." Spilling more paper came instructions for communications channels; navigational aids; details for dispensing Chaff and the assignment of call-signs; then a peremptory silence. There would follow more cascaded commands originating from "Pinetrees" — HQ of the Eighth Air Force — but, for now, the disembodied authority was silent.

From the recipient Operations Buildings on B-24 bases, orders fanned out. Scenes usually depicted in darkness today occurred in daylight as target folders were pulled and specialists prepared their briefings on weather conditions, navigational pinpoints, flak areas, bomb-loads, formations and, from senior officers, the purpose of today's assault on Hamm. Outside, ordnance, oxygen and fuel trucks trundled to Liberators, dormant on their hardstands for these infusions of modern warfare. On 11 airfields, the squat slab-sided bombers received homage from overalled technicians tasked with transforming them into armed and laden war gods.

At 1305, annex number one to Field Order 269 arrived giving fighter support information before clarifying routes and timings. Forty minutes later came further details on using GEE and flares for "colours of the day". Firm advice was given that, "Briefing should stress adherence to prescribed route to avoid defence between IP and target". In other words, avoid the Ruhr valley defences. Some minutes later, Tibenham's telex confirmed the 445BG's distinction as leader of the 2nd CBW and the entire Second Air Division. Green and red flares were to be fired from the 445BG lead ship as an assembly aid at 14,000 feet over the airfield. Assembly and formation order signals were also received by other groups — the 389BG to form over Hethel at 13,000 using red flares; the 453BG over Old Buckenham at 15,000 on green flares. All three would begin merging into Wing formation over buncher 6. Other CBW allocations rattled off the printer, easy on paper but a continuing challenge for the skills and experience of the airmen involved. 14CBW: the 392BG from Wendling to lead the neighbouring 44BG from Shipdham. 20CBW: the 448BG from Seething to lead, stacked high right would be the 93BG, Hardwick, and the 446BG aloft from Flixton flew low left. Finally, the 96CBW, the Norwich area groups lead by the 458BG from Horsham St Faith with the 467BG "Rackheath Aggies" high right and the 466BG from Attlebridge flying low left in the familiar slanted wedge formation.

The signal from 20 CBW headquarters even named the colourful "assembly ships" used by its groups to facilitate formation assembly. These were war-weary B-24Ds stripped of armaments and given garish, high-visibility colour schemes for their flocks to easily follow. *You Can't Miss It*, brightly checkerboarded by the 448BG, would lead followed 1,000 feet above by the 93BG's *Ball of Fire*, striped like a black, white and yellow circus marquee. The 446BG's lemon yellow contribution, *Fearless Freddie*, would position himself 1,500 feet lower and astern of *You Can't Miss It*. The 448BG was allocated the bombing altitude of 22,000 feet, with the 446BG at 21,000 feet, and the 93BG at 22,500 feet. After release, groups would make a descending starboard turn and shed 4,000 feet in a flak evasion tactic. Similar manoeuvres were transmitted to other CBWs, and all groups were provided with fuel load figures, typically 2,500 gallons per aircraft. Division assembly was advised as "Buncher 5, Splasher 6, Lowestoft 15,000 feet altitude. Order

Garishly-coloured, war-weary Liberators were used to aid mission assembly. The 93BG's Ball of Fire *was striped like a circus marquee.* (USAF Official)

of Wings will be 2nd, 20th, 14th, and 96th. All Wings flying in trail at three minute intervals. This will put the 96th Combat Wing nine minutes behind the Lead Wing".

Such planning detail did not deserve the divisional disarray which followed. Nor does the author wish any discredit for those leading the Second Air Division. The researcher's perspective is comfortably distanced from the drama and decisions facing men in combat conditions.

The troubles that initiated many subsequent problems occurred in the 2 CBW lead ship. Its radar apparently failed, the flux-gate compass became unserviceable and the pilotage and dead-reckoning navigators disagreed over their position. Because of this, the Combat Wing IP was missed and the leading 445BG took some of the force within range of deadly artillery defending the industrial Ruhr Valley. When the author contacted the pilotage-navigator, he also alluded to the effect of wind strength and a short dog-leg in the planned course prior to the IP as mitigating circumstances. The subsequent confusion was summarized by Colonel Charles B Westover, Chief of Staff at HQ 2nd Bombardment Division in a report dated 16 May 1944: "The 2nd Combat Wing, in lead of the Division, entered the enemy coast slightly south of course, and, due to an error in judgement of distance on the part of the pilotage-navigator, turned south short of the Combat Wing IP with the 14th Combat Wing in trail. Upon reaching what was believed from pilotage observation to be the Combat Wing IP, the formation was over the Ruhr Valley and exposed to heavy flak. At this point, the 2nd Combat Wing split up into two sections; the first composed of the 445th and one half of the 453rd Group turned left to attempt an attack on the primary from the southwest; the second section, composed of the 389th and the remainder of the 453rd, made a 360° turn to the right to make its run on the target as briefed. Upon entering the Ruhr valley, the 14th Combat Wing broke off from the 2nd Combat Wing and made a run on the primary from the west. The 20th and 96th Combat Wings flew the entire route as briefed.

"In the 2nd Combat Wing, the 389th and the first Squadron of the 453rd Group bombed Hamm with good to poor results. Due to other Combat Wings coming into the primary, the 445th Group and the 2nd Squadron of the 453rd Group could not bomb Hamm and attacked the last resort target at Koblenz with fair results. In the 14th Combat Wing, the 44th Group and the Second Squadron of the 392nd Group bombed Hamm with poor results. The first Squadron of the 392nd was forced to give way to the 20th Combat Wing coming in on its briefed run and bombed a target of opportunity at Swevecelle with unobserved results. Hamm was attacked with good to fair results by the 20th Combat Wing, the 467th Bomb Group, one squadron of the 466th and one squadron of the 458th. The other squadrons of the 466th and 458th Groups experienced difficulty in picking up the target because of smoke and haze and bombed the last resort target at Koblenz with fair results . . ."

Hidden between Westover's unemotional lines are stories of airmen facing the vicissitudes of war with typical courage and stoicism. First Lieutenant Edward W Sadlon and crew's 26th mission promised to be as rough as any since their first with the 445BG four months earlier. Leading the Group, and the Division, Colonel Robert H Terrill's crew had realized their navigational error and banked the formation to approach Hamm from the Dusseldorf area. Now, within range of the Ruhr's notorious defences, the embattled bomber crews rode in defiant procession through flak-riddled skies. German gunners of the 4/Flak Division could see their targets silhouetted against the high cirrus but the enemy aircraft seemed frustratingly impervious as repeated fire left barrels hot and soldiers sweating. Suddenly, one of the bombers faltered, as if tripped. Then it began to fall.

Sadlon's ship was slammed by the exploding shell and he knew almost instantly that the blow was fatal. Their intercom had malfunctioned earlier in the mission but, even if the bale-out alarm was unheard, the Liberator's steepening fall signified the end. From the rear fuselage, all four gunners emerged safely as other crewmen simultaneously leapt from the forward hatch. Delay meant death and the navigator, Second Lieutenant Marlin F Kulp, left it too late. He may have been wounded or stunned by flak and uncertainty surrounds his departure from the doomed bomber. One unsubstantiated story claims Kulp was blown clear when the aircraft exploded just prior to impact but his body fell into the burning wreckage. This may account for the German authorities taking several weeks to identify his remains which were originally interred as an unknown airman in the community cemetery at Willich. The destruction of the Liberator was so complete that it was first thought to be a Flying Fortress. Of the other crew members, only First Lieutenant Erwin J

Carle was injured when he fractured his right foot on landing.

For another 445BG crew, flak also set in motion a train of events leading to murder — and accounts of tremendous courage shown by airmen shot down on their first mission. Staff Sergeants Robert M Varty and John F Mahoney were respectively the radio operator and a waist gunner on the more experienced First Lieutenant Francis C Sneed's crew. The two tiros could be forgiven for their agitation that day, but even Frank Sneed felt uneasy about the mission. The radio's cheerful rendition of "Mairzy Dotes" appeared mocking as they left Tibenham's operations building and the confusion en route did nothing to bolster morale. Frank was further dismayed to find his group's approach to Hamm baulked by other groups, because the 445BG's late arrival now conflicted with groups keeping time. To avoid the risk of collision, the truncated 2nd CBW turned towards Koblenz and bombed at 1956 hours. Shortly after release, Sneed's foreboding flashed into violent reality when his Liberator shuddered from the punching blast of shells erupting in close proximity. Shrapnel scorched viciously into the starboard wing taking out their number three Twin Wasp which surged uncontrollably and had to be feathered. Seconds later, the number one engine quit but would not feather, its three weighty Hamilton-Standard propeller blades now dragging like anchors. From anxious waist gunners came the ominous news that both gasoline and oil were leaking.

First Lieutenant Frank C Sneed felt uneasy about the mission — he had every reason to. (Susan Sneed-Bailey)

Increasing the manifold pressure on his good engines, Frank Sneed sought to hold formation, but it was hopeless and he dropped astern calling for fighter support. Shepherded by P-47s, he felt reassured until the number two engine ran away and was feathered. Their rate of sink increased. Even discarding guns, ammunition and other equipment failed to alleviate the relentless pull of gravity overwhelming their last good engine. Straining all 1200 hp was proving too much as cylinder head temperatures ascended the scale. Near Spiere in Belgium, Sneed admitted defeat when a small fire developed in the right wing. Transmitting to his departing group, he wished them well and announced his intention to bale out. Thanking the Thunderbolts for their help, he gave the order to abandon aircraft and an orderly departure ensued. Sneed's last conscientious act of concern for his crew was to set the B-24 on auto-pilot and personally check each had departed. There was nothing he could do about the problems into which Varty and Mahoney would descend.

Frank Sneed landed near Otegem and was quickly captured. But finding some other members of his crew proved difficult for the Germans because they were spirited away by the underground. Sadly, collaborationists penetrated elements of the Resistance and Varty was arrested on 16 May near Arras. With him were Second Lieutenants Charles L Riddle, the co-pilot, Ray O Hargis, navigator, and John W Bryant, the bombardier. All were in civilian clothing and confined to the same cell at the Luftwaffe headquarters in Arras. Later that day a German officer removed Varty for interrogation but returned alone stating that the radio operator had been taken sick suddenly and sent to hospital. A weekly report for the Wermacht Information Centre from Army Field Hospital 9/XI (Arras) shows Robert C Varty being admitted on 16 May 1944. Translated, the record reads, "shot through the chest and belly. Bleeding into right chest-hole. Shot through cardiac region, milt, liver and stomach". He died the following afternoon. As he had been taken from his comrades, alone, unarmed but in good health, the strong conclusion to be drawn is that he was murdered during a ghastly process of interrogation.

The fate of John Mahoney illustrates his tenacity in continuing to confront his adversaries, not from the relative detachment of a B-24 but at very much closer quarters. Accompanied by the tail-gunner, Sergeant James R Cockriel, Mahoney evaded capture and was hidden by the Resistance near Ingooigem in Belgium. Father Rathe, priest for the community, later related how both men took up arms with their Belgian comrades until 6 September 1944. That day, Mahoney tried warning an approaching British Army spearhead about the proximity of strong German forces but was discovered along with other men of the Resistance. They were surrounded and out-gunned. A bitter battle ensued during which Cockriel was wounded, but survived. Captured with the brave Belgian freedom-fighters, Mahoney stood proudly with their number who were lined up in the Spitaal woods at Waregem and executed. For him, the sequence of events originating in a navigational error on Mission 311 had taken six months to reach a tragic denouement in a Belgian ditch.

When the 2nd CBW split, the rift occurred through ranks of 453BG bombers leaving some attached to the 445BG and others with the 389BG. *Cee Gee II* led the second element of the 453BG 'A' Squadron and kept with the 445BG. Further problems were encountered on the bombing run when this squadron found itself nipped away from its parent wing by other bombers converging on Hamm. Still managing to strike the primary at 1940, the now isolated 453BG Liberators attempted to catch a formation they believed were the 445BG but were unable to catch up so linked with another CBW for protection. The second section of the 453BG also experienced difficulties when they found the low left element of the 389BG obscuring their sights and in

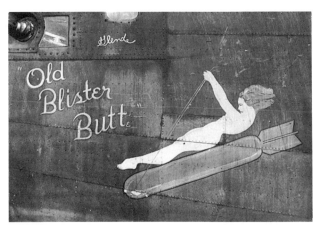

Smoke was too dense to observe results when the 389BG released over Hamm. 42-40776 Old Blister Butt *was one of only three B-24Ds in the 389BG formation.* (M J Bailey)

danger from the fall of "friendly" bombs. Aborting their release over Hamm these 453BG aircraft attacked the marshalling yards in Koblenz at 2008. Those 453BG ships which adhered to the 389BG were led by Lieutenant Colonel Paul T Burton as 389BG Command Pilot on Captain Willard P Stotter's crew. With mounting apprehension, Lieutenant Colonel Burton loyally maintained position after his Combat Wing Leader's navigational error until they were some 30 miles south off course and already in the clutches of guns protecting the Ruhr. Increasingly intense flak had damaged several ships and killed Staff Sergeant James R Rowland, a photographer on First Lieutenant C D Van Horne's crew.

Rather than run the gauntlet of continuing along the Ruhr, Burton advised Colonel Terrill of his position and stated he was withdrawing the 389BG to return to the approach briefed for Hamm. Wheeling a full circle right, the 389BG avoided further torment, but Burton's own ship now sustained severe damage making unlikely his chances of reaching home. Most of the crew baled out near Dortmund. However, Burton, Stotter and the bombardier, First Lieutenant Myron Gins struggled to accomplish their mission. Flames streamed from the number four engine as they neared Hamm still valiantly holding formation. One minute from release, the battle-worn bomber slid wearily aside, an ageing thoroughbred beaten near the line on its last race. Descending in a broad circle beneath the following bombers, Burton's ship was soon lost from view as the deputy lead, Captain Max E van Benthuyser, sought to take over. They were only a minute from release when bombardier, First Lieutenant W E Fowler found thrust upon him the responsibility for the accuracy of the Group's bombing. Hastily manipulating his AFCE, he triggered their release into the cauldron over Hamm. Smoke was too dense to observe results. Surprisingly, Stotter, Burton, and Gins kept aloft as far as Antwerp where they abandoned the burning bomber.

Heading westwards, the main 389BG was nearing the coast when there was a hint of things to come. Staff Sergeant Vernal L Boline, tail gunner on *Sack Warmer*, recalls, "Over enemy territory after leaving the target, I happened to see two fighters with the blue sky behind them between two clouds going towards 6 o'clock. As I was in the tail turret, they were higher than us and to my right. I knew they were Germans but, to alert the crew, I asked the navigator (Second Lieutenant Frederick A Heckmann) if we were supposed to have any fighter escort. He, of course, answered 'no' so I told them on the intercom about the two fighters and I would have everything set to fire at them if they turned round and came back at us. It seemed like eternity and the thought crossed my mind that they might have been low on fuel and were returning to their base. All of a sudden I saw behind us two wings light up and knew the fighters had turned around to attack us, but they were actually firing at the three planes of the three plane element to my left. Big round flashes of light were exploding near the three planes — 20 mm cannon I believe — so I started firing though I could not see the two fighters. I changed my firing, a little higher, and level, and a little lower with each burst. It wasn't long before I saw one German diving out of the darkness a little to my right. I gave him a large lead and slowly closed it with burst after burst and knew he would have to fly into it. When I believed my lead was correct, I followed him down until my twin .50 calibre machine guns hit the gun stops. Just then I noticed the other German fighter coming out of the darkness and I did exactly the same thing. After flying about two or three minutes there came into view two fires on the ground so I knew I had got them and hoped they were able to bale out. I never put in a claim for the two German fighters I am sure I shot down".

B-24s in subsequent CBWs were to suffer not only flak but more seriously from fighter attacks over Europe. Now entering the arena came the 14 CBW structured from the 392BG and 44BG with Lieutenant Colonel Warren A Polking, 392BG, as Command Pilot. Polking became increasingly dismayed with his Group's performance and that of the Division itself. His misgivings began when he observed the 2 CBW ahead "become badly stretched out and considerably right of course". This irritation increased when some 2 CBW aircraft, realizing the error, now swung left so their flight paths interfered with his own 14 CBW which he felt was on course and on time. To alleviate the situation, Polking was forced left of course into an area charted relatively flak-free, his intention being to uncover on the first right turn. However, the 2 CBW's next error solved some of his problem when it turned right early, enabling Polking to continue untroubled by errant aircraft from the preceding Wing.

However, it was now clear the 2 CBW were leading them straight into the Ruhr's explosive embrace. Polking started to call Terrill but heard Lieutenant Colonel Burton warn the Division Leader. Flak from the Ruhr's fringes was already intensifying and Polking now decided to break from the Division Leader's erroneous route, but he needed navigational confirmation for his decision. A quick conference with his navigator

The crew of Sack Warmer. *Standing L-R: Frederick A Heckman, Navigator; Leo J Oras, Pilot; William W Garrett, Bombardier; William H Rooney, Co-Pilot. Kneeling: Frederick H Potter, Waist Gunner; Donal W Cutter, Engineer; Martin M Weinstein, Radio; Wilford Brown, Waist Gunner; Vernal L Boline, Tail Gunner; James W Braa; Ball Turret Gunner.* (V L Boline)

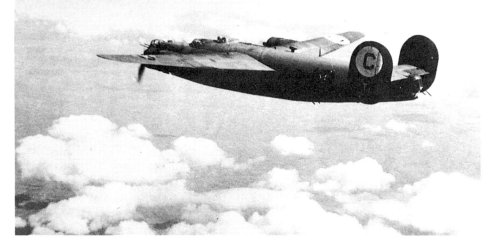

B-24J 42-100190 Princess Konocti *389BG was flown by First Lieutenant Vivian M Jerrold and crew. Attacked over the continent,* Princess Konocti *escaped damage. Pictures show nose art carried on port and starboard sides.* (M J Bailey)

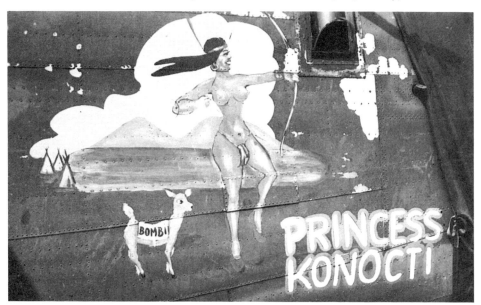

ensued and the dead reckoning navigator, First Lieutenant W F McShane, calculated that a 300 mph groundspeed had carried them beyond the combat wing IP, and felt an immediate alteration of course was essential to avoid altogether missing the primary target. Perched as pilotage-navigator in the nose turret, First Lieutenant Q C Hurdle pinpointed their position and agreed with McShane. Further confirmation came from flickering images on the scope of their ground-reading radar. Making his decision, Polking issued instructions to his CBW and banked steadily to port. They were now only two minutes short of the Group IP, and Hamm lay dead ahead. Transmitting the IP code-word and firing red flares, Polking signalled for bomb doors open and they rattled apart allowing the gentle evening light to expose the bomb bay's ugly brood. Second Lieutenant Orland H Hasselbach now assumed control via the A5 autopilot and began the bomb-run. In greeting, ferocious flak tore away the evening's touch of tranquillity and made the air writhe as shockwaves shuddered through the air frame. Suddenly Polking's B-24 was slammed violently from course, the number four engine spat flames and a large hole appeared in their starboard wing. Fighting for control, they were fortunate the fire did not take hold, but his crew were understandably shaken and Polking could get no response from anyone aft of the cockpit. Several attempts to raise his formation control officer proved fruitless and he then saw his deputy lead pull up and over to port giving Polking the impression the other B-24 was going out of control.

Events were swift and chaotic. Still unable to raise the crew, Polking and Captain L J Barnes were fully occupied getting back on the bomb-run. This was achieved but less than five seconds from release the bombsight itself was struck. Hastily salvoing their bombs, Hasselbach was unable to prevent the damaged bombsight's link to the autopilot from throwing the B-24 into a steep, starboard peel off. A sickening 1,000 foot drop occurred before control was regained and, as the ship levelled off, Polking finally raised his formation control officer only to learn they were alone. Flying to the rally point, Polking circled like a perplexed shepherd who had lost his flock. Somewhat irate, he instructed the radio operator to transmit their situation to Division but the Technical Sergeant pleaded that his hands were frozen. Finally, the disconsolate commander set a lonely course homewards until able to link with a B-17 formation for security. After the mission, he questioned both the formation control officer and radio operator about their lack of response. The officer said, "When I saw all that flak, I pulled my helmet down over my head and ducked into the bottom of the airplane and starting throwing out chaff". Polking's conclusion was that "all personnel in the back of the ship were suffering from a bad case of fright".

Fear and confusion in those flak-scarred skies can be understood. The 392 BG's approach was so disrupted that the first squadron failed to release on Hamm and Polking's abrupt departure created the impression he was going down. Assuming control, the deputy leader was too late to

The 392BG's approach was so disrupted that the first squadron failed to release on Hamm. Amongst those aircraft was 41-29433 (nearest camera) flown by First Lieutenant W E Mathias and crew. (J Bailey)

effect an attack on the primary and they eventually bombed the aerodrome at Chievres leaving large fires and a pall of smoke from burning fuel or ordnance stores plus one hangar in ruins. The second 392BG section which did release over Hamm was led by Captain Wyeth C Everhart. He would soon have his own serious problems.

Having trailed the 392BG towards the Ruhr, the 44BG also acted independently and turned away from the dense flak to make a second run on Hamm from the south. Three Liberators strayed during this process and eventually linked themselves to the 446BG. The main 44BG encountered only meagre flak when they released over Hamm at 1938 hours, eight minutes after the 392BG.

A homeward heading into the setting sun might seem picturesque but it disadvantaged the Liberators whose crews feared a classic "Hun from

Axis Grinder *was taken over the target by Lieutenant Johnson and crew.*

The Schildknecht crew in front of their regular aircraft. Rear L-R: Riley Sadler, Engineer; Al Hersh, Navigator; Hal Schildknecht, Pilot; Jesse Long, Co-Pilot; Marion Wasowicz, Bombardier; George Gegere, Waist Gunner. Front: B P Reed, Tail Gunner; Harry Reid, Ball Turret; J F Begley, Radio; "Jnr" Reade, Waist Gunner. Piloted by Second Lieutenant C Slafka, Double Trouble *was forced to abort Mission 311 when a dynamotor failed.*

the Sun" attack by enemy fighters. The Me109 and FW190 pilots of JG3 would ensure they would not be disappointed. To pilot, First Lieutenant Harold E Schildknecht, the distant dots appeared to be P-51s but he was puzzled by their odd weaving and strung-out formation. Manning the controls, his co-pilot, First Lieutenant Jesse D Long Jr, had no doubts. They were Me109s — over 30 of them, preparing to attack like fast ponied Indians against a wagon train. Alerted by the pilots, Second Lieutenant Marion V "Paddy" Wasowicz squeezed off the opening rounds from his nose turret as the first fighters curved and came slanting in. Paddy's discouraging tracers arced outwards intending to deter and encourage the selection of a target less alert. Keeping the B-24 a steady gun-platform, Jesse watched the tracers race sunwards and jumped as a deafening crash close overhead announced the first contribution from their top-turret gunner, Staff Sergeant Riley E Sadler.

As formation flying in a Liberator was tiring, the two pilots had established a 10 minutes each routine. This now left Hal Schildknecht with no immediate role other than to burrow into his seat, exposing as little of his body as possible above the instrument panel. Crouching as low as he could, he saw the swarm spread into line abreast, selecting

their intended victims. Two '109s clearly chose them. Calmly, Jesse told
Paddy to take care of the first, 12 o'clock high, while he would evade
the second speeding in high from 12.30. Closing at some 600 mph
demanded nerve-wracking judgement on both sides. At 800 yards, Hal
saw rapid blinks of light from the leading edge of the first fighter and an
array of greyish coloured bursts appeared above and ahead. Perhaps
deterred by Paddy's challenge, the first '109 missed. Pulling up to
correct, the pilot had no time and dived abruptly, narrowly avoiding a
collision. Paddy was confident he hit it — could Jesse elude its partner?
A microsecond's miscalculation might now hold their lives. Not yet. Not
yet. *Now.* As the '109 fired, Jesse shoved full right rudder then rammed
the control wheel forward, brutishly forcing the ship to slew and dip. In
testimony to the close timing, vicious lines of tracer whipped over their
starboard wing, cutting only sky where it had been. The fighter skidded,
trying to increase his dive and counteract the manoeuvring bomber. Too
close. Too late. It vanished. Then they were hit. Six cannon shells
smashed along the port side.

Avoiding one assault, they had seemingly slid into the line of fire
intended for someone else. With an ear-splitting roar, the first shell burst
through the cockpit window on Hal's side; number two exploded in the
port outer Twin Wasp causing flames to flash back over 60 feet beyond
Technical Sergeant Burwin P Reed in the rear turret; the third ripped
into the fuselage near Sadler's position; number four tore in forward of
Staff Sergeants George P Gegere and George J Reade in the waist; the
fifth gouged in just behind them, and the sixth slammed in near Reed.
Somehow, the reeling ship levelled and stayed airborne as its crew
reacted to damage and injuries. Schildknecht had been severely wounded
in the left back and shoulder when the first shell blew shrapnel, glass
and fragments of window framing into the cockpit. Jesse saw Hal thrown
forward, striking his head on his control wheel as the flight deck filled
with swirling, grey smoke. Dazed and shaken, Schildknecht strove to co-
ordinate his senses against an increasing awareness that he had been hit
— and the engines' howl seemed closer but screechingly discordant. Like
a man in his own nightmare, Hal wanted to reach for the intercom
button on his control-wheel but his left arm stubbornly refused to
respond.

Through the haze, he saw Jesse trying to maintain formation and did
not realise his co-pilot had also been wounded. Although shielded by
Hal, Jesse was peppered with debris and one dime-sized fragment of
window frame embedded itself in his upper left arm. Luckily, the injury
was slight and Jesse's response to their situation was unimpaired. Hal
saw him take his hand from the throttles and gesture towards the
instrument panel. Still dazed, Hal took a moment to comprehend, and
he struggled to distinguish the instruments indicated by Jesse. Focusing
through waves of shock and pain, Hal understood why the engines had
de-synchronised — manifold gauge readings confirmed one was dead
and another pulling only partial power. He knew the necessary actions

but still his left hand remained lifeless. Recognizing that Hal was badly wounded, Jesse reached for the mixture control and closed off the fuel supply to number one just as Hal reacted using his good right hand. Stretching across, Hal pressed the feathering button but, bewildered by his injuries, he pushed the wrong one, feathering their still-functioning number two engine. For a few, grim seconds, port-side power faded completely. Knocking aside Hal's hand, Jesse hit the correct button for number one, unfeathered number two, compensated for yaw with rudder and advanced power on the starboard engines. Already, they had fallen even further from the formation's protection. Straining on the rudder pedal with his right foot, Jesse attempted to set trim but there was no response from the trim wheel on his control console. At best, its mocking freespin meant flying would be difficult, but it might also indicate control cable damage further aft. Thankfully, the fire in number one engine had blown itself out and the fighters had vanished allowing some respite for assessing injuries and damage. Hal had taken the brunt of the blast. There was freezing air now whipping inboard from a three inch diameter hole punched through the armoured glass of his side window. Although cracked and crazed, this protection had clearly saved his life, but he had been grievously wounded by shrapnel. One possible benefit from the frozen air hitting Hal's back was faster coagulation of the blood. All Hal could feel was a numbness and detached sense of frustration over the failure to respond of his left, upper arm. When he pivoted his head to view the extent of his wounds it proved impossibly painful, creating an inward terror of permanent paralysis. Concentrating his actions, Hal was profoundly relieved to be able to manipulate his left hand and forearm, although the hand itself was now completely numb. With his crew in no immediate danger and cognizant that his injuries impaired judgement, Hal calmly reported his wounds and relinquished command to Jesse after requesting a status report from each of his crew.

Aware that learning both their pilots were wounded might worry the crew, Jesse said nothing about his own shoulder, even though blood now trickled down the inside of his jacket. No other wounds were reported, but the radio operator, Staff Sergeant John F Begley, had been donning his flak helmet when they were hit, and suffered a line of tiny pellets in the nape of his neck, unprotected below the rim of his helmet. His back-pack parachute, now riddled with fragments, had provided some unorthodox protection. Despite absorbing six cannon shells, the battered bomber held its rivets together and continued puffing along on two-and-a-bit engines. Then, from the rear turret, Reed reported enemy fighters approaching from 6 o'clock. Another damaged Liberator had also fallen behind the formation and Jesse knew two stragglers were easy fodder for a pack of '109s. Not wishing to advertise his plight, he unfeathered number one allowing its wind-milling propeller to simulate a good engine while increasing power on the others. Bracing themselves, they prepared for a one-sided combat as the fighters pulled into range — and transformed into robust and friendly Thunderbolts. Even the ship seemed relieved as Jesse re-feathered number one to continue the aching application of constant right aileron and rudder, at times using both feet on one pedal. Now able to leave his guns, Sadler came forward with a morphine syrette for Schildknecht. The diminishing numbness and shock produced spasms of increased pain, giddiness and nausea accompanied by a raging thirst. His wounds needed urgent, professional medical attention so the decision was taken to set the straightest course across northern Belgium to the English channel, then opt for the narrowest crossing.

Still flying nearby was their companion invalid, now identified as 42-52605, GC-E, piloted by Captain Wyeth C Everhart, also from Wendling. Leading the second 392BG squadron, Everhart had been caught in the same attack and his number four engine was still burning. Four of his crew had already baled out leaving eight on board including two passengers. Comforting each other, the two cripples crawled coastwards, slowly erasing each uncertain mile. A combination of morphine and full-rich oxygen stupefied Hal, inducing behaviour akin to inebriation. His renditions of *Show Me The Way To Go Home* became increasingly slurred, as did some accompanying expletives although, even now, the more extreme profanities were censored by his inherently polite personality. That morning, the crew had heard of a new policy whereby crews volunteering for a second tour of combat duty became immediately eligible for 30 days "R and R" (Rest and Recuperation). Several times, Hal loudly announced his intention of volunteering, defiantly proclaiming that, "those Jerries can't do this to me" as the morphine wore off, his pain increased and his mind wandered in the dream-like realms of semi-consciousness. His condition created anxiety. So did the evidently ailing flight of Everhart's B-24. A homebound P-47 provided limited escort and, before diminishing fuel reserves forced the fighter's departure, Everhart asked the Thunderbolt pilot to check over his B-24, especially the still-burning starboard wing. The fighter pilot's prognosis confirmed there was little time left, the fire was gnawing through the wing and its fuel tanks would explode at any second. There was no alternative. Everhart ordered those remaining on board to bale out. The two B-24s were now approaching the Belgian coast and Reed again became alarmed by the approach of another unidentified fighter. The tail gunner called for evasive action and, despite fears of control-cable damage and the Liberator's basic structural integrity, Jesse corkscrewed — a twisting stomach-churning tactic timed to evade fire from an attacking fighter. This action shed some 500 feet height only to establish their potential assailant as a P-47. The manoeuvre also distanced them from Everhart's B-24 and, shortly after crossing the coast, they witnessed his right wing flare into a mass of yellow flames. Banking to starboard, the defeated aircraft swung majestically towards land and began its final flight. Everhart was captured near Oostkerke, close to the crash site of his Liberator.

Outbound, Jesse always regarded the channel as cold and treacherous. But its demeanour was transformed into "as friendly as a back-yard pool" on the homeward journey and he felt pleased to see it glistening in the late evening sun as he began letting down towards the black landcast ahead. The long, blinding sun dazzled into the cockpit making it impossible to read the flight instruments, so Jesse asked the navigator, First Lieutenant Alfred Hersh, to call in with height and airspeed from duplicate instruments in the nose. Thinking the flight deck's instruments had been shot out, Al overdid the input, his voice tinged with alarm until Jesse explained the problem and called for a heading to the nearest airbase. In calmer tones, Al directed Jesse towards the grass-surfaced RAF fighter field at Hawkinge, just across the Kentish coast. Begley established radio contact. He also picked up r/t communications from anxious aircrews further north, afraid they were being stalked by intruders. The nervous chatter claimed German fighters could be seen taking off and calling for fighter support, but there was little that could be done to offer protection. American fighters were not equipped for night flying and echoes from the returning bombers swamped British radar.

Jesse realized their own course spared this anxiety. But he now faced landing a battle-damaged bomber which *might* have brakes, in semi-darkness on a postage stamp airfield with his pilot seriously wounded. Refusing further morphine, Hal fought the pain, struggling to gather his wits and contribute to the landing. Jesse was reluctant, however, because Hal still seemed dazed and disorientated. Worried about the potential loss of hydraulic fluid, Jesse asked Sadler to hand crank down their undercarriage and not to select flaps, hopefully preserving hydraulic pressure for their braking system. This decision meant a high approach speed, touching down close to the perimeter because Hawkinge had precious little space for a bomber, let alone one without brakes. Nursing the ship into a right-hand base leg, Jesse was concentrating on landing when, intending to point something out, Paddy tapped him on the shoulder hitting exactly the metal embedded in his undeclared wound. Jesse's yell and stream of invectives startled the engineer who stepped back looking aggrieved, quite unaware of the pains now lancing through Jesse's shoulder. Then Hal abruptly announced he would land the ship if Jesse would line it up. The airfield was still hidden from Hal's view when he said he would "take it" — meaning assume control — but Jesse was convinced his wounded pilot was still dangerously disorientated. Rather than risk Hal taking over, Jesse let him believe the ship was his but carefully supervised the landing, shadowing Hal's actions where necessary. Lowering towards the murky landscape, they were relieved when the airfield's lights appeared and switched on their powerful landing lights. The beams eagerly leapt trees and hedgerows, flashing on a rolling-drum of landscape below, closer and faster until the last hedge vanished and Jesse judged the touchdown. The instant tyres touched turf, Jesse and Hal hit the brakes, Jesse shoved the mixture controls into idle cut-off to stop engines and gain the braking effect from windmilling propellers. The rest was prayer and brakes. They held. But the bomber was still travelling too fast when it veered from course straight towards the watch tower from which building issued numbers of distinctly disconcerted airmen. Jesse, feeling their fading momentum, knew the building was in no danger and felt some amusement when the bomber lurched to a halt about 50 yards away. As it stopped, Hal slumped forward. Within seconds, British medical personnel boarded, gently easing him onto a stretcher beneath the port wing. Why, wondered Hal, was it so dark? He felt himself being lifted. An ambulance. Doors closing. Darkness.

As Hal began weeks of hospitalization, his crew were taken to the airfield's infirmary where, with some welcome Scotch, they received reassurances about their pilot and treatment for lesser wounds. Jesse kept the metal fragment removed from his shoulder. Next morning, as he taxied the B-24 out of harm's way, he found it had no brakes, so the hydraulic system had been damaged and, it seems, the ship was deemed beyond economic repair. Transported to Manston, they were collected by a 392BG B-24. Only then did they learn of their division's other misfortunes during the remainder of Mission 311.

Leading the Mission for the 20 CBW were the Seething-based 448BG. They were spared serious fighter attack over Europe — their reckoning came later. At wing IP, Major Heber H Thompson transmitted the code word "Black Jack" and bombs were released within two minutes by aircraft from the 448BG, 446BG and 93BG, with many hits observed around the MPI. Flak had abated and was only meagre and inaccurate, although the formation still carried out the briefed,

Prior to take-off on 22 April 1944 the crew of Vadie Raye, *448BG, posed for pictures. Pilot Alvin D Skaggs smiles from the cockpit.* (E Gaskins)

L-R Elbert Lozes, Bombardier; Francis Sheehan, Waist Gunner; Ray K Lee, Waist Gunner. Command Pilot Captain William G Blum is kneeling. This would be the last mission for Vadie Raye. (E Gaskins)

evasive turn and descent. Some minutes later, in the Cologne area, a gaggle of about 35 Me109s were seen approaching from 11 o'clock high and seemingly intent on attack. One 93BG crew reported seeing them release belly tanks as they closed in. Some felt their markings were deliberately schemed to resemble P-51 paintwork, while others went even further and reported the fitting of fake airscoops to give closer resemblance to the Mustang. Anxious eyes also noted a small number of

The afternoon sun slants across Vadie Raye *as Francis Sheehan and Ray K Lee ready themselves for take off. Lee is wearing patches on his cheeks to prevent frostbite.* (E Gaskins)

Focke-Wulf 190s and this force was almost certainly the 27 Me109s of IV/JG3 and eight FW190s of the Sturm Staffel which had taken off from Salzwedel at 1830 hours. For the first time in several missions, American aircrews also reported twin-engined Ju88 and Me410 "Hornet" fighters, but the author has found no record supporting this, and both types were already considered too vulnerable to operate unescorted although the "Hornet" would soon sting with memorable viciousness.

Nervously, crews of the 20 CBW waited for the attack. Crossing above the 448BG, the enemy swept through the 93BG and 446BG exchanging fire. For the 3,050 rounds of ammunition expended, the "Bungay Buckaroos" claimed six destroyed, but German records hold no verification. On the other hand, some German bullets found their mark and Second Lieutenant Sidney Hodgson, navigator on Lieutenant Kasnia's aircraft was badly wounded in one leg. Applying a tourniquet to staunch the blood, Hodgson held his post, as did Staff Sergeant Herbert A Johnson who was blown out of his tail turret but clambered back to continue the fight. The crew made it home. Rockets were reported during this skirmish and First Lieutenant Benjamin L Schaefer of the 44BG felt the fighters fishtailed to fan their fire into the Liberator formation. His ship was one of the three which had earlier wandered from its parent Group when the division occurred in the 14CBW. Continuing through the 20 CBW formation, JG3 now bore down on the 96CBW which was already in some disarray.

Concluding the Second Air Division's assault on Hamm, the tail-end 96 CBW suffered a combination of problems which segmented the Wing near Hamm. Ushered towards the target by a 389BG PFF ship commanded by Major Donald C Jamison of the 458BG, the 458BG, 466BG and 467BG also experienced navigational difficulties. These the Lead Bombardier, Flight Officer Herman Lodinger attributed to the pilotage-navigator's decision to sit in the bombardier's compartment instead of riding in the nose turret for better visibility. Missing their checkpoints and the Group IP, the 458BG over-ran some 10 miles to the edge of Dortmund before the error, claimed to stem from "confusion in the lead ship", was realized. Communications on board the PFF ship were handicapped because there were not enough interphone points and, following Divisional SOP (Standard Operating Procedure), the Dead Reckoning navigator had ceased navigating to operate the bomb doors. This meant he was not readily available on the flight deck or intercom when concern arose about their position. Twice changing direction, they eventually approached Hamm on a 360° heading compared to the briefed course of 136°. Adding to the 458BG's woes, they encountered flak which damaged the PFF's A5 autopilot at a critical point on the bombing run. There was no time for a smooth transition to the deputy lead — and yet more mayhem arose when their formation meshed with late-arriving Liberators from the formerly lost 2 CBW. Luckily, alert aircrews avoided collisions, but this chaotic catalogue of events climaxed when strong sunlight hampered the lead bombardier's attempts to pin-point their target.

On board *Dream Boat*, First Lieutenant Richard O Alvestad's crew were poised with a present of their own for the enemy. That morning Alvestad had scrounged from the Mess a gallon can of sauerkraut to drop on Hamm. This seemed an appropriate gesture for the Krauts and went well with Hamm. With take-off delayed, the crew occupied their time soldering on a wire hook and attaching a large rag to act as a banner for their secret weapon. Now, with the wind whipping his clothing, Technical Sergeant Elmo R Fikes balanced by the open bomb bay waiting for the bombs to clatter from their shackles. Twenty thousand feet below, the landscape slid by as if on a gigantic screen. Then Hamm appeared, a distant, dirty rug with huge palls of smoke reaching over half-way to their altitude. Still, the steel shackles clutched their prisoners. It was too late for them to find their mark, but Fikes had no intention of leaving the sauerkraut anywhere else and threw it clear, the only "weapon" the first 458BG section dropped on the primary. Beset with problems and uncertainties, the lead ship failed to release. *Dream Boat* and her sisters now followed Jamison towards Koblenz — a fatal decision for one in their midst.

Guiding the second 458BG section, First Lieutenant K C Barton encountered his own difficulties when he was unable to set up the C1 autopilot for his bombardier, First Lieutenant Carl J Beasly. With seconds ticking away to release, they opted for a manual run and Beasly guided Barton via the intercom. Peering into his bombsight, Beasly found the smoke impenetrable so he synchronized on a reference point clear of the smoke, adjusted his cross-hairs onto the still obscured

The most threatening contribution from the 458BG over Hamm was a can of sauerkraut dropped by the crew of Dream Boat. (H Armstrong)

objective and cross-checked for satisfaction with his target charts. The bomb release safety guard was uncovered, Barton held steady — Beasly's hand poised over the release switch. In his bombsight, still only smoke then, two seconds to release, a patch cleared revealing the marshalling yards. Beasly's squadron bombed Hamm. Anxious to record the results, Beasly switched on his camera but this reward was frustrated, the camera to intervalometer link had failed. No pictures were taken although his deputy confirmed their bombs were on target and the unladen Liberators faithfully followed the first section towards Koblenz with the Group leader still experiencing problems.

An earlier hiccup also cost part of the 466BG their mission value. Following the 458BG towards Hamm, Colonel E Anastasio commanded from the lead 466BG ship, *Nobody's Baby*, and was somewhat uncharitably blamed for the navigational error. "Toured the Ruhr with Anastasio" was the cynical comment from one crewman. As Anastasio's formation approached their IP, his bombardier moved a lever on the bombing control panel to choose the method of release — in this case, fully forward to salvo. When moved into "select" the apparatus malfunctioned, prematurely releasing not only the lead ship's bombs but prompting similar action from several other aircraft. The unfortunate recipient of these bombs was the hamlet of Olfen, some 15 miles west of Hamm. Even worse, the 466BG then overshot its IP and, lacking time to co-ordinate an attack on Hamm, most of the remaining aircraft released on a target of opportunity at Neiderfell. For such inconclusive results, the 466BG suffered 18 ships damaged by flak. The crew of *Gallopin Ghost* were particularly fortunate to remain temporal when a shell went through their port wing without exploding. Staff Sergeant William J Kent, tail gunner on Lieutenant Brown's B-24 was wounded, but there were no other serious casualties.

Third in the 96 CBW were Lieutenant Colonel Albert J Shower's 467BG, the *Rackheath Aggies*, named after the village near their Norfolk base. Early assembly problems had been resolved by the time they reached the Dutch coast, although there was some tendency for the Group to over-run its Wing position during the approach to Hamm. This prevented them from easily uncovering at Wing IP. Shower chose to execute a 360° left orbit south of Munster to improve their positioning for the bomb-run. This decision, combined with the 458BG's difficulties, separated the 467BG from the 96 CBW and increased the risk of flak damage during the detour. This point was emphasized to Lieutenant Kenneth L Driscoll's crew when their ship was hit and lost power in its number two engine. Feathering the propeller, Driscoll increased RPM on his good engines and regained formation. Otherwise, Shower's gamble paid off and his lead bombardier, Second Lieutenant Kenneth S Penoyer, was properly positioned to exercise his skills. Target recognition was easily provided by smoke from previous attacks, but Penoyer realised his MPI (Mean Point of Impact) had already been well bombed. Another problem arose when the lead ship's autopilot failed, forcing Penoyer, Shower and the regular pilot, Second Lieutenant Richard J Campbell, to make the run using PDI (Pilot's Directional Indicator). This was a back-up method demanding excellent co-ordination between bombardier and pilot who responded to the former's corrections by keeping the PDI indicator needle perfectly centred — not easy if flak infested their route. Calmly, Penoyer requested small adjustments, gently turning the formation northeast to a section of the yard as yet comparatively unscathed. Dispensing chaff, they encountered only light flak and their bombs tumbled into the twilight at 1937 hours. One aircraft suffered a bomb rack failure and released late on houses in a village beyond the target.

Guiding the second 467BG section was bombardier First Lieutenant John K Gile who sighted for range and deflection on what seemed to be goods wagons in the yard's southern end. A two-minute bombing run at 23,500 feet on A5 autopilot went smoothly for his 14 ships, with only minor problems encountered. Another rack malfunction delayed release from Lieutenant Goldsmith's ship but at least they fell in the target area, whereas those from Lieutenant Perry's aircraft merely started fires in woodland because his bomb bay doors stubbornly refused to open in time. Most crews were pleased with their bombing results — but, departing from the target area, the 467BG realised they had lost the 96 CBW. Careful calculations by Second Lieutenant Morton Deutsch, the lead navigator, established that continuing their southerly course would see them rally with the 458BG near Koblenz. His flight record was used for both navigational and general observations and, at 1950 hours, he noted the sighting of a parachute. Other Liberators came so close to the

On board Snooper *of the 467BG (42-52571), calculations by lead navigator Morton Deutsch plotted a rendezvous with the 458BG.* (M J Bailey)

hapless airman that they almost spilled his parachute. Like Deutsch, their crews had no way of knowing the descending flier was one of four from a 458BG Liberator about to become the 200th "kill" for the famous Luftwaffe fighter ace, Heinz Bär of JG1.

Almost minced by the Liberators, Staff Sergeant Herman A Peacher swung frighteningly in his harness, buffeted by prop wash and wincing as another on-coming bomber swerved to avoid him. As it thundered by, Herman longed for the security of his own tail-turret, homeward-bound as he had been 10 times before. True, there had been some rough trips, but Herman's faith in his pilot, First Lieutenant George N Spaven Jr, remained unshaken — even now he could hardly believe what had happened. Twice before, George had pulled their damaged ship home against almost impossible odds and his prowess inspired confidence within his crew. Today, that reputation helped settle their waist-gunner, Sergeant Robert L Allin, a replacement flying only his first mission. Spaven seemed indestructible. He had flown P.39 Airacobra fighters, twin-engined B-25 bombers and now handled the heavy B-24 with renowned deftness and sensitivity. But even Spaven had little choice against flak. En route to Koblenz, the inherent challenge in the name of their ship, *Flak Magnet* would prove fatally apt.

Southwest of Hamm, their top-turret gunner, Technical Sergeant James H Wedding, saw on their starboard side a crippled B-17 being encouraged homewards by a fussy P-47. Tucking in near his charge, the "little friend" played cub-scout helping an old lady cross a dangerous street. Wedding was comforted by the sight. It was a relief to see their escort and he inwardly wished the pair well as he powered his turret to

En route to Koblenz the inherent challenge in her name proved fatally apt for Flak Magnet *of the 458BG.* (A North)

view forward. Suddenly, his concern became acutely personal — a box barrage of flak spattered the sky almost dead-ahead. Obscene red flashes in the evening sky left an ugly, black afterbirth. This first box was low, dead ahead — then a second, also dead ahead but high in the evening sky like devil's spit in heaven. The third box ensnared them at 8, 11, 2 and 4 o'clock with the fifth shell hurtling diagonally right through the front of the bomb-bay into the centre wing section, exiting unexploded just aft of the liferaft hatch. It had bayoneted *Flak Magnet*, peeling back a large section of top-fuselage, its skinning now flapping wildly in the slip-stream. Inside the fuselage, the wound was grievous, with a torrential downpour of gasoline from three ruptured main fuel cells which fed their number two engine.

Flying off *Flak Magnet*'s right wing, the crew of *Dream Boat* saw the other B-24 veer alarmingly towards them then drop from formation, the gash in its upper wing clearly visible. Also evident was a haze of vaporizing fuel streaming from the stricken ship. Inside, some 500 gallons of gasoline pouring from burst tanks turned them into an enormous Molatov cocktail needing only one spark to eviscerate aircraft and crew in a fireball. Dropping swiftly from his turret Wedding operated the bomb door auxiliary control valve releasing clouds of fuel into the air behind *Flak Magnet*. The engineer's actions would not only reduce the fire-risk but his reactions had to be rapid if *Flak Magnet* was to stand any chance of reaching home. Checking the fuel gauges, Wedding confirmed three seriously damaged tanks were empty and quickly set the transfer valves, started the bomb-bay booster pump and cross fed the number two engine from their undamaged tanks. By his calculations, they had lost about 550 gallons of fuel but he felt there was still sufficient on board to reach England. Further aft, the situation was more confused, causing reactions which helped seal the fate of *Flak Magnet*. The bombardier, Second Lieutenant James F Mortinson, had hastened astern to get his parachute which he had left in the waist when boarding that afternoon. To do this, he had grabbed a portable oxygen bottle and disconnected himself from the intercom. Passing through the bomb-bay, he found the stench of high octane fuel almost overpowering despite his oxygen mask. Crawling into the waist, Mortinson saw Sergeant Allin gesturing at him to bale out and, being off intercom, Mortinson assumed Spaven had given the order to jump. Reaching for his parachute, he saw Allin hastily clip his own parachute on before leaping from the right waist window. The gunner's action convinced the bombardier who soon followed, as did Staff Sergeant Lawrence J Scheiding, emerging from his ball turret into this hectic scene.

Still in his tail-turret, Herman Peacher watched with mounting alarm as leaking fuel streamed off the starboard stabilizer. Like many Liberator tail gunners, Herman kept open his turret doors. The blast of air from the waist was now moistened by a spray of neat fuel sucked in the left waist window, and dousing the bomber's interior. Glancing round, Herman saw a figure vanishing through the right waist window, glimpsing only a pair of vanishing feet. Herman had not heard the bale-out command but the empty fuselage told him everyone was leaving, his intercom must be out. Hunching into a ball, he released the power control handles for his turret and rolled backwards off his stool on to the fuselage catwalk. Eighteen months ago he had been building B-24s in San Diego so he knew how to move fast inside one. As he rolled, his oxygen mask and microphone tore off and the action snapped the quick release tabs on his flak jacket which fell away as he stood up. Inside the fuselage, he saw gasoline streaming along the aluminium corrugations and pouring out of the camera hatch. The ship was an airborne tinder-box.

Grasping his parachute, Herman clipped it on as he hastened to the camera hatch. *Flak Magnet* seemed empty and could explode at any second. Reaching the hatch, he forced his way through, only to be caught when the door snagged his knees. For an instant, Herman hung inverted beneath the bomber then, kicking himself clear, he parachuted into the path of Liberators lower down.

Having heard confused voices on the intercom, then silence and no response, Spaven told Staff Sergeant James L Fittinger to leave his nose turret and check what was happening. All guns on *Flak Magnet* were now unmanned. Regaining control, Spaven now pulled back into formation, but being bound for Koblenz was increasing the distance home on their drastically depleted reserves of fuel. A few minutes later, other 458BG crews watched *Flak Magnet* shed its position and turn on a lonely western heading.

Left *Major Heinz Bär of II/JG1 hastened from his base at Stormede hoping to catch the unescorted B-24 and claim his 200th kill.* (E Mombeek)

Right *Flying FW190 RED 23, Bär and his wingman rapidly caught up with* Flak Magnet. (E Mombeek)

Other, less compassionate, eyes also saw the solitary bomber. Major Heinz Bär of II/JG1, with Oberfeldwebel Schuhmacher flying wingman, hastened from his base at Stormede hoping to catch the unescorted B-24. On board *Flak Magnet*, Fittinger reported the absence of the bombardier and other gunners before setting about the release of their bombs by hand because the standard release and jettisoning systems had failed. This process entailed leaning over a vast, slowly moving panorama of German landscape while jockeying with a screwdriver to trigger the shackles individually. Breathing on a walk-round oxygen bottle, Fittinger, aided by Wedding and the radio operator, Staff Sergeant Cedric C Cole, managed to free several bombs, each one increasing their chances. Cole had already attempted raising American escort fighters on the radio but heard only a mocking silence and felt he was of more use helping to dump their bombs. As the three fliers wrestled to release each ugly 500 lb burden Bär's FW190, *Red 23*, was closing rapidly from astern. Seeing the bombs fall from the Liberator, Bär assumed it was a "solitary scout" smoke marking the area. As a farmer's son, Herman Peacher was adept at shooting crows on the wing and those skills translated neatly into his Liberator turret — but now it was empty. Diving on the B-24 from 5 o'clock, Bär expected retaliation from the tail turret. None came as the Liberator loomed larger in his Revi reflector sight. Judging his moment, Bär squeezed the firing button.

Fearful of anoxia, Fittinger had just requested a replacement for his portable bottle when Bär struck. A storm of destruction erupted in *Flak Magnet*. Cannon and machine gun bullets riddled the tail then strode towards the bomb bay. Miraculously, the first enfilade missed all three airmen in that section, even though some rounds ricocheted alarmingly off the bombs themselves. In the cockpit, the co-pilot, Second

Lieutenant Robert L Zedeker thought they had taken another hit from flak as exploding shells and a fury of bullets blasted pieces of perspex, glass and aircraft into the cockpit. Again fate spared both him and Spaven, but *Flak Magnet* was doomed as the number two engine burst into flames. Even Spaven's skills were overwhelmed. Yet the courageous pilot still had a duty to his crew and struggled to keep the B-24 level while they escaped. In the bomb bay, Fittinger had become groggy so Wedding and Cole snapped his parachute on for him then pushed him off the catwalk before themselves following him into the void. Exerting all his expertise and sheer willpower, Spaven kept *Flak Magnet* flying as his navigator, Second Lieutenant Peter Kowal opened the nose wheel doors. From the shattered cockpit, Spaven and Zedeker could see Bär's FW190 peeling off to the right as he swept round for a frontal attack. Releasing his seat harness, Zedeker hoisted himself clear, yelling at Spaven, "Let's get the hell outta here!" Moving between the armoured seats, the co-pilot saw that Spaven had not moved so he turned and slapped him on the shoulder. Spaven knew Zedeker could escape but what about Kowal? Hesitating, he nodded at Zedeker, released his harness and began leaving his seat. At that instant, Peter Kowal was about to pitch himself through the nosewheel exit but was startled as lines of spiteful red tracer cut viciously across his view of the green landscape beneath. The second they ceased, Kowal leapt for his life.

Zedeker was shielded by the back of his armoured seat when the final torrent of fire tore into the cockpit. George Spaven had half risen. Then the instrument panel disintegrated and his body convulsed in a storm of bullets before slumping lifelessly across the controls. Zedeker threw himself clear. Seconds later, swinging beneath his parachute, he still hoped Spaven would appear but the once-proud *Flak Magnet* had

At Stormede, a crowd surrounds RED 23 and Bär is helped from his flying suit to celebrate his 200th victory.
(E Mombeek)

become a funeral bier for its pilot. Wreathed in flames, the bomber dived steeply until an explosion blew both wings to pieces and the shorn fuselage carried George Spaven to earth near the community of Hoetmar. He was interred there the following day. His crew survived, although Herman Peacher broke his right ankle on landing in a field near Balve. Worse was to follow.

Spilling the air from his parachute, Herman awaited capture by people seen running in his direction as he descended. First to arrive was an armed civilian, ominously pointing his pistol at the injured aviator. Herman was unarmed. The 458BG discouraged the wearing of .45 automatics because being armed might provide an excuse for the Germans to shoot. Even so, someone yanked his helmet off and violently clubbed the back of his head. Still stunned, he was hauled up and manhandled roughly towards the village. During this agonizing journey, one of the four men carrying him took fiendish pleasure in tormenting the injured flier by deliberately manipulating his broken leg. In the village, he was interrogated by an ugly fat "Gestapo" female and a police sergeant before being taken to hospital in Balve where his arrival was at least treated with gentler curiosity. He was the first American shot down that close to town. Soon a variety of locals were trooping past his bed — school children, mothers, wounded soldiers and others curious to see this "terror flieger". There was no serious attempt to treat his injured leg and, after two days, he was given a pair of crutches and ordered, unassisted, down three flights of stairs to a waiting truck. Every stair was a torment and, on reaching his transport, the excruciating pain had left him in a state of shock. Only pleading by a B-17 pilot on the truck got Herman a shot of morphine from the syrette in the first-aid kit on his parachute harness. It was three weeks before his leg was set but Herman has always considered himself fortunate that his only physical legacy was lameness in one leg.

A few minutes after *Flak Magnet* left formation, the continuing difficulties on board Jamison's lead ship finally forced him into relinquishing the lead slot at 1957 hours when he transferred command to Elwood T Clagget. Navigating for Clagget was First Lieutenant I R Burton, who immediately gave his pilot a new heading towards their last resort target, the marshalling yards in Koblenz. Clagget's bombardier, First Lieutenant James C Smith was already preparing for the bombing run and found the optics on his bombsight were fogged. Unflustered, he calmly dismantled the unit, polished the glass and reassembled it before continuing his search for suitable reference points. An evening haze hid many ground features but rivers shone like strands of burnished silver. The confluence of the Rhine and Mosel in Koblenz provided a prominent feature and Smith synchronized on a distinctive section of river bank. Troubles with the C1 autopilot dictated a run on PDI and, nearing the target, Burton noted how the enemy appeared to "set off a field full of dummy bombs on east side of river opposite city". Undeterred by this deception, the 13 laden bombers concluded a four-minute approach and released on the target at 1938. An almost flawless example of co-ordination was only slightly marred when Smith forgot to turn on the camera so lost his ship's pictures of the attack. However, crews could now go home feeling something had been salvaged from the purpose of their mission.

Turning to starboard as it left Koblenz, the 458BG was 13 miles south of its briefed course and abreast of the Division formation. Earlier, Burton had used GEE transmissions as a navigational aid but then it succumbed to enemy jamming and was still of little use as the Group withdrew. Their radio compass was "meaconed" — tuned for directional signal strength from known beacons — but Burton felt his radio operator, Technical Sergeant R V Hanson, a last-minute substitute, lacked the necessary lead-ship experience and training to reliably fix their position. However, the region's many glistening lakes and waterways were distinctive markers as the 458BG merged with the course briefed that morning.

Leaving Europe, some Second Air Divison Groups encountered radio communication problems because of the skip effect when higher frequency radio signals ripple between atmospheric layers. Enemy gunners also put on a display of "peculiar" pyrotechnics, "resembling pom-poms and rockets" near Ostend. Some ships suffered flak damage on the way out and, over the channel, several crews became wary of one B-24 which they suspected was enemy-flown and tracking their movements. In the gathering darkness, repeated bursts of tracer sparkled from this aircraft — seemingly aimed at nothing. This behaviour alarmed other crews. Eventually, the strange craft ceased firing and faded into both the night and historical mystery. Its identity remains unknown.

There is no doubt, however, about the identity of the enemy unit which *was* preparing a reception for the returning Liberators. Kampfgeschwader 51 *Edelweiss* had been one of the Luftwaffe's most distinguished bomber units, fighting in the Battle of Britain, on the Eastern Front and in other war-theatres. Faced with increasingly superior Allied bomber-power, the Luftwaffe was forced from the offensive role towards increasing its defensive capabilities and elements of KG51 converted from bombers to fighters using the Me410. By April 1944, a special long-range night fighter Staffel of KG51 had been formed under Major Dietrich Puttfarken, himself a holder of the Knight's Cross. Based at Gilze-Rijen in Holland, Puttfarken's II Gruppe had only recently achieved operational status but, on 22 April, he recognized the circumstances facing American airmen and sought advantage from this unusual opportunity proffered by US planners. Only a handful of aircraft and crews were available — but this small force would wreak such havoc that its size became many times magnified by those on the receiving end.

•CHAPTER SEVEN•

Fighters: Escort and Sweep

CONTRARY TO ANY impression that US fighters were thin in the air at vital moments, Bombardment Group records for 22 April 1944 praise the quality of escort. The significant contribution made by sweeps was invisible to bomber crews but arguably more effective in their protection. True, there were some occasions when Luftwaffe controllers got it right and positioned their interceptors where escort was weak, and the segmenting of the bomber force handed German tacticians benefits which were not really pressed to their fullest advantage. USAAF commanders did note how the Luftwaffe apparently sought to calculate the endurance of American fighter escort and time its assaults at the end of one fighter Group's endurance, just prior to the rendezvous of a relieving Group. In

American Thunderbolts, Lightnings and Mustangs were not designed for nocturnal operations and the P-38 Lightning shown here also had other difficulties operating in the European climate.

Left *Unharnessed Mustangs clearly demonstrated their potential during Mission 311.*

Right *US fighters waged a relentless campaign against Germany's transportation network and the rugged Republic P-47 proved its prowess on 22 April 1944.*

all, losses to enemy fighters over Europe were relatively few — more bombers would be destroyed in the darkness over England where USAAF fighters were impotent.

The Thunderbolts, Lightnings and Mustangs were not designed for nocturnal operations, nor were their pilots trained. Their entire modus operandi was based on action in daylight. On 22 April they performed magnificently in their prime role and the day's events became more stepping-stones in a series culminating in almost complete air superiority. Faced with this onslaught, the quality of Germany's fighter force ultimately haemorrhaged in a cycle of casualties creating the need for early replacement by pilots less well trained who in turn fell victim even more swiftly creating another demand — and so on into extinction. This inexorable process had already begun. It increased proportionately with the increasing numbers of unharnessed Mustangs which clearly demonstrated their potential during Mission 311. Not only would the Luftwaffe be scourged from its own skies until there existed comparatively few experts in a fuel-starved force, but US fighters also waged a relentless campaign against Germany's transportation network. Nothing was left unscathed by foraging Allied fighters eager to shred trucks, trains, barges and boats — vital elements for a nation supplying its troops and workforce.

Supporting Mission 311, the 22 American fighter Groups and four RAF Squadrons involved were assigned tasks under the broad headings of escort and sweep. Both terms adequately describe their functions although duties could intermingle depending on the exigencies of combat. Sizes of Groups and squadrons deployed varied and, in some cases, a unit's strength allowed the use of 'A' and 'B' Groups from the

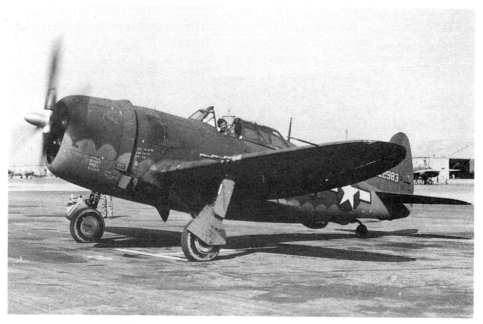

same parent, as with the bomber force.

For the escort groups, timely rendezvous with the bombers was essential. On reaching the bomber combat wing box, the fighter group would position its three squadrons to provide effective protection based on experience and local conditions. Two sections of eight from one squadron would usually divide and fly above and about five miles ahead of the bombers to counter frontal assaults. The second squadron would also separate and position its sections on either side of the bomber formation, while the final squadron would split and provide top-cover some 4,000 feet above the bombers. One top-cover section would move sunwards to guard against the classic "Hun in the Sun" attack. For all the fighters, speed differential dictated weaving or broad circles and engines would be set to conserve fuel with fighters frequently flying to the limits of their endurance.

The 395FG from East Wretham in Norfolk had the distinction of escorting the vanguard Third Air Division during the penetration stage of Mission 311. Briefing was called for 1600 hours. As the young fliers jostled and bantered nervously into the briefing room, they recognized the short stature of Major General William Kepner, commander of Eighth Air Force Fighter Command. "Bill" Kepner's slight figure belied a truly tall, tough personality. He drove his men hard but earned their respect. One of the pilots present, Captain John H Oliphant, had only recently returned from special detachment with "Bill's Buzz Boys" — a unit nicknamed after Kepner and formed at his initiative especially to develop strafing techniques. In less than three hours, Oliphant would put into practice some of those skills. Taking the podium, Kepner thanked the 359FG for their achievements during the past 73 missions and expressed his confidence that they would continue their success this evening. Captain Daniel D McKee, the Operations Officer, inwardly endorsed Kepner's wishes with personal fervour — he would be leading the 359FG for the first time.

As the briefing continued, the background rumble of heavy bombers straining for altitude emphasized their purpose and contrasted with the closer, sharper crackle of a Pratt & Whitney R2800 Double Wasp as a crew chief fussed over the rugged radial of his Thunderbolt. Nearly 50 of Republic's portly product were being similarly cherished. The base bustled with fuel bowsers, oxygen carts and bicycles as ground personnel hastened through a multitude of tasks necessary for the 359FG's operational status. The big Curtiss Electric propeller on each P-47 had been "pulled through" — manually cranked to avoid the fire hazard created when gasoline gathered in the lower cylinder heads of an idle engine. Armourers had carefully snaked long linkages of .5 calibre ammunition into gaping wing bays and attentively adjusted gun-feed mechanisms for each of the eight machines guns. The Thunderbolt was aptly named. Its formidable firepower could achieve a combined rate of 6,000 rounds per minute and each shell, gleaming like brass on a widow's mantlepiece, had its own deadly task. Black-tipped bullets were armour piercing; red were tracer; bright blue for incendiary, and silver for armour-piercing incendiary. Some 16,000 gallons of high-octane fuel would be consumed by thirsty engines given greater range by drop-tanks tucked beneath the belly of each tubby fighter.

It was 1730 when McKee, call sign "Tailor 31", lifted from the turf at East Wretham and climbed away with the rest of his flight in close attendance. A few minutes later he had the satisfaction of knowing his first mission leading the Group had begun without serious mishap. Three pilots turned back — one with frozen controls, another suffering from a leaky oxygen regulator, and the third as escort. McKee's force rendezvoused with the Third Air Division's Fortresses at 1823 hours, 24,000 feet over the Zuider Zee. For over an hour, the escort was uneventful and the P-47 pilots witnessed some "excellent" bombing by their "big friends". In retaliation, the flak seemed to increase. One, huge white burst was later thought by some pilots to be an attack or sky-marking signal for German fighters because, moments later, at 1850 hours, a gaggle of enemy fighters were seen positioning to attack the B-17s. Criss-crossing overhead as top-cover, Yellow Flight's leader, Lieutenant Ralph E Kibler spotted about 20 bandits on the far side of the Fortress formation and already beginning to attack. Calling for top-cover from his Red Flight counterpart, First Lieutenant Raymond B Lancaster, Kibler winged his flight over to starboard in a steep, diving turn as the enemy, now seen to be Focke-Wulf 190s, swooped on the bombers. At that instant, First Lieutenant Robert M Borg called in bogies — unidentified fighters — at 9 o'clock. Lancaster's help would be needed, but Yellow Flight's priority was to protect the bombers. Hurtling to intercept, Yellow Flight risked their own safety and Yellow Two,

Second Lieutenant Earl W Thomas Jr, had additional problems because his P-47 unaccountably fell astern as the four Thunderbolts raced towards the enemy. Reacting to Borg's call, Red Flight had seen the bogies — four FW190s — spurring after Yellow Flight and towards the bombers. Lives lost and saved depended on who got there first. It was already too late for one B-17 which keeled over and fell burning — five parachutes were seen. Yellow Flight's action saved others because several FW190s broke to engage the P-47s and one that did not was torn apart by return fire from the bombers, its pilot baling out. The four Focke-Wulfs closing on Yellow Flight caught up with the trailing Thomas. First Lieutenant Harold D Hollis, Red Two, had seen some German fighters sweeping round to port for another dive on the bombers. He chose one to attack but it fell to fire from the Fortresses before he got close enough and Hollis lost his position as wingman to Lancaster in the melee. Catching up with what he thought was Red Flight, he found himself behind Yellow Flight and one P-47 had an FW190 on its tail. Hollis thought it was Yellow Four, First Lieutenant John L Downing, but it was most likely the unfortunate Thomas who was overhauled by Downing in the dive to defend the B-17s.

Using his P-47's superb diving speed, Hollis hurtled after the FW190 which continued attacking the P-47, apparently oblivious of vengeance at hand. Ignoring diving limitations, Hollis was determined to deflect the FW190 and built up such speed he made sighting difficult. Then, at 3,500 feet the FW190 pilot either saw him or felt his own victim had no hope of recovery. Rolling out of its dive in a steep turn, the Focke-Wulf disengaged and for an instant was in the P-47's gunsight. Hollis fired. Most rounds probably missed but some did not and there came a brief sparkle of strikes on the tail and top fuselage of his turning opponent. Shuddering at well over 400 miles an hour, Hollis overshot and sped past the German less than 50 feet away, so close he could see yellow and black markings and a red badge on the German's port side which identifies the aircraft as an FW190 of JG1. By now, the enemy pilot had opened his canopy and his engine was smoking badly. Rolling into a dive, the FW190 then split his turn to confuse Hollis who was pulling up to port and sensibly checking his own rear-view mirror. Banking sharply to confirm his tail was clear, Hollis saw the FW190 continue its dive. Making no further effort to pull out, it hit the earth and exploded. Having expended 1,654 rounds of ammunition, Hollis climbed to rejoin the Group and met Kibler who, for only 548 rounds of armour piercing incendiary, could claim his two victories.

Diving to cut off the attack on the B-17s, Kibler had curved neatly on to the tail of an FW190 when Lancaster's speeding P-47 sliced across his path. Heaving back on his stick Kibler cleared his companion by mere feet and lost his intended victim. Reefing round, he glimpsed another FW190 diving from the fray and power dived in pursuit. At 5,000 feet he had closed to 250 yards and a short burst blew off a large piece of the FW190's engine cowling and caused its right undercarriage leg to droop. Instantly, the cockpit canopy whipped away and the pilot leapt clear. Kibler had no time for elation. He knew well enough the risks in a seemingly empty sky and became an adept swivel-neck with a fox like alertness, seeking opportunity and sensing danger. Pulling out, he saw below another P-47 overshoot an FW190 and apparently lose it. Winging over, he fell on the FW190 which plummeted earthwards hoping to outrun the American. Six tons of gravitationally eager P-47 stood no chance of being out-distanced and, as Kibler closed in, the German took violent evasive action, racing across the rooftops of Hamm itself. Several times Kibler was poised to fire when the FW190 swung steeply into him using its excellent, low altitude dog-fighting features. Crammed into his seat by "G" forces, Kibler found the deflection angle so large and the need to "lead" — fire ahead of his opponent — that he lost sight of the enemy beneath his P-47's nose. Taking a chance, he fired blind from less than 250 yards and kept firing until he mushed past the FW190. Downing, Yellow Four saw Kibler's bullets shatter the FW190's canopy and watched as it slewed then, slowing down, it failed to roll out of its turn and nosed down to dive vertically into the ground. Noting the rooftop race, Kibler's second victim was most likely Gefreiter Heinrich Born of II Gruppe JG1 who was killed when his FW190A-8, "White 8", was shot down at Rhynern, near Hamm. Kibler's first intended victim had been pulverized by Lancaster in three five-second bursts, 1,811 rounds of armour-piercing incendiary. Chasing another FW190, Lancaster followed it through a series of "split-ess" manoeuvres which prevented any proper deflection shots although a few rounds hit the German's wing root. After almost colliding with his quarry, he realized he had lost Hollis and was isolated so, choosing his moment, he broke off and scuttled homewards.

Corresponding combat reports with times and locations enables some incidents to be linked, but the confusion of combat at hundreds of miles an hour makes precision impossible in all cases. One encounter, clearly established, involved homeward bound elements of the 359FG following their relief from escort duties. Finding no airfields not already pitted with bomb craters, they went train-spotting on the line to Munster. Near Ostbevern, White and Blue flights observed several locomotives and peeled off to attack. For the next few minutes, chaos was created in and around the station of Ostbevern, then on the nearby Dortmund-Ems Canal. Captain Carey H Brown, Blue Leader, raked one train and, gaining altitude, saw a selection of engines both north and southbound of his position. Further machine-gunning blew up at least one boiler before, heading west, he and his wingman paid unwelcome attention to six canal barges and an oil tanker.

Blue Four, Lieutenant Ross O Major found a stationary freight train in Ostbevern, between the station and its switch tower. He later reported, "I opened fire at 800 feet and held a seven or eight second burst on the station, the locomotive and finally the switch tower. I observed heavy strikes on the station, loco, a switchtower and quite

accidently 'creamed' a German switchman trying to climb down out of
the switchtower when I went by. I chandelled up and watched the loco
go sky-high in a big cumulus type cloud of steam or white smoke. I
started a second pass to confirm destruction via camera when a box
opened and covered my windshield with black oil. I ran into another
flight of two P-47s coming down the track and had to pull up to avoid
collision. The Huns were tossin' lottsa flak by this time so I joined up
with this other squadron, climbed up to 12,000 feet and came home".
Major had lost his leader, Lieutenant Ray S Wetmore who would
eventually rank among the higher-scoring American aces — but an
embarrassing experience on 22 April could have curtailed this career.

   After calling in to Brown the sighting of several more locomotives,
Wetmore strafed three trains — one exploded and a second was severely
damaged. Pulling up, Wetmore lost his comrades but, seeing two fighters
about five miles away, he hastened to join them for the journey home.
Flying in trail about 1,500 yards apart, they apparently saw his approach
because the first ship entered a gentle right turn making it easier for him
to catch up and formate. Relieved at the prospect of company, Wetmore
slid neatly into formation on the lead ship's starboard side, about 60 feet
away. Intending to wave his appreciation Wetmore looked cheerfully
across at his companion to meet the startled gaze of another pilot —

*Captain Ray S Wetmore (left) with his armourer, Sergeant Locklyn Sangster. The
fighter ace's career could have been curtailed on Mission 311 because of a simple
mistake.* (USAF Official)

Left *JG1 was heavily involved against Mission 311. From L-R: Oberfeldwebel Piffer; Leutnant Eh; Leutnant Berger; Hauptmann Schnoor and Leutnant Ehlers. Herbert-Konrad Eh engaged Ray S Wetmore in combat.* (Eric Mombeek)

Right *Lieutenant Robert P Guertz over-turned on take-off and was lucky to avoid serious injury.* (USAF Official) *Engineers set about retrieving his broken 353FG Thunderbolt.* (G Cross)

only this time in the Luftwaffe! Wetmore had formated alongside Leutnant Herbert-Konrad Eh of 3 Staffel, Jagdgeschwader 1. For one strange moment neither reacted, then both leapt like startled cats, each fighter breaking violently away from the other and manoeuvring swiftly to attack. Wetmore, marginally faster, took the initiative and curved back towards the Focke-Wulf. Realizing the danger, Eh hit the deck, weaving hard to prevent Wetmore from aiming as he used the FW190's better low-altitude acceleration to pull away. Anxious to slow his adversary, Wetmore calculated Eh's next weave and chanced a long burst from 300 yards. A sprinkling of hits registered on the FW190's fuselage then, at first unseen by Wetmore, two more P-47s appeared on the scene — First Lieutenant Harry L Matthew, White Three, with Oliphant as his wingman. Both had just strafed a passenger train in Ostbevern station and, increasing height to avoid small-arms fire, Matthew met Eh's silvery-grey Focke-Wulf pulling up in front of him about 800 yards away. His escape route closed, Eh dived desperately into a sharp, low altitude right turn, now being chased by Matthew and Oliphant who had already halved the distance. Suddenly, the Focke-Wulf surged upwards and Matthew punched two brief bursts into the cockpit area and port wing root. Like an injured hare hemmed in by hounds, the wounded Eh hauled his "Yellow Two" heavenwards, bidding for his life as more bullets tore pieces off his soaring fighter. As he reached 1,500 feet, the canopy detached and his FW190 rolled on its back. Hit in the left leg, Eh tumbled clear, his parachute opening unnoticed by the prowling P-47 pilots who saw only his fighter nose dive to destruction. His defeat was shared by both Wetmore and Matthew, both of whom now registered

the intensity of groundfire and hurried from Ostbevern with the remainder of White and Blue flights. For the loss of one pilot, the 359FG had given good account of itself and kept its commitment to Kepner, as did other fighter Groups involved that evening.

Overlapping the 359FG's escort was the 353FG from Raydon led by Lieutenant Colonel Ben Rimerman. Their departure saw one mishap when Lieutenant Robert P Guertz over-turned on take-off and was lucky to escape from his inverted Thunderbolt without serious injury.

Making landfall north of the Hague at 1815 hours, the 353FG met its four combat wings of Third Air Division B-17s 24 minutes later. Passing along the majestic ranks of Fortresses, the Group's squadrons separated

LeFebre led his 351FS, 353FG in YJ-L. (C W Peterson)

near the leading CBW's and took up their positions. Now spearheading
the force, the 351st fighter squadron's Red and White flights were taken
unawares by a mixed force of some 30 Me109s and FW190s from JG1.
First Lieutenant Herbert "Shorty" K Fields, later killed in action,
submitted an encounter report relating what happened, "I was leading
Lawyer Red Flight on penetration support to our big friends. As the
bombers turned into their target run, our squadron made a left orbit.
Shortly thereafter approximately 20 FW190s flying in Groups of five
abreast broke out of the clouds in front of us and were on us before we

realized what they were.

"I immediately made a fast climbing left turn making two or three orbits. '47s, '51s and '190s were going in all directions. Seeing two FW190s heading northeast and for the ground, I did a fast wing over and started in pursuit. I lost my flight during these violent manoeuvres and the enemy aircraft, evidently seeing me, started in a tight, left orbit. We were at about one or two thousand feet by this time, going round and round and still losing altitude. I kept peppering away at the tail-end enemy aircraft who was on the inside of the turn, but never observed any strikes because my plane blocked out my view.

"I finally ran out of ammunition and was down at about 100 feet when the enemy aircraft on the outside of the Lufbery (a tight defensive circle named after a World War I ace) tried slowing down by pulling his nose up and to get on my tail. Instead, he stalled out and spun into the ground. After the next orbit around I saw a big puff of black smoke on the ground where he went in. Out of ammunition, I decided to straighten up, throwing everything to the fire wall and heading for home. The remaining FW190 evidently had enough by this time because he did not follow me".

None of the 2,000 rounds fired by Fields had apparently found their mark but he was credited with the FW190's destruction because he manoeuvred it into the ground. First Lieutenant Harry F Hunter also claimed a FW190 which he diverted from an attack on Lieutenant Crampton whose P-47 reached home scoured by such unwelcome attention. Following this engagement, 351FS pilots proceeded homewards while the remainder of the 353FG, relieved by Lightnings of

Left *First Lieutenant Herbert "Shorty" Fields stood tall when it came to courage. He manoeuvred an FW190 into the ground after his ammunition was exhausted.* (C W Peterson)

Right *First Lieutenant Harry Hunter claimed an FW190 which he diverted from an attack on Lieutenant Crampton.* (C W Peterson)

the 20FG, had a shooting spree against trains, buildings and an oil storage tank which was set on fire near Dorsten. En route to Raydon, 352FS pilots saw Stotter's 389BG Liberator and noted the crew baling out near Soesterburg having concluded there was no hope of crossing the North Sea.

Speeding out of Europe in the 353FG P-47, *Boston Bulldog*, First Lieutenant Paul J "Mickey" Trudeau unexpectedly found himself facing a similar predicament. Trudeau had been wingman to "Shorty" Fields but became separated during the skirmish and found himself alone. He recalls, "We got into that mess and by the time it broke up, we were scattered all over the sky and you don't know where anybody is so the usual process is just to head for home and see if you can join up with others on the way out. When I got within sight of the North Sea, I switched from my auxiliary tank to the main tank and got no response from the engine so I switched back to the auxiliary and she'd start up again. Every time I switched to the main tank, the engine went dead. Switching back and forth only proved that my main tank was empty or a gas line had been cut. I immediately gave out the words 'Mayday, Mayday' to let anybody know I was in trouble. I was still over Holland and was contemplating that there wasn't much left in that auxiliary tank and I'd never make it across that water. I thought I'd have to bale out over Holland. At least I'd still be alive — hopefully — afterwards, even if I was a POW. I did not look forward at all to crossing 90 miles of sea.

First Lieutenant Paul "Mickey" Trudeau's Mayday call told comrades he was in trouble. Pictured later in the war, he had experiences which proved invaluable when he served with the 5th Emergency Rescue Squadron. (P Trudeau via S Harvey)

Fortunately, or unfortunately, Captain Frank Emory and Lieutenant Bob Strobell heard my Mayday calls. I told them my problem. I didn't know whether to bale out over dry land or keep going for it. Emory said, 'Try it. Try it. Go as far as you can. Go as far as you can.' Easy for him to say but I did keep going. He was trying to catch up and find me before I got too far. I didn't get too far. I thought it was kinda ridiculous how little I got out there but I was not surprised". Emory takes up the story. "I heard him calling when I was a little east of Utrecht with my wingman. We advised him to fly as far out as possible before baling out. We then hurried out the coast, crossing out at the Hague, 15,000 feet, and turned south towards the Dutch Islands. Trudeau advised that he was crossing out at 6,000 feet so we dove down to 6,000 and, when we got in this area, spotted him just off the coast. I sent my wingman up to 9,000 feet to relay radio messages and stayed with Trudeau trying to coach him along as far as I could".

Trudeau continues, "The idea as I got down to 6,000 feet was to jettison the canopy, which I did, and climb out on the wing and get the hell out of there. I was at 6,000 feet when the engine gave up completely. When I tried to climb out on the wing, I found I wasn't even strong enough to get out. The windstream was too strong. I only weighed 136 lbs at that time. I used to sit on a cushion to fly so that I could see out through the windshield of the plane. I got back in the cockpit and dove the plane for 1-2,000 feet then rolled it over and tipped the nose up. Of course, I'm supposed to pop out. Unfortunately that didn't happen either — there was no popping out. The plane was falling upside down and pinning me in the cockpit. Fortunately, there was a rear-view mirror just above the cockpit so I grabbed that with both hands and physically hauled myself up and out of that cockpit. There I am, like a sheet on a clothes line thinking, 'My god. Now the tail's gonna smack but I can't stay here'. It was only a couple of seconds. I let go and cringed, braced myself for the blow. It never happened and the moment I knew I was clear I pulled the rip-cord of my 'chute. When the parachute opened, I didn't even have time to look down at the water and think how I was gonna do it. I was in.

"Having always been a good swimmer the water did not scare me although I must admit it took a long time before I surfaced. I expect the weight of my flying clothes, the life vest and the dinghy kept me down longer than normal. I popped off the English-style parachute. That's not too great an experience treading water with your Mae West on and trying to get your dinghy open and hoping it inflates. Fortunately, it did, then the difficulty of getting in was not an easy task. Eventually I got in and sat down and contemplated my fate."

Emory, watching events relates, "His 'chute soon sank leaving only Paul in his dinghy in the middle of a large oil-slick. I circled at 1200 feet and called the Air-Sea Rescue people by use of Lieutenant Strobell as relay. Several planes tried to find us, but could not find us in the haze and dusk. A Walrus that had been despatched to pick up Trudeau stopped 20 miles west of us to pick up a B-17 crew and could not help us. They (Air-Sea Rescue) got several good fixes on our position, which was 17 miles off Overflakke Island. Strobell finally got so low on gas that he had to go home. He left about 2130. I stayed with Trudeau, dropping down almost to the water to keep him in sight. Finally, it got so dark that I couldn't see him any more and I had to leave. It was about 2230 then and I was almost out of gas. I climbed to 3,000 feet and started home mostly on instruments. The last of our bombers were leaving the enemy coast near Ostend and I could see the flak bursting all over the sky to the south of me. It made big red splashes in the sky with long streaks where tracer was being used. I kept flying through bomber prop wash, and still couldn't see any bombers, except now and then a big, black blob would cross in front of me. I finally got over England, coming in at Orfordness light. There were lots of searchlights around and then I began to locate various bombers as they turned their running lights on. I got a homing to Raydon, where the field lights had been turned on for me. I nearly missed it in the haze, but saw a marker flare that the tower shot up. I landed at 2300 hours and had to leave my airplane at the end of the runway as there was an air-raid alert on and all the lights had to be turned off the minute I was on the ground . . . I got to the mess hall just in time to see the tail-end of our first party at Raydon. Some Saturday night party".

Sitting forlornly in his dinghy, Trudeau would have agreed with Emory's sentiments. He had no way of knowing that a Walrus sent for him had chanced upon a B-17 crew whose bomber had crashed on 20 April. Fully laden, the Walrus could not continue its original mission and had to taxi home. Trudeau continues, "I sat there and sat there. For some reason the heating pad did not seem to work, or perhaps I did not do something right. I already had the green dye-marker over the side but decided to pull it in and put it in the bag that came with the heating unit. I did not want to lose that dye-marker. I tied the package together well and again put it overboard. I could see that it was working very well. Finally it gets dusk and finally it gets dark — and it's a lonely place. I never did sleep. That was impossible. I recall sitting there during the night hearing RAF bombers come over and bomb the coast. I could not see land from the dinghy but I did see bomb blasts and some fires, lots of them to the southeast of my position. It was quite a show and you can't see that stuff unless you're pretty close to land. So I sat there through the night and the next morning comes up — a nice bright, sunny day, blue sky and no clouds. Thank the lord for that, I felt encouraged but I sat and sat and sat for what I thought was the whole day. My high hopes faded as the day wore on. I saw a few planes to the south of my position and usually much too high to spot my dinghy. I had my green dye out but was finally thinking, 'I'm in big trouble. They can't find me out here, perhaps I'm too close to the enemy shore!' I had little feelings — if any — in my lower extremities, the only warm thing in that dinghy was my urine so I let it go and sat in it for warmth. The sea cooled it off in a hurry. I concluded, if I make it through the night, my only way was to paddle with my hands towards the rising sun and get back to the enemy shore.

"Fortunately, finally — zingo! I see two planes come down, lower and lower, off to the south east of me. I knew immediately when they turned towards me that my wait was over. Boy oh boy — they found me! They dove over me and then got altitude to relay my position. Another long wait took place but, eventually, what shows up is an RAF Walrus seaplane which landed and taxied round to me. There was the pilot and the co-pilot who was reaching out of the door with a pike on a pole to pull my dinghy over to the plane so they could help me get in. What happened was the pike punctured the dinghy. Zap! The dinghy immediately deflated and I was back in the water! I thanked the lord for the Mae West. They looked at me and said, 'Sorry about that, Yank — we've got to make a big circle and come back at you!' Since I knew that rescue was imminent, my sense of humour returned and I rather enjoyed the co-pilot's expression. I said 'OK, I'll be right here. I'm not going any place!' They came round and did well the second time — they came up close enough that they got hold of me and I got hold of them. So, I'm in the plane in a small compartment behind the pilots and they attempted to take off but couldn't as the sea was too rough. I guess they tried three or four times and the pilot said to me, 'Are you scared, Yank?' I replied 'No. Not now I'm not, I got company — I feel a lot better!' The plane got buffeted so badly, I got nothing to hang on to back there so I'm hanging on to some object which turned out to be the radio which finally ripped off the wall of the plane. We then began a

"What shows up is an RAF Walrus." Countless aircrew owed their lives to this doughty old amphibian. (H. Quinton)

long, slow taxi westwards and, to the best of my recollection, it was
hours — one, two, maybe more before a Royal Navy high speed launch
found us and put a tow on the plane, after getting me on board and
into a bunk. What a relief! We did have fighter cover so I was sure we
would get home some time. I was in a boat with hot soup and thawed
out. The launch towed us 90 miles back to England and didn't get back
until dark. After a night at a hospital I was taken to my unit. They
preferred that I go and spend a week R and R (Rest and Recuperation)
in the country but that did not appeal to me. I had already recovered
from my adventures and took a three-day leave to London instead where
I had a good time".

Trudeau's Walrus drivers were Warrant Officer R C Whittaker and
Flying Officer P J Roy of 278 Squadron, Coltishall. Trudeau himself
later transferred to air-sea rescue duties with the USAAF's 5th
Emergency Rescue Squadron. Air-sea rescue featured in the activities
of the 20FG on 22 April when four of its P-38s accompanied RAF
Warwicks searching for aircrew downed during the previous two days.
However, this was secondary to their 54th mission when Major
Herbert E Johnson Jr led 47 Lightnings aloft from Kings's Cliffe to
overlap with the 353FG. Contrary to the 353FG the P-38 pilots
found matters far too dull, so two squadrons — the 55FS and 77FS
— were detached early from escort duties and sent hunting for ground
targets. Major Johnson destroyed a train at Dorsel while Captain R M
Scrutchfield shared another plus a flak-tower for the tally board on his
P-38, *Jeanne*. In return for one Lightning damaged, the 20FG also
shot up river-steamers, factories and electricity pylons, all set to
relieve their frustration over lack of more suitable spoils. The 79FS
stayed longer than expected with the bombers, and pilots reported too
much chatter on channel 'C' which was intended for important
bomber   to   fighter   dialogue.   Compounding   their   grumbles,
Thunderbolts from the 361FG, Bottisham, were late and left the
Lightnings no time for freelance excitement. Even tempting the
Luftwaffe proved pointless. Lieutenant Jim Bradshaw remembers,
"While returning to England after leaving the bombers, we saw some
'109s flying quite high and it appeared they might be looking for
crippled or straggling bombers. Bob Meyer and I and the pilots in our
flights split up and flew under them on the same course trying to
entice them to take a 'bounce' on us, but they either did not see us
or had no interest. There was no need for us to try and climb up to
them as they could maintain a greater altitude or just roll over and
depart and I believe we were getting a little low on fuel so we gave up
the game. I guess the reason I remember it so well is that I was the
bait. Bob assured me he could bail me out if they attacked — could
have been interesting".

Travelling inland, Major Roy A Webb Jr of the 361FG contacted the
bombers and steered his fighters towards Koln. There they found one
Fortress Group, before locating the majority of the Third Air Division

Top *Captain R M Scrutchfield shared another locomotive to add to his tally board. Pictured here with his groundcrew and their P-38* Jeanne. *(USAF Official)*

Above *Thunderbolts from the 361FG were late. Lining up on the steel mat runway at Bottisham, aircraft prepare to take-off. (S Gotts)*

Right *Lieutenant Jim Bradshaw acted as bait. (J D Bradshaw)*

Major Roy A Webb Jr contacted the bombers and steered his 361FG fighters to locate Third Air Division Fortresses. (S Gotts)

25 miles northeast of Koblenz at 1923 hours. With no sign of enemy aircraft, Captain John W Guckeyson's flight dropped below the bombers to see if poking a stick in the hive might stir some reaction from the Luftwaffe. Gaining no response, he vented his spleen on yet another hapless locomotive pulling freightcars eastbound out of Dorsel. Dissatisfied with just one pass, the P-47s blew up the boiler on their second run, then repeatedly raked the wagons when the train was halted in a gorge. Appetites sated, they ascended to 22,000 feet and resumed the role of escorts.

Few enemy aircraft were seen by the 361FG but, near Bonn, they chased a mysterious Me109 with white wings and its Balkenkruez on the wings trimmed in red. Even more puzzling was its escort — two yellow-cowled Thunderbolts! Preparing to attack, the 361FG were seen and the strange trio took swift evasive action, speeding away on a southerly course. Near Brussels, a more conventional Me109 was pursued but also evaded. Still in the area, the 361FG responded to a plea from First Air Division B-17s apparently being attacked but found them in no trouble and returned to the Third Air Divison, now crossing the coast at Ostend. It is possible that the Germans were transmitting spurious signals because the next call drew them to a disastrous outcome for one pilot. A B-17 allegedly under attack by four enemy aircraft, called for help and claimed to be on the deck near Zeebrugge. This caused Captain Charles H Bergmann Jr's Red Flight to descend and investigate

Right *Captain Charles H Bergmann Jr took his Red Flight down to investigate — a decision that proved fatal for one of their number.*
(S Gotts)

Below *Flames streamed from First Lieutenant Jim Norman's Thunderbolt.*
(S Gotts)

but they found no bomber, nor did subsequent research identify this B-17. Now at a lower altitude, Red Flight risked hits from small-calibre fire as they searched to aid a big friend in trouble. Cutting across Zeebrugge, First Lieutenant James M Norman's Thunderbolt was hit by light flak. Trailing slightly behind Norman on his starboard side,

Bergmann saw Norman's P-47 veer sharply from course, rearing like a frightened pony in a climbing curve. Flames streamed from the Thunderbolt as it crossed in front of Bergmann, arced into the sea and disintegrated in a spume of fire and foam. Shocked at the suddenness of their comrade's death, Red Flight fled homewards, the last of the Third Air Division's escort to leave Europe.

Chaperoning the First Air Division during penetration support were 48 Thunderbolts from the 356FG headed by Lieutenant Colonel Philip E Tukey Jr. These P-47s had an extra contribution because, in addition to their 108 gallon belly-tanks, shackled below each mainplane was a 100 lb ANM30 demolition bomb. Meeting their charges near Deventer, they accompanied the B-17s to an area southwest of Munster. During the 25 minutes of their escort, the only "hostile" aircraft seen were some of the B-17s themselves. Understandably nervous, certain gunners tended to fire first and identify later. In fairness, fighter pilots were warned about approaching in any manner that could be interpreted as unfriendly, and a deferentially slow slide in, showing your most prominent recognition features, was considered wise. However, there was no damage this time and the 356FG were superseded by the 364FG.

Relinquishing the monotony, the men from Martlesham Heath split into their three squadrons — the 359FS, 360FS and 361FS — to set about disrupting Hitler's train timetables and water-borne traffic delivery schedules. Descending from 22,000 to 7,000 feet, the 359FS found a sizeable gathering of tugs and barges in a five mile stretch of the Dortmund-Ems canal, near the bridge at Senden. These were left to Red Flight because White Flight had spotted their own tasty morsels on the railway track between Haltern and Munster. Making their initial approach from 90°, Red Flight peeled off in classic style from 5,000 feet. Screaming earthwards along the length of the canal, pilots picked their targets and released bombs between 1,500 and 2,000 feet. First Lieutenants G B Peet and R G Vossler each hit a barge. To his slight embarrassment Tukey missed, but other hits were scored on a house and bridge. Increasing altitude to swing round for another pass, Red Flight saw First Lieutenant R A Rann's White Flight swooping on a long, slow-hauling freight train of 40 wagons chugging towards Munster. They were on it with the enthusiasm of gulls finding a newly-spilled garbage can. Rann took the engine with Lieutenant W H Wood while Lieutenants W C O'Barr and R B Warren shared the freight cars. O'Barr got more than he bargained for. Squeezing only some 20 rounds from each gun at a freight car, he was startled when the whole thing simply vanished before his eyes in a massive explosion. Flames, smoke and debris hurtled some 700 feet into the air. Flying at only 75 feet, O'Barr was too close to avoid the foul, grey black geyser roaring skywards and his fighter hurtled into a wall of surging smoke and lumps of locomotive — then, amazingly, hurtled clear. Checking himself and his aircraft, O'Barr could scarcely believe his wings were still those of a P-47 and not empyrean. Somehow, his Thunderbolt had swept through the blast with only minor damage. Even Red Flight at 5,000 feet were tossed aside like corks in a fountain. Skidding away from the explosion, Rann's P-47 was also slightly damaged and, looking back, he saw a huge crater in the railway bed, the tracks were torn up and several freight cars were now scatterings of matchwood smouldering in the surrounding countryside. Lieutenant Warren had been so startled, he had no idea if his own bullets had made any more contribution but, gathering his wits, he pummelled a nearby switch-house. Continuing with their piscatorial pursuit, using ordnance instead of rods, Red Flight remustered and went "fishing" in the nearby canal, pouncing repeatedly on their selection of barges and tugs, one of which exploded and began settling rapidly. Content with their catch, ammunition spent, the P-47s pulled up, re-formed and set off westwards.

Further along the Dortmund-Ems canal, the 360FS also bombed and strafed barges, then set about some trains but with less spectacular results. Being a bargeman or train driver in Germany was proving a risky occupation because the 361FS were giving similar treatment to river and rail traffic between Gutersloh and Bielefeld. The sky over Germany was plagued with pilots prowling for targets — the 361FS found itself competing with green-nosed P-47s of the 359FG as both units sought pickings in the same area. With most of their bombs expended, the 361FS departed. Off the Dutch coast, they saw Trudeau but contact with Strobell confirmed matters were in hand. Further out, an inconsiderate B-17, that must have seen them, jettisoned bombs which whistled through their formation "too damn close for comfort". Back at Martlesham Heath, someone else either had a warped sense of humour or failed to appreciate that pilots may have had enough of matters German for one day because they sat down to a late dinner of . . . frankfurters!

Returning P-47 pilots of the 356FG were disenchanted with their evening meal.

Pictured later in the war, Colonel Osborn, left, discussed a point with Bill Kepner. Roy Osborn's misadventures with a P-38 on 22 April 1944 caused consternation decades later when wreckage of his Lightning was found near Thetford. (D Engle)

Earlier that evening, one ranking fighter pilot was annoyed over his failure even to reach Germany. Colonel Roy W Osborn, commanding the 364FG, had over 3,245 hours flying experience and, when things went wrong, he drew on every minute of it to keep his P-38 aloft. Leading his Group of 46 Lightnings from Honington to replace the 356FG escorting the First Air Division, Osborn had reached the Zuider Zee when the port Allison engine of his P-38J began running rough. Leaving Major John H Lowell in charge, Osborn turned homewards with an escort in case he was forced to ditch. His Group had a relatively uneventful mission. Blue Flight of the 385FS were inconclusively bounced by about 40 Me109s at 1945 hours, south of Hamm. Hitting the deck, the P-38s evaded damage and took token revenge by shooting up three oil barges on the Rhine. The Me109s carried on into the Second Air Division but the outcome of this was not seen by the 364FG. Meanwhile, Colonel Osborn had crawled steadily homeward on one good Allison and one which continued to falter until it gave up decisively by exploding with such force it blew pieces off and left a large chunk of torn cowling impeding the aerodynamics. Luckily, Osborn was now over the English Coast and in contact with Honington's control tower. Skilfully, Osborn only just kept control but found it impossible when he slowed the ship down in a landing configuration. Crossing the airfield at 5,000 feet, he notified control of his intention to bale out and circled cautiously overhead. Concerned about local communities, Osborn directed the miscreant fighter towards empty heathland used by the British Army for mortar bombing practice and baled out. His only injury was an ankle sprained on landing but, over four decades later, his Lightning caused some anxiety for East Anglian aviation archaeologists.

Shuttling over Belgium to replace the 364FG came 23 Thunderbolts of the 56 'A' FG led by Lieutenant Colonel Francis S Gabreski, one of the Eighth's most famous aces. His task today provided no scope for additions to his score and the Group broke escort at 2038 hours near Ostend. Flying home to Halesworth at 20,000 feet, they witnessed the sobering spectacle of Norman's P-47 plunging into the sea.

The 78 'A' FG also had a placid day and took the First Air Division Fortresses from east of Namur at 2015, out over the North Sea. Comfort was given to five crippled B-17s but there was little drama for the Duxford Group — some of whose fighters escorting the Second Air Division's Liberators would have more exciting tales to tell.

On 22 April 1944, the 352FG were in transition from Thunderbolts to becoming a Mustang unit. They operated a 'B' and an 'A' Group with each type, albeit of markedly different sizes. The 352A Group's eventful sweep with Mustangs will be described later. The 352FG, essentially the 328FS, still flying P47s were assigned to penetration support under Field Order 309. Lieutenant Colonel Clark took off at 1805 hours followed by 15 Thunderbolts. Rendezvousing with the B-24s, they found them in only "fair formation but strung out". The bombers' problems were only just beginning. The 352B FG reported little else of interest. Some large, white bursts of flak at 35,000 feet in front of and above the bombers were thought to be marking their course. Later, Stotter's ship was seen near Hamm with one propeller feathered and another engine smoking. Eight parachutes were counted but there was little the P-47 pilots could do to help. Unlike the unfortunate Stotter, they all made it home, landing at Bodney at 2105.

Tracers scorching close over his cockpit canopy confirmed First Lieutenant Clair A Penners' premonition that he would not make it home. He felt his P-38 shudder under the marksmanship of an unseen assailant. With its drop-tanks still attached, *Little Man* instantly torched into a funeral pyre threatening immolation for its pilot before merciful termination 22,000 feet below. Sheer terror and searing heat spurred the survival instinct. Within seconds, he jettisoned the canopy and followed so closely, he hit it as he departed. This collision ripped the dinghy's red sail from its pack and Penners tumbled clear with it flapping frantically in his face as he fumbled for his rip-cord, found it, and tugged. Terrifyingly in his mind was the spectre of a parachute being swiftly consumed by flames from the cockpit, but such anxiety vanished in the breath-taking jerk and beauty of a white dome overhead. Across the

Left *First Lieutenant Clair Penners of the 55FG is still looking for the guy who identified the approaching fighters as "friendly".* (C A Penners)

Above *Close up of the mission board on Penners' P-38* Little Man. *The brooms indicate a sweep and the broom and bomb denotes escort and sweep.* (C A Penners)

evening sky came sounds of the continuing aerial contest. Blending with the distinctive notes from Allison engines came the unfamiliar beat of Daimler-Benz and BMW power-plants, all orchestrating the choir of cannon and machine guns. Penners, contemplating what had happened, admitted his Yellow Section of the 343FS had been effectively bounced by about 20-25 Me109s. What a mistake. Just before *Little Man* was hit, he heard the rapidly approaching dots called in and then dismissed by a pilot on the port side as "little friends". How wrong. Several decades later, Penners commented, "I am still looking for that guy and if I find him I'll break his neck!" Facing a 15 minute descent into captivity, he was at least alive and he wondered how others in his 55FG had fared.

Fifty-one P-38s took off from Wormingford to escort the Second Air Division, but numbers soon depleted with engine and other mechanical problems only too familiar to Groups operating Lockheed's creatively-styled configuration. Comfortable in warm climes, the Lightning suffered a loss of operational efficiency in the damp operating environment of northern Europe. Adding to the 55FG's woes, they found the Liberator formation spread over a distance of nearly 20 miles making comprehensive cover impossible. Splitting his Group, Major Jones apportioned protection as best he could — the 338FS went forward with the 38FS and 343FS escorting the centre and rear bomber units. The 38FS and 338FS saw "50 to 60" FW190s and Me109s bounce one box of B-24s but were too far away to intervene. Spread too thinly to defend all the widely scattered bombers, the 343FS had further divided into Red and Yellow Flights with Penners as "tail-end Charlie" — a

55FG pilots gather in the parachute room. L-R: Lewis; Gordon; Mearns; Welch; Buttke; Moore; Courtney. Buttke claimed an Me109 destroyed as pilots tried to protect a widely-scattered bomber force. (E Giller)

notoriously vulnerable slot which again lived up to its reputation.

Flying as top-cover, Captain Eugene E Ryan squinted into the setting sun knowing enemy fighters could use this to advantage during an attack. His concern became reality when about 20 unidentified aircraft emerged from the glare. Convinced they were hostile, he ordered tanks dropped and his flight split left and right, climbing as they turned towards the enemy who swept overhead without apparently seeing his Lightnings. Tanks tumbling away told Ryan they were also preparing for combat, probably hoping to hit the bombers or possibly Yellow Flight further back. With Ryan's White Flight climbing in pursuit of what they now recognized as FW190s, Yellow Flight were pounced on by Me109s and Penners' P-38 spun away in flames as aircraft on both sides whipped into a series of vicious dogfights. Seeing an FW190 closing on Blue Three, Ryan fired to frighten it and the Focke-Wulf broke away. Giving his P-38 full boost, Ryan gained, firing again and causing an explosion in his opponent's engine. Smoking badly, its pilot apparently wounded, the FW190 tried to evade in a split "ess" turn but only slithered round, verging on a stall. Grasping the opportunity, both Ryan and his wingman, First Lieutenant Norman J Bartz fired, knocking the FW190 into an erratic fall from which there seemed no hope of recovery. Its destruction was claimed.

As the combat scattered across a magnificent evening sky, First Lieutenant Arthur L Thorsen felt it was "the most graceful scrap I was ever in. It was a beautiful aerial ballet". But death was one of the dancers. Far below, Siegfried Vetter also felt the splendour as he stood watching through binoculars with his family from their garden in Eiserfeld, east of Siegen. Looking north, he saw fighters defending the Fatherland confront their adversaries, then heard gunfire exchanged as the aircraft writhed into the frequently-exchanged rhythm of hunters and hunted. Anxious and excited, the family saw a Messerschmitt open fire on the tail of an enemy machine which immediately flipped over and spun vigorously to earth trailing flames. Seconds later, its funereal screech ceased abruptly and a pall of smoke plumed heavenwards from the direction of Siegen. The Vetters' jubilation was brief. Unable to warn their pilot, they saw an American fighter speeding in to attack. As it fired, the Messerschmitt lurched over, cork-screwing towards the ground. Down and down until it seemed their hero was doomed then, not many metres high, it recovered and spluttered away southeasterly, still losing height. Suddenly the ailing engine ceased. Too far away to see if the pilot had escaped, Siegfried Vetter quickly telephoned his brother, the mayor, to alert the relevant authorities. Later that evening the family were delighted to learn that the pilot, Uffz Heribert Doering of 3./JG3 "Udet" had landed safely by parachute. Testimony by the Vetter family confirmed Doering's claim which was officially credited in June. Doering never knew: he was killed in action on 24 April.

Sadly, Doering's victim, Captain Bernie V Guthrie, also perished. Accounts by his comrades describe the ferocity of the combat in which he lost his life. Firstly, the 55FG ace, Captain Robert L Buttke, 343FS: "I was leading Tudor Blue Flight on the escort mission to Hamm. Tudor Squadron was to act as top-cover. We rendezvoused with the bombers about five minutes before they reached the target at 25,000 feet and continued on with them. About 20 miles from Hamm, my Flight was bounced by 15 or more Me109s. I called them into the Group Lead and then my radio went dead. I turned into the first four head on as the Flight split up, opened fire with no visible results. I had three on my tail in short order and, in reefing my plane in too tight, I went into a spin and hit compressibility before I could get it out. I lost the Me109s in the spin so I started climbing back up when I saw a P-38 at 11,000 feet with two '109s on his tail. The left engine of the P-38 was smoking so I charged in head on trying to chase the Me109s away. I couldn't get a good shot on the first pass and the '109s didn't scare worth a damn. On my second pass at the two, they broke left of the P-38 they were attacking and I got about 70 % deflection shot at the first one, observing strikes round the wing roots and cockpit. This '109 fell out and went spinning down which I claim as a probable. I pulled up a little and saw the other '109 a little below me and about head on. We charged each other head on but didn't observe any strikes. He went over me and tried to split S on my tail. I zoomed up, did a 180° turn and met him head on again. After we passed, he did a split S for the deck. I climbed up to about 16,000 feet and saw a P-38 below me with two '109s on his tail, very close. I came into them from almost a 90° angle doing better than 400 miles. I had to lead the P-38 about a radii thinking I would hit the first '109. I opened fire, observing many strikes on and around the canopy of the second one. He slowly turned over on his back and resembled a falling leaf. I claim this one as destroyed. I hit compressibility again and had a hard time pulling back up. When I got to climbing again I found that I had collected the other '109 on my tail. I tried turning with him but he put a burst of tracer right under me to I kicked top rudder and started a tight spiral upward. After about three turns, the other P-38, Lt Fair, came from underneath and slapped a bunch of slugs into the '109's belly. The last I saw of him, he was smoking and spinning. Lt Fair joined me and we came home. I claim one Me109 destroyed and one probably destroyed".

Buttke's claim was supported by First Lieutenant Gene R Fair who came close to becoming another casualty.

"I was fourth man in Tudor Blue Flight and flying at 25,000 feet when we were bounced from above by 15 or more silver and blue Me109s. We dropped our belly tanks and tried to turn into them. After completing about a 90° turn there were four '109s closing in on my tail. We were turning to the left so I tightened my turn and turned inside of the Flight. I could see that I wasn't turning sharp enough so I kicked into a spin. After making four or five turns, I recovered and started back up, collected two '109s as I did. My air-speed was down so I couldn't turn so I kicked it into a spin to the other side. I think my left engine had been hit before this. When I tried to recover, I saw that I had no control of the plane, my airspeed was over 500 mph then, and I was at 20,000 feet so I released my canopy but couldn't get my hands on the safety belt to release it. When I couldn't get out, I started kicking the ship all over the sky. Finally, I got some response from the ship so I started to pull it out. In doing this I buckled the right wing of my ship and raised the right engine up about four or five inches in the mounting. As I was flying straight and level, CY-J came by and called me to let me know my flaps were down. He turned to the right and I to the left and that was the last I saw of him. I believe that was Capt Guthrie. While turning to the left two '109s bounced me and closed in to about 50 yards, firing all the way. I then saw a P-38 coming in from about 90° and firing, Capt Buttke hit the second man from behind and crossed in behind the first man. The '109 Capt Buttke hit seemed to slowly roll over on its back and fluttered down in that attitude. I confirm the '109 destroyed by Capt Buttke".

In all probability, Buttke's second kill was 19 year old Lieutenant Peter-Paul Presbar of 1./JG3 who was hit and apparently leapt from his Me109 "White 8" without a parachute. Perhaps it caught fire or his parachute had been rendered useless. His broken body was found several days later near Helmeroth. German records also show that Unteroffizier

Karl Schnitzler of 1./JG3 was slightly wounded and force-landed "White 5" in a field near Waltershausen which lay between the combat area and his base at Burg.

Support for the sorely-pressed 55FG arrived northwest of Koblenz at 2000 hours in the welcome shape of 24 Thunderbolts from the 56B FG. To their disappointment, Colonel Hubert Zemke's Group found skies empty of the Luftwaffe but fear of their presence was clear when jittery gunners fired on P-47s approaching the strung out formations of Liberators. Explosions, fires and smoke billowing from Koblenz testified to some success for the bombers, and evidence of other fighter activity glowed from a hangar and aircraft ablaze on Wevelghem airbase, but the 56B Group pilots had to content themselves with policing the bombers to the Belgian coast. Near Liege, one flight of the 61FS saw flares and heard a bomber calling for help. Descending to investigate, they found no sign of the distressed ship. Later, a B-24 was seen to crash near Brugge. No parachutes were reported, and the final act of malice was intense flak thrown at the force by guns near Ostend, Knokke and Walcheren.

Closing the door on the departure of Mission 311 were 26 P-47s of the 78B FG and 54 Thunderbolts from the 405FG, Ninth Air Force. The experience of each Group was similar to that of the 56B FG, although the 405FG had a little more excitement under Type 16 Ground Control. Essentially, this was the use of high-definition radar peering from Beachy Head and other southern locations into the closer areas of the Continent and offering a more-detailed picture of air activities. Although able to control only one or two units simultaneously, Type 16's RAF personnel could vector Allied fighters in either an offensive role or defensive response. En route to patrolling the Charleroi area, one squadron of the 405FG were diverted to rescue a straggling Fortress from attack by two enemy aircraft which they drove off before playing consort to the cripple until it crossed the enemy coast. The remaining aircraft flew an uneventful patrol before returning to Christchurch at 2156 hours.

Encountering far more excitement were those fighter Groups flying sweeps, particularly the famous 4FG from Debden. That morning, pilots had been practising dog-fights wearing recently received RAF issue "G" suits. These water-pressure Frank suits were effective in reducing black-out during high speed manoeuvres. But, being uncomfortable to wear, they proved unpopular and were not used operationally, soon being discarded until an effective "G" suit became available later that year. After lunch, Colonel Donald J M Blakeslee called a meeting of squadron leaders and flight commanders to impart a tough, no-nonsense, core message — pilots would fly "from dawn to dusk" — reiterating words spoken by General Eisenhower during a recent visit to Debden. No doubt, the Supreme Allied Commander in Europe had invasion plans in mind when addressing his eager young fighter pilots and warned they would "forgo much eating and sleeping" in the forthcoming weeks. The

Colonel Donald J M Blakeslee masterminded a classic bounce by 4FG Mustangs against JG1.
(USAF Official)

4FG had a reputation to maintain and Blakeslee's stance permeated the afternoon briefing for Field Order 309, a sweep through the Hamm/Kassel areas at 1757 hours. His audience listened attentively. The respect shown for Blakeslee had been earned by example, and he made the point by deciding to lead this sweep himself.

At 1625 the powerful beat of Packard-Merlins reverberated over the Essex countryside as 33 sleek Mustangs slid into formation behind Blakeslee and began their thrust towards Europe. Extending their range, a new type of compressed paper drop tank was being evaluated, but there were difficulties and six Mustangs were forced to abort because of fuel supply problems. The remainder prowled into enemy airspace, hunting north of Hamm at 25,000 feet before descending towards Kassel. Isolated inside his aluminium shell, each pilot was alone, yet not alone, and the comforting undulations of nearby aircraft cresting the same invisible currents would be enhanced with the occasional friendly gesture from a pilot who also understood the anxious solitude. Teamwork was essential and pilots segmented the sky in repetitive search patterns as well as frequently checking rear view mirrors mounted on the canopy arch. Good guys in a Western classic, they strode down main-street, alert against ambush, hands poised for the swift draw.

The group's sharpest marksman would ultimately be First Lieutenant (later Major) John T Godfrey. His keen eyes were first to detect a cluster of over 25 enemy fighters against the landscape. Responding to the bomber threat, III. Gruppe of Jagdgeschwader 1 were aloft from Paderborn and forming up at 4,000 feet near the Eder Lake and small town of Korbach. Rapidly assessing the situation, Blakeslee ordered retention of drop tanks to avoid the risk of them being seen tumbling to earth — they would be jettisoned at the charge. Telling the 334FS to remain and provide top-cover, he led the 335FS and 336FS down to

attack in a diving, starboard turn, swinging up-sun with his two squadrons spreading out to box in the enemy. During this manoeuvre, they lost sight of IIIJG1 and released tanks in case they themselves were bounced. Several anxious minutes elapsed until the 335FS, at 8,000 feet, spotted the enemy some 3,000 feet lower and at 9 o'clock. The 336FS had descended to 6-7,000 feet and were out of position so a hasty climb to 10,000 feet ensued and the German fighters were soon observed on the squadron's port side. By now IIIJG1 had seen the threat. Caught at a height disadvantage, they winged steeply into a tight, defensive circle — the Lufbery — each fighter protecting the tail of the one in front. Realizing his cover had been broken, Blakeslee also recognized the professionalism of his opponents. Their tactics made individual attacks by his pilots very risky, and the two forces now circled like wary pugilists, each with his guard up, waiting for the other to move first. Someone would either snatch a chance or lose their nerve.

Nearest the enemy was *Becky* Red Flight of the 336FS commanded by First Lieutenant Willard H Millikan. Circling cautiously, he eased closer, flying alongside the Lufbery, taunting the enemy out to fight. His three sections kept a compact formation, offering a tempting but viperous target. Then, abruptly, the German circle broke. Curving out towards the P-51s came two Me109s intent on a swift, darting attack — but the Mustangs were ready. Millikan called a break to port. Merlins whining, power surging on, the Mustangs reared up and round. Seeing the two Me109s Blakeslee promptly raced for the gap created by their audacity and, in his own words, "the fight was on". In seconds, the sky was a seething turmoil of fighters, each twisting, turning, climbing and diving, all entangled in the tumult of merciless combat. Millikan saw the first '109 out of the Lufbery banking steeply to attack Red Four and he tormented his P-51 into an accelerating turn, dropped flaps and contorted the protesting fighter into the Me109s turning circle. Responding, the German pilot tightened his own turning radius, gaining on Millikan. Sweating hard, Millikan kicked his Mustang into a stomach-churning, nose up corkscrew, wrenching himself from the '109's clutches. It worked. Momentarily outwitting his opponent, he reversed their roles and Millikan's guns snapped a burst into the '109, flicking it out of its turn. Desperately striving to regain the initiative, it started a sharp, split-ess but Millikan's tracers streaking across its nose proved a potent dissuader, forcing it back into the original manoeuvre, just as the American anticipated. Hit again, the Messerschmitt skidded, slowing down — now a more compliant victim. Dropping more flap and throttling back, Millikan still found himself overshooting so he side-slid the Mustang and fired, raking the '109 from close quarters. Slithering violently made sighting impossible but he was now so close that aiming was unnecessary — he simply blasted the '109 getting closer and closer until fear of collision forced him to pull up over the German. With all fight gone, his bravado blasted by 50 calibre bullets, the German baled out as a triumphant Millikan soared by. Somewhat cruelly, the American later commented, "I wished I could have hit the pilot for he was extremely good and his loss would mean a lot for our cause". His first victim was probably Leutnant Kurt Ibing or Feldwebel Gerhard Reimitz, both of whom baled out during this engagement. Reimitz was found paralysed, his back broken but Ibing suffered only a slight head wound and, bearing in mind Millikan's remark, quickly returned to combat.

Millikan's next kill was more literal. Pulling up into a left hand climb,

he noted a Mustang on the wrong end of a '109 and pounced. Seeing him, the German fighter left its intended target and reefed into a series of very tight turns with Millikan chasing hard, even blacking out as he pulled high "G" through one manoeuvre. Grimly, Millikan traced the '109 pilot's every action then, calculating his moment, he hit the German in one turn forcing him to frantically jink the '109, but Millikan's burst hit him again. Smoke streaming from its engine, the '109's dive steepened then, threatened by another Messerschmitt, Millikan lost sight of it but his wingman, Second Lieutenant Joseph A Patteeuw, saw it crash and burn. The attacking '109 cut between Millikan and Patteeuw, swiftly getting Millikan in its sights before his wingman could intervene. Urging more stress on body and airframe alike, Millikan realized it was too late. This '109 was about to mete out vengeance and the shark-like snout could not be shaken off. Closer, ever closer — any moment its 30 mm cannon could recite his requiem.

Glancing over his left shoulder, First Lieutenant Robert H Norley had already destroyed an Me109 and was wisely checking his own tail when he saw Millikan's plight. Tugging hard into a diving turn, Norley charged in, his guns ripping out a long, warning burst. Some rounds hit their target — not seriously — but enough to discourage the German who rolled on his back and went straight down, quickly distancing himself from Norley. Almost mesmerized, Norley realised something his adversary seemingly did not. Their height was only 1,500 feet. The '109 plummeted into the ground and exploded. Still more strange behaviour would follow as Norley curved round to confront another '109 closing from 8 o'clock. Amazingly, its pilot appeared not to see the Mustang and levelled off almost lazily in front of its guns. Provided with such an opportune target, Norley promptly missed, not once but five times. The

"Glancing over his left shoulder, First Lieutenant Robert H Norley had already destroyed an Me109 and was wisely checking his own tail . . ." (L Nitscke)

unwary German's slipstream was bouncing his P-51 about too much to be accurate. Edging out of the turbulence into less disturbed air, Norley was squeezing the trigger again when he sensed another aircraft astern. Dumping flaps, he leapt into a sharp, port turn losing both intended victim and suspected assailant. Identification was difficult as fighters mingled in the melee. At one point, Blakeslee called for all his Group to break starboard, the assumption being that anything going port must be German. The speed, confusion, tension and peaks of sheer terror were exhausting. Seconds stretched into aeons as the complex drama of kill-or-be-killed continued.

To Millikan, having been rescued and just dispatched a third prey, "things were certainly mixed up, and it seemed like we had been fighting for hours. Fires were burning everywhere . . ." Tackling another '109, it put up "an amazing demonstration of aerobatics" but, ignoring the showmanship, Millikan thumped it between stunts and the demoralized Messerschmitt straightened out then gracefully slow rolled. Hitting it again, Millikan half-admired another beautifully-executed slow roll but still fired as it levelled off. Fire now dressed the circus performer, but what seemed like yet another slow roll ceased and the burning '109, remaining inverted, entered a shallow dive. The finale, as it struck the ground, was a gruesome cascade of flames and burning debris.

Other 4FG pilots were making their own contributions to the carnage over Korbach. Blakeslee and his wingman chased one Me109 into a shallow, wooded valley. At some 350 mph, the three fighters skimmed the tree tops. Two bursts from Blakeslee concluded the conflict and he zoomed past only 15 feet above the Messerschmitt as it churned into the ground. Air combat might appear to offer a deadly grace and beauty, somehow removed from war's more grisly features but Captain Winslow M Sobanski was starkly reminded of its horrors as he flashed over Blakeslee's first kill. Sobanski's fleeting glimpse of the pilot's torso torn in two and splattered grotesquely from the cockpit by the impact, haunted his soul with the ugly reality. Distracting moments of compassion could kill, however. Sobanski swiftly dispensed with such emotions as he climbed to rejoin the battle. Meanwhile, Blakeslee had also winged up to 5,000 feet before sighting another Me109 being harried by a pack of P-51s. Using height for speed advantage, Blakeslee sprinted after the '109, closing in as it lifted and straightened to avoid some trees. Two seconds of death hammered from his guns. With its wings and cockpit riddled, the fleeing German clipped into the tree tops then cartwheeled to destruction. Still the slaughter of IIIJG1 continued.

First Lieutenant Kendall E Carlson originally found himself in the centre of the first Messerschmitt carousel, briefly firing at four or five different aircraft in the mad merry-go-round. Results were inconclusive. Then, seeing two more vulnerable Me109s below, he flicked out of the circle and bounced them. Seeing him, they climbed steeply to starboard but it was too late for the second machine, Carlson's bullets smashed into the engine and cockpit, setting it on fire. Rolling over, the pilot

Second Lieutenant Donald R Emerson flew with a lucky rabbit's foot as a talisman from his girlfriend. It prevailed during combat on 22 April 1944. (R A Freeman collection)

baled out just as Carlson's number two, Second Lieutenant Donald R Emerson, opened fire. Seeing the pilot leaping clear, Emerson ceased fire but these circumstances might account for the loss of Lieutenant Joachim Göhre. German archives say simply, "after an attack with P-51 he baled out and was shot at 800 m in the chest and died. Attack planes not recognized. Body was recovered and buried in home town of Eberswalde".

Starting to climb, Carlson heard Blakeslee's command for a starboard turn. This helped him identify three or four Me109s scuttling over the terrain. Diving in pursuit, Carlson and Emerson saw Blakeslee in WD-C get one and another P-51 destroyed a second before they got there. Climbing again, Carlson glimpsed a lone Me109 sneaking down a ravine and, once again, both P-51s powered down in pursuit. Firing, Carlson got a few hits, so did Emerson. Throttles fully open, they streaked low over the countryside. Firing again, their bullets scythed into the rooftops of a small town. Emerson's ammunition was exhausted, Carlson had only a few rounds left and could not help but admire the German pilot's skill, weaving and dodging, hugging the landscape. Firing again as the '109 flitted across his gunsight, Carlson used the last of his ammunition — then, momentarily, he lost his opponent. A second later, he saw the '109 curve earthwards, crashing into a large clump of trees. A morbid pyre of black smoke burgeoned skywards as the victorious P-51s swept upwards to rejoin the Group.

Flying number three in Carlson's flight, First Lieutenant Reuben Simon had gone for one of the first Me109s to break from the Lufbery and his bullets sent it screeching vertically towards the ground. Staying close, Simon shot off more pieces from the '109 as it plummeted earthwards, then he had to pull out with his P-51 now registering over 400 mph. His wingman, Second Lieutenant Donald J Patchen kept with him and saw the Me109's impact. There was no parachute.

Credited with first sighting the enemy, Godfrey relates his contribution to the fray. "I was flying White 3 in Becky section. As we let down from 25,000 to 15,000 feet I reported bags of fighters forming up below us. They were in a gaggle flying in three's so we orbited and took the bounce. For a while we lost them but finally caught sight of them in a Lufbery. I split up from my number one, and orbited the outskirts of the circle. I could not get inside the circle without getting a couple on my tail. One broke off and tried to break away. I closed to about 350 yards and gave about a 15° deflection shot. I got a lucky hit and he straightened up for me. I clobbered him really good and noticed strikes in the cockpit and engine. He pulled up and rolled over with flame and smoke pouring from him. This '109 went straight in.

"On my second '109 I caught another one trying to sneak away. I fired at about 300 yards at this one with 10° deflection. I did quite a bit of shooting and noticed strikes in the cockpit and engine. The kite began to smoke and I overshot to starboard and pulled up preparing to make another attack. The Jerry was smoking and losing altitude, I guess he figured he didn't stand a chance for he bailed out at approximately 1,500 feet. These two aircraft were confirmed by my wingman Lieutenant La Jeunesse, who stuck behind me during the fight. He did a very good job.

"On my third I saw a '109 turning on the deck. I gave flap and dove down in a steep turn. I got very close to this one and started firing, allowing quite a bit of deflection. He got lower and lower, above the trees. I had quite a job keeping on his tail as I would get in his slipstream and nearly flicked into the deck. Two of my guns jammed but I still kept firing. I saw a good strike in his cockpit and he lost speed. I overshot him, sliding up to port. He seemed to flick and went straight into a bunch of trees. I wanted to get a picture of him burning so I made a port turn. I looked back and found out that I had a '109 on my tail instead of my wingman. My wingman called up that he had lost me but I did not hear him. I dropped flap and made a tight turn. The '109 could not get deflection on me so I kept up the turn. Fortunately another Mustang came in and shot him off my tail. I was too shaken to get a picture of my last Jerry so I hot-footed it for altitude. I claim three Me109s destroyed. Ammunition expended: 734 rounds incendiary".

Blakeslee's decision to leave Captain Sobanski's squadron providing top-cover proved doubly sensible. Firstly, the orbiting Mustangs swooped on several retreating Me109s, forcing them back into the piranha-pool. Sobanski hit one himself and confirmed both Blakeslee's victories. More importantly, the need for top-cover became evident when First Lieutenant Paul S Riley, wingman for Captain Albert L Schlegel, saw two Me109s preparing to attack from above the protective umbrella. Dropping their tanks, the German fighters peeled off and, this time, forced the Mustangs into a Lufbery. Seeing no opening in the defensive circle, they broke off their attack, diving away very steeply. Boosting his

Harried by Jones, its pilot finally misjudged . . . (Ian Z Garstka)

Merlin, Schlegel gave chase with Riley in dutiful close attendance. The
rapidity of descent caused condensation to mist over Schlegel's screen
and he lost sight of his '109 close to the tree tops. Suffering similar
misting problems, Riley managed to wipe his canopy and chased the
other Messerschmitt down to 50 feet where it whipped into a sequence
of sharp turns. Swinging wide to follow, Riley was startled when another
Me109 slid neatly in front of him during one of the turns. Working
quickly, he hauled his control column well back, dropped 20° of flap
and, with G-force crushing him into his seat, edged into line for a
deflection shot. Realizing the danger, one Messerschmitt spurted out of
the deadly dance, vanishing northwards in the knowledge that Riley
risked being hit by the second '109 if he followed. The whirling tail-
chase had now drifted into a small valley with Riley nibbling pieces of
his opponent in short bursts but wary of the sloping ground which
prevented a decisive hit. Finally, he called for help from other P-51s
who still provided top-cover.

Hearing Riley's appeal, First Lieutenant William B Smith and Second
Lieutenant Preston B Hardy dived on the Messerschmitt. Smith's first,
long burst savaged the German and the still-pursuing Riley saw hits in
its cockpit and large pieces torn off. Straightening up, the Me109 was
obviously badly damaged. Racing towards the valley slope, Smith and
Preston pulled out, surging skywards over the rim then curving swiftly
back on to the '109 whose pilot was now jettisoning his canopy, perhaps
injured, struggling to escape. No chance. Like wolves on an injured stag,
the P-51s pounced again. Smith's next burst pierced the German's port
wing before his Mustang soared again out of the valley, turning to repeat
his assault. Riley was also closing in. Then yet another Mustang, flown
by First Lieutenant Frank C Jones, cut in front of Smith, firing as it
approached. Jones had already been blooded. He had damaged a '109
before chasing it so close to the ground that it sent dust eddies swirling
from the soil in its race for survival. Harried by Jones, its pilot finally
misjudged, caught a wing and somersaulted in a ball of dust and
disintegrating aircraft debris. Seeking his deuce, Jones now joined in the
chase after Riley's '109. Firing as he dived, Jones missed but the hapless
Messerschmitt had been hounded to exhaustion. As if appealing for
mercy, it straightened out to crash land but, catching some trees, had
one wing torn off and exploded, scattering wreckage across the
countryside.

Having demisted his screen, Schlegel climbed into the battle. He
"attacked a '109 from about 80° allowing a little over two rings
(100 mph sight), opened fire under 200 yards and saw strikes in the area
just above the wing root; it started smoking immediately". Carlson,
racing after the same '109, was so impressed with Schlegel's skilled
deflection shooting, he quipped on the intercom with "Damned good
shooting" but then was unable to prevent himself sliding in front of
Schlegel's nose forcing the latter to abruptly climb away. However,
Carlson was gracious in confirming the kill as Schlegel's while Schlegel,

still climbing, could see a P-51 having problems with the '109 it was chasing. Simulating a crash-landing approach, the Messerschmitt baited the P-51 into overshooting and now Schlegel saw the '109 nosing up after the unwary American. Spurring his Mustang, Schlegel swept down on the '109. Firing at long range, he diverted the German who now climbed towards him. Racing head-on, both aircraft fired then, as the Messerschmitt hurtled beneath him, Schlegel kicked his P-51 into a steep turn and gave chase. By now, the '109 was heading straight down but, cautious over its previous trickery, Schlegel throttled back, trailing and firing until it struck the ground.

As the remnants of IIIJG1 fled from the area, the 4FG assessed their situation, reorganizing their own ranks. Several pilots expressed anxiety about their severely stressed engines. Others had electrical problems, and many were now out of ammunition. One pilot, First Lieutenant Robert F Nelson was missing. During the dogfight, his aircraft either malfunctioned or sustained damage. Second Lieutenant Oscar F La Jeunesse had seen Nelson circling with glycol streaming from his engine and watched as his comrade parachuted near Korbach.

Extricating himself from a tree, Nelson evaded capture and lived on buffalo grass until caught four days later. Against his loss, the 4FG claimed the destruction of 18 Me109s later re-assessed to 17. German casualties indicate nine aircraft shot down and seven pilots of III. Gruppe/JG1 were killed, two wounded. In the fast-moving, fear-ridden ferocity of combat, some duplicated claims were inevitable but not deliberate. Of more importance was the demonstrable supremacy and teamwork of well-trained, experienced American pilots plus the potential of their P-51 Mustangs.

"Long live the Mustang" was a comment recorded on 22 April 1944 by First Lieutenant Quentin L Quinn who flew his recently-acquired aircraft on a sweep with the 352A FG. Their task took them into northern Germany and Lieutenant Colonel John C Meyer's force of 33 Mustangs reached the Hanover region just before 1800. Splitting into two forces, they foraged. Near Nienburg, the 486FS descended from a lightly-clouded evening sky to destroy six locomotives, damage several more and leave burning a number of oil-wagons. Further north, the 487FS, with some attached 328FS pilots, attacked Stade airfield. Approaching with the sun behind them, they destroyed or damaged several aircraft and blew-up a Ju88 caught taxi-ing out. Several pieces of this hit Captain B McMahan's P-51 but the damage was only slight. Blundering onto the scene, another unfortunate Ju88 was set upon by Yellow Flight, led by Major George E Preddy Jr. Seeing the Mustangs, the Ju88 veered frantically away but, with several fighters firing as they closed in, the larger, twin-engined type had no hope. Burning, and with one crew member visible as he clambered from an escape hatch, the Ju88 flipped over and plunged into extinction from less than 1,000 feet.

Setting a homeward course, the 352FG attacked more locomotives and airbases en route. Strafing airfields was hazardous and intense ground fire separated Quinn from his comrades after sharing in the destruction of an Me210 on an aerodrome near Bohmte. Returning alone, he was still pleased to have converted from a P-47 to a P-51. Somewhat less enamoured with his new mount was First Lieutenant Marion V Long whose aircraft suffered flak damage during the airfield attack. A superb air-combat fighter, the P-51 was, however, more vulnerable to light flak than the P-47 because its in-line Merlin engine needed coolant and even slight puncturing of the system soon caused seizure. Captain William T Halton found Long "just west of Dummer Lake at 14,000 feet. He was flying very slowly and seemed to be in trouble. I flew very close to him and observed that his coolant scoop had been damaged and that there was a thin stream of white smoke coming out of his scoop. About 15 miles west of Lingen, flames and smoke came out of his exhaust stacks and he called me and said, 'This is it, Bill, I've got to bail.' I told him that I would cover him, and he jettisoned his canopy and rolled his ship over on its back and bailed out. I circled him three times and saw him in his 'chute at approximately 3,000 feet before I left."

Being taken prisoner — or worse — as the result of attacking heavily defended airfields became all-too-common and fighter Groups increasingly learned to assess the likely benefits before strafing. Sweeping in an area close to the 352FG, the 355FG patrolled Brunswick, Celle, Minden and Einbeck from 9,000 feet to ground level but intense flak discouraged forays against airfields. One squadron was detached for bomber escort while the Group's remaining Mustangs struck at trains, barges and oil installations. Apart from a slight headwound suffered by Lieutenant McGinty, all 48 fighters settled safely at Keevil just before 2100.

Anti-aircraft fire accounted for all four empty seats in the Officers Club at Steeple Mordern that evening as the Ninth Air Force's 363FG rued the results of their first fighter sweep into southwestern Germany. Forty nine Mustangs participated, strafing airfields near Frankfurt, Badkreuznach and Karlsruhe. Two Ju88s were probably destroyed and the Group asserted damage to a trainer biplane, a glider, flak emplacements and even an enemy bulldozer. Attacking a flak-site proved detrimental to First Lieutenant John A Sharrock when return fire damaged his oil system. Climbing away, he found himself alone and, with engine temperature steadily increasing, he set his 380FS Mustang on a homeward course.

First Lieutenant Ward F Miller of the 381FS was given no choice when the first burst of an accurate barrage achieved a direct hit on his Mustang at 15,000 feet over Ludwigshafen. Luckily, he leapt clear and his parachute opened at 8,000 feet. Also damaged was Captain George R Doerr's *Pegasus*, but he too tried taking his ailing aircraft home until forced to parachute into captivity near St Dizier in France.

Sharrock also failed to get home. His misfortunes were further compounded by a partially-opened parachute, but providence

Right *First Lieutenant John A Sharrock tried to make it home but his engine gave up and his parachute only partially opened.* (W E Sharrock)

Below *Captain George Doerr had to abandon* Pegasus *over France.* (S Blake)

compensated with a well-placed grove of trees to arrest his descent uninjured. The burning wreckage of his aircraft some 300 yards away attracted the initial attention of the Germans enabling him to cut his

parachute harness and clamber down unseen. An athletic former football star, he added speed to his departure as German soldiers began their search. Diving into undergrowth near a stream, he concealed himself and waited. Fortunately, the Germans did not search in his direction but his whereabouts had been detected — by the French Underground. When darkness fell, they gave him civilian clothes, including the obligatory beret, three hard-boiled eggs and some bread, but could not yet take him into their system. For three days, Sharrock successfully concealed himself before they returned and, risking their own lives, absorbed him into a network of hideouts until the area was liberated.

Parachuting into occupied Europe offered at least the chance of a friendly reception. Landing in Germany seriously reduced the likelihood of escape. Nonetheless, the fourth 363FG flier lost that evening did his best as Second Lieutenant Paul R Maxwell recalls:

"We had gone in an hour before target time and split up the triangular area surrounding same by Squadrons. Our side of the triangle was from Frankfurt to Karlsruhe and was supposed to have based some 600 fighters. Our Mission was to sweep these fields and to get as many of them airborne as possible (without engagement) so they would be on the ground refuelling at the bombers' target time over Hamm, Germany. At least this was my interpretation of the briefing. We had further broken down into flights upon departing Frankfurt and I was flying Number Four, or second element wing position of 'C' Flight. Our lead was trying to stay at or near 15,000 feet and we were tracking down a river with a low sun to our backs while diving on targets of opportunity (river barges, RR trains etc), climbing back to altitude after each pass and exposing ourselves to heavy flak. This was totally against my limited experience and training (when you commit yourself to the deck, stay there) plus, the most lethal altitude for flak was about 15,000 feet.

On our last such climb-out, straight ahead and setting sun to our back, I strained my eyes toward the ground along our projected flight path and was able to make out smokestacks and buildings of a large city through the purple haze of sunset, whereupon I notified flight lead with no response. (I talked to the other two members in this flight a couple of months later in Luft III and they verified hearing my transmission.) Anyhow, from where I was sitting in the formation, we caught plenty of flak as we continued our climb-out over what I've always claimed was Karlsruhe. I took a hit on the left wing, losing tip and damaging aileron; however I was still flying and was able, with some effort, to hold formation. My instinct told me to hit the deck and go for home; but, again, my training to never break formation took over and I hung in there.

The next thing I remember we were scooting along over heavy forest around 2,000 feet and I was watching muzzle flashes about a mile or so left and seeing flak bursts about the same distance right. Almost at that same instant, I took a hit behind the seat which felt to me like someone standing on my shoulders swinging a 16 lb sledge hammer right into the middle of my back. The next few seconds seemed an eternity. The cockpit filled with smoke, the engine over-revved as I watched the tachometer go off scale, and it suddenly became very hot around me. Not knowing my altitude at that moment, but realizing it was marginal for 'chute deployment, I simply reacted to my instinct (or my tremendous fear of fire) and proceeded to unhook, dump the canopy and dive over the side toward the leading edge of the left wing. Had I been in level flight, this would have been proper procedure and would have carried me behind the trailing edge ahead of the horizontal stabilizer. Much to my chagrin, the next instant found me lying on my left side with my body nearly parallel to the trailing edge, facing forward and glued fast to the wing. With considerable effort, I moved my free top (right) arm behind me, reached for the trailing edge, tugged myself off the aircraft with all my strength and pulled the "D" ring with very little hesitation.

I had very little time to enjoy my one and only bail-out! It seemed that the 'chute had only just popped and I found myself scooting across the top of a heavy pine forest dipping in and out of the tree tops at a very high rate of speed. Several scratches and gouges later, I came to a stop and fell down through the foliage, stopped by the canopy of my 'chute snagged above. Looking down, I found I was still a long way from being on the ground and swinging free between two trees.

If I live to be 100 I will never forget the next instant . . . I looked at my watch to see 7.00 pm . . . target time! Then I heard the distant rumble of bombs impacting. On time, I thought . . . good! Then the next sound I heard was three Packard engines fading off into the distance . . . my buddies heading back to England . . . more than 300 miles away! I suddenly felt very old (at 22), very, very tired and most of all, terribly alone!

Enough feeling sorry for myself. I next took inventory of my physical condition and, surprisingly enough, I was in good condition with the exception of several scratches and bruises. (I must thank 'Pop' Woods, our intelligence officer, for advising us to wear two of everything on a mission.) Next my situation . . . not so good. I was swinging between trees, unable to grasp anything to pull myself to the nearest tree trunk which appeared to be 20 feet away. The first thing I would have liked to have had was about 100 feet of rope. These trees were all about 125-150 feet tall with foliage only at the top fifth, with the bottom half made up of mostly rotten snags. After several attempts at swinging, I managed to grab the trunk with my legs; but, when I unbuckled and the 'chute swung back, I lost the use of the 'chute, its shroud lines and the fine evasion kit it contained. To top everything off, at this moment I heard many voices yelling back and forth in a language I couldn't understand . . . again I remembered what Pop had said about hiding up a tree from a German soldier because the design of their helmets wouldn't allow them to look directly overhead. He was absolutely right! I watched three waves of soldiers go under me over a two hour period. Not one of them stood near the base of the tree I was in and looked straight up, which is what they would have had to do in order to see me in such a thick forest.

Everything quietened down about dark, which came around 9.00 pm, and I started thinking about finishing my trip to the ground down the long, utility pole-like tree. I also thought of another tidbit that Pop told us often, 'If your first hiding place is a good one, stay there at least 24 hours'. However I was having problems. There were no large limbs to sit on, only three to four inches, and most of those were dead snags which would break if I put all my weight on them. I was sitting astraddle these limbs and hugging the tree with my arms. I was napping on and off and became concerned that if I went to sleep I'd release my grip on the tree and down I would go. (The tree let-downs in the current service 'chutes would have certainly helped about now.) Besides, in the dark it didn't look nearly so hairy or so far down that 'utility pole', so down I started. Shinnying went pretty well to start; but the farther down I went, the harder it became as the tree got larger, until finally I had to push out and drop the remaining 10-15 feet.

I pulled off the top of my evasion boots, turned my A2 jacket wrong-side out and, as I had a dark pair of civilian trousers on, I thought I appeared very continental. I only wish I had a mirror and a flashlight. What I didn't know was that while lying on the wing in the exhaust wake and all the material it was spewing (oil, soot flame etc), when I took off my helmet and goggles I looked like a pet racoon — white around my eyes and forehead with the rest black and burnt!

This got me caught about two hours later on a compass heading south through the woods. I was planning on Switzerland. I knew I was closer to France but from what 'Pop' was telling us, the resistance was selling airmen to the highest bidder after considerable stalling in country . . . besides, he always told us the Swiss border was easy to cross if you were a good swimmer because the Germans didn't patrol the river too heavy due to its swiftness. Anyhow, sometime after midnight while walking along this path (another no-no) through the forest, two soldiers suddenly appeared coming toward me. They were pushing a bicycle between them with a light on the handlebars which, of course, generously played over me. I mustered up my best German (another Pop tidbit) and grunted 'Guten Abend'. They returning the greeting sounding very much like I did (surprisingly enough!) and we passed. However, after passing, they immediately came up each side of me with rifles ready and said 'vor zie der krief ich fertic' laughing and pointing at my face. Of course, I didn't understand them and it wasn't until the next day and my first look into a mirror that I realized what had given me away!

The two soldiers took me to their headquarters which was nearby and consisted of a few, small, tar-paper buildings (still deep in the forest) and turned me over to their officers. (I'm nearly certain this was some sort of Luftwaffe unit. At that time I wasn't too familiar with uniforms and, besides that, I was scared to death.) They proceeded to insist that I strip down to my birthday suit. None of them spoke English so there was considerable roughness on their part in trying to make me understand. At one point I took a lick on the head from a handgun used as a club which laid me out on the floor for a spell. They seemed to be searching for something and would become quite irate each time I couldn't respond to what sounded to me like a bunch of grunting. (It was procedure in our Group that, before each mission, we would each file by our intelligence officer with our pockets turned wrong-side out, place all personal items in a pigeon hole, and pick up a small evasion kit which fits in our shirt pocket.) The evasion kit contained a silkspan map, a button sized compass, pencil clip compass, K-ration candy bar, three benzedrine pills and a few other things I can't remember. I ate the candy in the tree and took the pills so that I might stay awake and not fall out of the tree. I was using the map and compass when caught by the soldiers. They kept those plus anything else I had in my pockets. I guess I will never know what they were looking for so intently and why they became so irate when they couldn't find it.

I was at this location probably an hour or two before being picked up by two Luftwaffe officers in a fine, big car in which the driver sits outside and the rear seat is enclosed. They put me in the sidecar of a motorcycle and we went with them following very close behind in their fine car. Man, I thought I would freeze to death and I don't think they went less than 50 mph. This continued about an hour until we came to a small town and stopped near its centre where we entered some sort of government office. Here a man recently awakened from a deep sleep and who seemed to have some authority grumbled with my captors in German. After arriving at some sort of decision, the two officers and myself departed with me between them in the back of that fine car. After perhaps 30 minutes, we came to a very large and beautiful old estate-type home. They explained to me that this was exactly what it was before commandeered for an officers club. We entered and, with very little delay I was led up a beautiful winding staircase to a large dining room. Man, I was sure glad to see this! I hadn't eaten since about noon except for the K-ration bar and it was now about 3.00 am on the following day (23 April). We sat at the end of a beautiful, long, white table with white tablecloth and all the trimmings. I thought 'wow, bring on the fancy chow!' It turned out to be black, sour, soggy bread, Liederkranz cheese and ersatz coffee. I turned up my nose and told them we wouldn't feed this to the dogs back home, whereupon they laughed at me and, after eating theirs, ate mine and told me I would soon be glad to eat so well.

They locked me into a small closet downstairs by the front door and that was the last of I saw of them. I must say they were gentlemen. Before going to sleep, I took off my shoes and stockings and found that my right stocking was glued to my leg due to dried blood from an injury on the front of my shin just above my shoe top. Since it wasn't bothering me too much at the time, I decided to leave it be.

I was awakened some time after daylight by a boot gently prodding me in the stomach. It was a Luftwaffe sergeant who spoke some English. After getting my shoes and being allowed to use the bathroom (where I saw myself in the mirror and was able to wash off my racoon mask), we were off again. On foot this time. After some time had passed (two or three hours), *we came to a streetcar track and boarded the first car that came along. We rode all the way across a large city which I am reasonably sure was Mannheim. This was my first experience to see first-hand all the terrible devastation of the British and American bombardment. The suburbs weren't too bad, but the city proper was completely destroyed. The only traffic were the streetcars which were very busy running both ways down the centre of the street. All of the bombed out buildings had been neatly cleaned out and all the debris was neatly stacked out to the tracks which prohibited all auto traffic. Nevertheless, most of the businesses appeared to be open and folks were hustling to and fro, both walking and riding street cars. I was sure glad to be with the sergeant at this time. I believe some of those folk would have torn me apart otherwise.*

Shortly before dark, we arrived at an old prison of some sort and the sergeant left me. I was locked up in a small cell and I could see through the window that we were on an airdrome. I could also see two airplanes (an Me109 and a single engine trainer) sitting on the ramp probably 300 yards distance . . . Man, if I could only get to them! No chance.

Before going to sleep, I read some of the graffiti on the walls (some of which was in English) and then quickly dozed off. One in particular stayed with me and was of great value during my year of captivity. 'The only friend you have here is God.'

I was picked up the following morning (24 April) by another sergeant who tried to feed me bread and cheese from his pockets. I still wasn't hungry enough to eat it. After another walk through a residential area, we came to a large railroad station and boarded a train whose destination was Frankfurt. Having been told by Pop many times that the best time to escape was early in the capture while en route, I made my one attempt on this portion of the journey while my guard, who seemed very tired, was napping. We were alone in a compartment and he was sitting across from me with a 'grease gun' on his lap pointed at me; however, he kept nodding off, and much to my surprise, he actually fell off into a deep sleep, snoring and all! I was able to get the door open (platform side) and outside the car. Here I goofed again! I should have hit the cinders immediately but I hesitated hoping to find a softer place to land. I felt a tap on my head and turned around to find a Luger pressed firmly right between my eyes . . . it looked like a cannon to me. I would never have thought anything could be so magnetic! The officer holding it slowly pulled his arm back into the compartment and I was glued to the muzzle like a puppy dog on a leash. After chewing out the sergeant and finding another Luftwaffe enlisted man on the train to accompany him in his mission to guard me, the officer departed the train at the next stop. That was my last chance to escape on this journey. We arrived at Frankfurt, Dulag Luft, late that evening.

I was placed in a small cell, probably eight by eight, with a wooden bench on one side to act as a bed and, believe me, it felt like a feather bed as I quickly fell into a deep sleep.

Upon awakening the next morning, I was led down the dark hall to a latrine where I was permitted to wash up and perform other necessities with the only toiletries supplied being four or five pieces of newspaper about the size of a cigarette paper. As near as I can remember, I was fed twice a day — a ration consisting of thin soup and some more of that wet, soggy, sour bread. Ugh!

Sometime during my stay here (nine days), a boy came into the cell next to mine and we were able to talk some through the wall before the guard would shut us off. I was never sure if this was another trick of my captors or not, but he sure had a sad story to tell. He told me that he was still burping ham and eggs when they first brought him in to Dulag. It seems that his crew departed New York right after breakfast, flew directly into Germany via the bent radio beam the Germans put out for this purpose, and delivered a brand new B-17 with full crew to them. I can't remember his name but I do recall him saying he was from Texas.

As for interrogation, I can only say that we had the best source of intelligence available in our Pop Woods. He had addressed every situation which we might encounter here and our proper response to it. I simply followed his instructions and everything happened as he proclaimed.

First day — 25 April. A Red Cross representative came to my cell with a flowery, home-baked appearance and a long, long form which I was to fill in completely before he could notify my loved ones that all was well. As per Pop's instructions, I completed name, rank and serial number and ran a heavy, wavy line through each and every other blank on this form. This made him very angry and I was promised that I would probably rot here, after which he stormed out.

Second day — 26 April. As expected, he returned with the same forms completely filled out by two of my 'comrades' who were shot down the same day, Captain George Doerr and Lieutenant Ward Miller. I was not acquainted with them but I did meet them in Luft III later on. As per Pop's instructions, I refused to fill out his forms and that was the last I saw of this character.

For the next days, I was left alone in the dark with my only contact being the guard as he led me to the latrine or slid a pan of soup and a slice of bread (I was finally eating the bread) in the door once or twice a day. No conversation. Next came the interrogation sessions. I was led out into the light of day, morning and afternoon, which was blinding after the darkness but was also a joy. Again, every move and every ploy I was aware of from Pop's teachings.

My interrogator spoke fluent English, slang and all, as he had been a waiter at the Waldorf/Astoria Hotel for 17 years until he was forced to return to the Fatherland in 1938 through threats on his father's life who was still living in Germany. At least that was his story to me which I took with a grain of salt. He seemed to know everything about me including my High School Graduation date, date of service, entry, cadet class, date of sailing for England and arrival port, the different units I was attached to in England, and, most of all, the names of the entire staff of my current group and squadron with only a couple of blanks. He kept insisting I would have to fill in the blanks to prove that I was whom I claimed to be so I could avoid being shot as a spy. My answer remained name, rank, and serial number.

Another big question was, What kind of black box did we carry to enable us to depart England many hours after the bombers and still rendezvous with a particular division for escort in the target area? Again — name, rank, and serial number. (Actually, I wasn't aware that there was such a box!)

I found it pretty easy to play dumb on the whole matter . . . being a second John replacement pilot, I don't think they expected too much from me, plus I kept thinking of another Pop Woods tidbit, tell them nothing. 'If you let slip one little bit of information, you will never get out of Dulag Luft.' I was out and on my way to Luft III in nine days. (On my last session with the interrogator, I asked him how in the world he had so much general information on all of us. He responded with 'from your stupid newspapers. We have been keeping such files for years'.)

We were transported by rail to Sagan, arriving there 4 May 1944, a short time after the big escape from centre compound. We were certainly made aware of it, the fact that 50 were shot because of it, and that we could most assuredly expect the same if any attempt to escape was made. They were quite proud of the fact that no American officer had ever escaped from inside any German POW camps.

After processing through outer Lager, I was assigned to west compound along with 15 others. This is where I spent the next nine months, followed by the winter hike to Spremberg and train ride to Nurnberg for another two and a half months. Next was the 120 kilometre hike to Moosberg (ahead of General Patton's army) where he caught up with us seven days after our arrival for return to American control on 29 April 1945.

Upon reflection, I suppose this short period of confinement has had more of an impact on the rest of my life than any other single event. I'm satisfied that I've been a better person because of it in some ways . . . but, in most instances, I'm not too sure. It's always been there in the back of my mind affecting every decision that I've made concerning family, career development, advice to my four children, etc, etc. Freedom has been so important . . . I've missed so many things through the years because of my fear of crowds, standing in long lines . . . anything that might threaten that freedom. I've never been able to stick my neck out an inch in a career decision for fear of jeopardising my comfortable little rut of three squares a day and a paycheck every two weeks.

Freedom, or the lack of it, has undoubtedly been the predominant factor in every decision I've made since my captivity.

A sweep in northeastern Germany was the second task that day for the 362FG, Ninth Air Force. An earlier dive-bombing mission cost one P-47 whose pilot also became a prisoner-of-war. Their second casualty was less fortunate. Near Biene, on the railway line between Lingen and Meppen, the 377FS attacked a train which halted, seeking protection from anti-aircraft positions protecting a series of radio or radar towers

"Freedom, or the lack of it, has undoubtedly been the predominant factor in every decision I've made since my captivity." Paul R Maxwell reminisces during the POW reunion in 1985. (Paul R Maxwell)

near the track. Flying an assignment with the 362FG to gain experience was Major Gene L Arth from the 406FG whose own Group was working up to its operational debut. Caught in a maelstrom of light flak when diving on the locomotive, Arth died when his P-47 plunged into a farmyard and exploded. A second 377FS Thunderbolt was hit but Lieutenant Roy D Tedards reached home safely. Suffering no losses, the 362 Fighter Group's 378FS flew an uneventful sweep while the 379FS emerged unscathed after the destruction of two locomotives and probably destroying a third.

Originally a Ninth Air Force unit, the 357FG had been traded to the Eighth Air Force in exchange for P-47s of the 358FG. Needed for long-range escort, the P-51 was more suitable for the Eighth's strategic requirements whereas the rugged durability of the Thunderbolt on ground-attack duties suited the Ninth's tactical demands. Fifty-two 357FG Mustangs left Leiston commanded by Captain Joseph E Broadhead on a sweep of northwestern Germany. Reaching the Quackenbruck area at 1750 hours, the Group's 362FS, 363FS and 364FS separated to cover territories designated during briefing. Flying north of Osnabruck at 1900 hours, the 362FS saw about 30 FW190s overhead, obviously heading to intercept the bombers. Broadhead gave chase but, as the enemy were positioning for an assault on the bombers, they ran into the 353FG's escorting Thunderbolts and the dogfight described earlier ensued. Seeing Lieutenant Crampton's P-47 dive away with an FW190 shooting at it, Broadhead urged his Mustang after both aircraft and the trio screamed down from 23,000 to 3,000 feet. Broadhead saw the '190 obtaining strikes on Crampton's P-47 as his P-51 gradually closed into firing range, opening up at 350 yards. The Focke-Wulf whipped into a right turn, split it to the left then, pulling up vertically, Broadhead saw the canopy detach and its pilot hastily depart. As he swung away, Broadhead found himself facing another FW190 which opened fire from head on but missed. As it dived beneath his P-51, Broadhead fired and clearly saw strikes through the red tail band denoting JG1, but the German vanished without serious damage. Another FW190 was claimed by First Lieutenant Gilbert O'Brien, 357FG, who hit it repeatedly in the fuselage and wings as he followed it down. Then, pulling out, it stalled and spun earthwards. At that instant, O'Brien himself was bounced by an FW190 which, speeding on him from out of the sun, put a cannon shell through his port wing before disappearing as swiftly as it arrived. Luckily, the damage was not serious and O'Brien climbed homewards from the combat zone. The Leiston group's other squadrons had to content themselves with an assortment of ground targets, eliminating six more locomotives from the Reich's rolling stock as well as damaging barges and tugs north of Nienburg. In addition, First Lieutenant Leonard K Carson's flight set three large oil-

Left *First Lieutenant Gilbert O'Brien received a cannon shell through his port wing.* (H A Aukeny via M Olmsted)

Right *Supporting the US Eighth and Ninth Air Force sweeps were RAF Mustangs of 19 and 65 Squadrons. FB113 was flown by Flight Lieutenant D P Lamb of Green Flight, 19 Squadron.* (Imperial War Museum) storage tanks ablaze as a parting gesture.

Droning into and out of Europe proved innocuous for the 365FG whose incursion protected the mission's northern flanks. To the south, things were similarly quiet for the 358FG who reported "another milk run" when they returned from patrolling Rheims, Metz and St Dizier in France. However, their fellow Ninth Air Force Group, the 368FG, had a livelier time.

Flying their very first mission into Germany the 368FG left Chilbolton and, reaching 20,000 feet, they ranged towards Bonn and Koblenz. At 1815 hours, near Bonn, a flight of the group's 395FS were ambushed by four FW190s which burst out of the sun from 7 o'clock high. The RAF Wireless Intelligence Service heard the trap being sprung as the German fighter leader ordered one section to attack from astern while he led a frontal assault. As the startled P-47s reeled to fight, another eight FW190s descended into the fracas completely surprising the inexperienced Americans. Their opponents were from JG26 — one of the Luftwaffe's crack fighter Groups but, determinedly, the 395FS retaliated as the fight fractured into smaller, deadly skirmishes. Captain Thomas N Montag duelled with one grey-coloured FW190 down to the deck. As they fought, Montag saw Captain James W Goodwin

apparently firing at the same target but Goodwin then pulled up and broke away while Montag finished off his prey, even taking a camera-gun picture of its parachuting pilot. Seconds later, he saw a P-47 crash and realized another FW190 had pounced on Goodwin — there was only one parachute and that belonged to his own victim. Oberfeldwebel Ellenrieder of 3./JG26 claimed two P-47s but, although Flight Officer Edgar M McCrone and Captain Leary were missing some tail-feathers, both reached England, one force-landing at Manston. Off-setting Goodwin's loss, the 368FG claimed two more FW190s, one to Captain Roy L Bowlin and the other to First Lieutenant John Lougee who chased it to Limburg before forcing its pilot to bale out.

Supporting the US Eighth and Ninth Air Force sweeps came an RAF and RCAF contribution of Mustangs and Spitfires. Firstly, operating from RAF station Ford, 19 and 65 Squadrons sent 23 Mustang III fighters to counteract any German interceptors reacting from the south. Departing at 1625 hours, they reached 20,000 feet heading towards the Strasbourg — Nancy areas with the 11 Mustangs of 19 Squadron as top-cover. Nearly an hour had elapsed when German fighters were reported crossing their route and, soon after, they detected about 14 Me109s of 7./JG2 and 8./JG2. Wing Commander G Johnston took 65 Squadron and one flight from 19 squadron to engage as the Messerschmitts characteristically half-rolled and dived to escape. Chasing them down to telegraph-pole height, Wing Commander Johnston proved the point by collecting some telephone wire round his spinner but, apart from interrupting phone calls, he also claimed one Me109 destroyed and one damaged. Flying Officer N E S Mutter of 65 Squadron claimed one as did Flight Sergeant B Vassiliades from 19 squadron. German losses confirm two of these aircraft — Unteroffizier Helmut Rätzer was shot down near Compiegne and baled out with grievous chest and stomach wounds from which he died in hospital later that night. Unteroffizier Erwin Will of 7./JG2 was killed in his burning Me109 when it fell near Soissons. A victory for JG2 came when Pilot Officer W A Chisholm radioed during the fight that he was force landing. After this affray, both squadrons returned to base.

Returning to base meant a different abode for the two RCAF squadrons involved. Taking off from Westhampnett in Sussex, their Spitfires staged through Manston for refuelling then left at 1745 hours on the deepest penetration they had yet flown. Anticipating combat, they were twice "attacked" by American Thunderbolts and Mustangs, but managed to get themselves recognized before any harm came. Real combat proved elusive apart from intense flak which damaged Pilot Officer P E Ferguson's aircraft, obliging him to land at Manston. Eventually, 23 dejected pilots flew in to their new home at Funtingdon, "in a completely browned off condition and with sore bottoms". That evening as the Canadians made their new tented accommodation more habitable, the Second Air Division returned to its "Night of the Intruders". The fighters that secured their safety in daylight were powerless to protect them from the nocturnal predators of KG51. Losses sustained would make USAAF commanders chary about further operations running into darkness. Before describing events which created this caution, a look will be taken at the bombers' achievements against their main objectives.

CHAPTER EIGHT

Main Targets

RAILWAYS REPRESENTED DIFFICULT targets because, although damage might appear massive, inflicting permanent destruction proved difficult and repair teams could rapidly reopen a network. Trains were running through Hamm within a few days, and Koblenz resumed receipt of rail-traffic on 24 April. However, damage to some of the installations was so severe that they were lost for the duration. Following Germany's surrender, the Allies assessed the damage wrought by aerial bombardment and the US Strategic Bombing Survey Physical Damage Division Report Number 67 commented:

Object of the Study: The railroad marshalling yard, Hamm, Germany, furnishes a typical example of the damage inflicted by a strategic bombing on a target which includes various structures scattered over a large area. Within this area, the freight locomotive sheds and repair shop and the bridges over Hafenstrasse and the Lippe Canal and River were the major

Smoke pots seek to defend the marshalling yards as bombs tumble towards the target early in the attack.

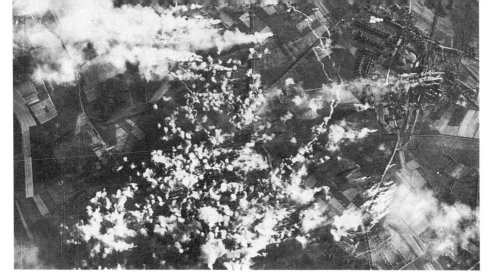

Viewed from over 20,000 feet, Hamm marshalling yard as seen by Liberator crews of the Second Air Division. (Norbert Krüger)

Taken a day after the attack on Hamm. Skilled teams move in to repair and reopen the lines. Twisted track would be replaced and craters filled within hours. (Norbert Krüger)

Photographed as part of the US Strategic Bombing Survey Physical Damage Report, a view looking north showing temporary repairs. Note hastily-daubed signal for Occupying Forces and the presence of several unexploded bombs. (USAF Official)

bottlenecks which affected the flow of traffic through the marshalling yard. The railroad marshalling yard at Hamm was the largest in Germany and dealt with general traffic between the Ruhr and N Germany. It had a capacity of 10,000 wagons per day — four main lines left from the southern and two from the northern end of the yard. At the extreme N end was the Lippe River and Canal Bridge over which passed all the northbound traffic. There were 23 attacks on the marshalling yard, the freight locomotive sheds and repair shop, and the bridges over the Lippe Canal and River were damaged during 12 of these raids, 11 by the Eighth Air Force and one by the RAF. The total tonnage dropped during these 12 raids was 6808.5 tons of HEs and 1456.5 of IBs. The first heavy attack on the bridge occurred on 23.3.44, and the first major raid on the m/y was on 22.4.44.

Analysis of Damage: 26% of the roof damage to structure, including the steel frame of the freight locomotive shed and repair shop, and 7% of the concrete slab floor, which was destroyed in these raids, had not been repaired on 30.4.45. On the bridges, there was a total of 45 square metres of floors and 60 square metres of abutment wing wall destroyed. Two direct hits and three near misses damaged the switch tower, including the electrical equipment, and put it completely out of action. 300 metres of railroad track were destroyed and never relaid. Despite all the damage to the bridges, however, repairs were made rapidly and the bridges kept open to traffic. Only on 23.3.44 was railroad traffic stopped for 24 hours. Rolling stock

Devastated loco shed and repair shop. The officer is standing in the centre of a 9 metre diameter crater, 3½ metres deep. (USAF Official)

suffered severe damage and this, in conjunction with track damage hampered the operation of the marshalling yard. The freight locomotive shed and repair shop on several occasions were cut down to 40% of normal operations because of damage to the sliding locomotive transfer tables and other equipment. Used against the freight locomotive shed and repair shop, the 1,000 lb GP bomb proved to be most effective. The 100 lb GP inflicted most damage on trackage and rolling stock but the 100 lb GP and 500 lb GP bombs were not effective when used against the Lippe Canal and River bridges.

Description of the target. General. The marshalling yard at Hamm was one of the busiest yards in the country and was called the nerve centre of the German rail traffic. The four main lines were:

1. *Dusseldorf via Schwerte, Hagen and Wuppertal.*
2. *Duisbrug via Dortmund, Bochum and Essen.*
3. *Duisbert-Ruhrort, either via Wanne-Eickel, Gilsenkirchen and Oberhause, or via Lunen, Recklinghausen and Botrup.*
4. *Soest and thence to Paderborn and Central Germany and from the northern end, A. Berlin via Bielefield and Hanover with branches to Bremen and Hamburg. B. Munster and thence to Holland, Bremen and Hamburg.*

The northeast end of the marshalling yard adjoined the town of Hamm, the yard was long and narrow with an overall length of more than three miles.

The northern portion measured 1,470 yards in length and its major axis in a north/northeast, south/southwest direction. Its greatest width was 630 yards, it had three humps which were in the centre of the area where a r/r passed under the yard. The sorting sidings in the centre of the target area dealt with traffic to the north and those in the southwest with the southbound traffic to the Ruhr. Main repair facilities were situated between the central sorting siding and the station. The most important of these was the freight locomotive shed and repair shop.

Description of the Attacks. General. The marshalling yard was the primary target for all attacks except that of the Eighth Air Force on 23.3.44 which had the city of Hamm and the bridge over the Lippe river as the target. History of Attacks: the first heavy attack on the bridge over the Lippe occurred on 23.3.44, the first major raid on the marshalling yard took place on 22.4.44. During the attack of 22.4.44, 1327.3 tons of HEs and 356.9 tons of IBs were dropped on the marshalling yard, which was the primary target.

Comparison of PRU Claims and Observed Damage. Repair Shops. Raid 22.4.44. PRU Statement, ref K2114: the target is obscured by much haze and cloud making a satisfactory statement impracticable. The W/E and E/W sorting siding and a portion of the yard to the north of them are dimly visible, however, and it is possible to state that a considerable dislocation of wagons exists. A number of craters are to be seen on the tracks, many of which are severed. Now that there is complete cover of this marshalling yard it can be seen that damage is considerable throughout the main part of the yard while craters are thick on either side, particularly on the southeast. There is important damage to the railway sheds at both ends of the yard and disruption to tracks and wagons is the greatest amongst the eastbound sorting sidings. Goods locomotive sheds and repair shops: three places damaged, one severe. Two bays of roof severely damaged on west side of building.

Vulnerability of Target. The freight locomotive shed and repair shop was vulnerable to direct hits and near misses of 1,000 GP or larger bombs. It was concluded that the building was not vulnerable to IB, although part of the roof sheeting was of wood covered with tar paper, because the roof was sufficiently high to withstand heat from incendiaries burning on the concrete floor. The bridges across Haffenstrasse and the Lippe Canal and River were not vulnerable to 500 lb or smaller bombs and r/r traffic was not seriously interrupted. Damage caused by 500 lbs was usually to the track and a hole through the bridge which could be repaired from 1 to 3 days.

On the human side, German sources show 230 people perished in Hamm including 30 "foreigners". Some 700 houses were completely destroyed, with 1,500 damaged, making about 10,000 homeless. Casualties could have been heavier but the city had numerous, ruggedly constructed air-raid shelters which were well used by a populace more accustomed to air attack than the citizens of Koblenz who saw no military sense in attacking their town. In fact, a contemporary local rhyme ran, "Koblenz they will

Lippe River canal and street bridge. View looking east. (USAF Official)

Destroyed during the attack on 22 April 1944, the locomotive transfer table was still unserviceable in May 1945. (USAF Official)

Bombs from the 458BG detonate in Koblenz. A picture taken from the aircraft flown by First Lieutenant L Andrew and crew. (USAF Official)

spare — then *they* will live there" — "they" being the Allies. So, when bombers were reported, many inhabitants felt it was another opportunity to engage in the pastime of watching and counting the aircraft overhead. Indeed, the first formations did fly majestically past, the evening sun glistening off the wings of many bombers, and fighters darting to-and-fro like silver fish. Air-raid wardens and police tried clearing the streets but many people stood, fascinated by the procession above. The first bombs swiftly achieved what the authorities could not but, for many, it was too late. Perhaps the experience of one anonymous young mother will symbolize the suffering she did not deserve but it also has to be said that none of the young airmen overhead would have deliberately wished her harm. She simply had the misfortune of living under a tyranny so cancerous that the free world was forced to expurgate whatever the cost. "As I was feeding Wolfgang, my baby, I heard the alarm and wondered shall I put him in his cot or not, then decided to undress him after all but put all his clothing and blankets ready. The already packed case with our papers and other emergency articles was in the cellar. I went to the kitchen and did some ironing, sometimes looking out of the window whenever the engine noise became louder. Then I saw a bright smoke signal, the sign for attack. I ran to the bedroom, collecting all the baby's clothes and blankets on the way. I tried to switch on the light but there was no power.

"The first bombs were already falling. I grabbed Wolfgang, ran back to the kitchen and saw through the window an enormous dust mushroom from a bomb hit close by. I quickly picked up my money, ration cards, candle and matches and ran downstairs. I didn't want to go to the cellar on my own, my husband had not arrived home yet, so I ran into the street to our neighbour's house but nobody answered the door. I ran to the next house and, just as the door was opened for us, I saw my husband coming down the street. I apologized to the people and we quickly went back home to our own cellar. It was quiet for a little while but as soon as we were in our cellar, the bombing started again. We were sitting close together on two chairs, our boy between us. We heard many explosions, they seemed to come closer and closer and the next detonation was massive and shook walls and ceiling. The noise was tremendous and the air was filled with dust and rubble and we thought we would choke. Many thoughts passed through my mind in those few seconds. My first thought: fate has caught up with us and this is the end for us, like thousands of people throughout the Rheinland. Our lovely flat, our furniture — everything, gone. My second thought was 'please god, don't let us die down here'. I once read about a woman who was trapped in her cellar with her child for hours. Standing injured, in water up to her chest, holding her child high, near to fainting many times. She was rescued in the end. That's what I was thinking". Luckily, in this case, the couple were rescued by neighbours breaking through the wall into their cellar to extricate them from beneath the rubble of their home.

In addition to the courage of neighbour helping neighbour, fire crews from surrounding communities responded although services were initially slow and not all were diligent. The crew of one fire-boat needed prompting at pistol-point. Covering the gamut of human behaviour, there was moderate looting, but 250 awards for bravery were later made including one to an academic, Dr Bellinghausen, who rescued numerous valuable books from the library. Many of the 350 buildings destroyed or seriously damaged were also part of the town's heritage but they could be re-built. The lives of 109 civilians and prisoners-of-war plus nine soldiers could not. Never again were the citizens of Koblenz complacent about air-raid warnings.

•CHAPTER NINE•

Wolves
in the Flock

. . . STILL GRASPING LIFE'S baton, Munsey and Crall kept *Cee Gee II* aloft as the stricken bomber raced for the coast. Mac McClure hurried back from the flight deck to help McKinney while Orlowski tended to Grady, calming the young radio-operator's rising fear of

Below left *Lieutenant James S Munsey kept the stricken* Cee Gee II *aloft as they raced for the coast.* (Don Olds)

Below right *Second Lieutenant Robert O Crall also remained at the controls despite flames searing into the cockpit.* (Don Olds)

blindness. Dropping from his top-turret, Technical Sergeant Grover G Conway ignored other methods of escape and concentrated on opening the bomb-bay doors to provide a speedier exit for the wounded. Both doors jammed, so Conway resorted to kicking and jumping on them, gradually prising them open.

Needing help with McKinney, McClure cranked up the ball-turret to enlist aid from the diminutive occupant, Sergeant Norman W Brown. As the turret hatch slapped open, the terrified gunner scrambled out, panic-stricken by fear of being trapped in his tiny capsule and now even more frightened by the sheer size, noise and proximity of flames from the burning wing tanks. For a few moments, his high-pitched voice squealed incoherently but, struggling within himself, Brown calmed when he saw McClure and realized McKinney was hurt. As the crew's largest figure, McKinney dwarfed both Brown and McClure and they quickly saw, with the bomb-doors stubbornly refusing to open, that there was no way they could bodily hoist him out of a waist window. Their only choice was dragging him to the rear hatch and attaching a static line. Even this option became stunted when the static line could not be broken loose. Hastily devising a plan, they decided to push McKinney through the hatch with McClure holding his rip-cord at arm's length so the weight of his falling body would tug the release mechanism of his parachute. Hopefully, an arm's length would avoid snagging any protrusions; if he was still alive, it would be McKinney's only chance. *Cee Gee II* was now lurching downwards making balance difficult but the two men managed to attach their own parachutes and one to McKinney. Slowly, they began dragging him towards the hatch.

Meanwhile, Orlowski had fastened Grady's parachute and was guiding him to the bomb-bay, praying Conway could free the doors in time. He did, but Munsey told Orlowski to keep the crew in as they were still over the sea. No-one would survive for long in the water, ditching was impossible, and the fuel tanks could explode at any second. Their lives were rolling dice as *Cee Gee II* thundered landwards.

McClure and Brown had hauled McKinney too far aft to retrace their steps when Conway cleared the bomb doors. *Cee Gee II* was falling even faster but still level and under control. Orlowski saw Munsey and Crall now sitting admist flames wreathing into the cockpit, still bravely holding her steady, urging all speed for the coast. A thin trace of foam flashed by; a change of tone in the darkness below. Land. Conway had gone, Helfand followed, then the right waist gunner, Staff Sergeant Kenneth G Laux leapt from the bomb-bay. Pushing Grady out, Orlowski glanced back to see Crall starting to get out of his seat. Then Orlowski jumped.

Standing by the rear hatch, McClure and Brown hesitated, pondering how to heave McKinney's bulk through the hatch while still holding on to him. Then the fuel tanks exploded blowing all three into space. McKinney disappeared leaving McClure still grasping his ripcord, their scheme to save him, now amended by an explosion, might still work.

Falling into the void himself, Mac had no time to think. Suddenly the heat and noise were gone. How high was he? Pulling his own ripcord, McClure felt his parachute stream out smoothly, swinging him only once before his feet hit the ground mid-way through the second swing and he tumbled into an involuntary, sideways somersault, ending up sitting in a marsh, surprised at the speed of his arrival. His acrobatics spattered mud on his flying suit but fortuitously doused areas where it had been smouldering. He was also surprised to find himself still clutching his own ripcord, McKinney's, and a flashlight which he could not remember picking up.

Pleased at this unintentional foresight, Mac unclipped his parachute and began searching for his crew. Stumbling across the marsh, he found his cries got no response, and his dazed condition made him unaware of other engines and combat overhead. Soon, a civilian found him. Taking the bedraggled gunner kindly by the arm, the man helped him to a very humble dwelling of two rooms, an earthen floor but at least the comfort of a warm fire. Mac was becoming increasingly agitated about his crew, and sympathetic tea did little to soothe his anxiety. The family bandaged his head as best they could and Mac began to feel extremely guilty about his imposition into their Saturday evening. Their daughter, a blond-headed toddler of about five, was fascinated by their peculiarly garbed, strangely speaking guest. Mac decided he must do something for the child and felt his silk parachute would make some pretty dresses. Realizing Mac was reacting in shock, the man calmly thanked him but said the parachute had probably been taken by now and, only after Mac insisted, would they accept his silk, inner flying gloves as a gift for their child. Shortly, an ambulance arrived and took Mac to hospital. There, further questions about his crew were quietly deflected — they were 'fine', he must not worry. Re-bandaged, his burns attended to, Mac slept.

Two days later a US Army Ambulance ferried him to the base hospital at Old Buckenham. Entering the ward, he found Laux and Helfand, both bandaged from shoulder to head-top, Helfand also had one hand bandaged and his arm in a sling. Only now did Mac learn what had befallen the others. Munsey and Crall were both dead. When the fuel tanks exploded, *Cee Gee II* rolled on her back and plunged into a coastal marsh near the Suffolk village of Reydon, entombing their bodies. Brown survived physically unscathed and summoned sufficient courage to complete his full 30 missions, but the emotional strain was deep. Soon after the war, he committed suicide.

Orlowski had only a sprained ankle. McKinney was found dead and had probably died in the initial attack. The unfortunate Grady never opened his parachute. Blind, he probably never realized their altitude, perhaps struck something when he left the aircraft or was unable to locate his D-ring. Conway's departure dumped him in the sea some 50 feet off shore at Southwold with Helfand splashing in about 20 feet away. The sea was slight, with a light southwest wind pushing them seawards.

Coastguards witnessed their descent and three auxiliary coastguards, aided by soldiers and Wrens, launched a small boat. Reaching Helfand about 200 yards out, they hauled him on board. Gasping for breath, he told them Conway was nearby but felt reassured to learn another craft was urging through the swell to his rescue. Only the dark glaze of an empty sea greeting the second boat. Conway was never found and is listed among the many whose spirit still invades the waves.

McClure was stunned by the loss of his comrades. It took tremendous willpower to fly three more missions — during which his stark terror proved a potential liability, so he was grounded as a turret maintenance technician. Laux never flew again, nor was he ever able to speak about the incident. Orlowski was sent home. Helfand became a lead navigator completing 30 missions before doctors took him off flying. For his courage, Munsey was posthumously awarded the Distinguished Service Cross which was later presented to his small daughter, the two and a half year old CG. It was her namesake, the intruders' first victim, which would stir this author's archaeological interests several decades later.

British radar had seen the intruders stealing towards the Second Air Division, and the RAF Wireless Intelligence Service heard radio transmissions from a Staffel of KG51 flying south from Soesterburg to shadow home the bombers. There was little that could be done to detect them if they infiltrated the bomber formations under cover of darkness. Secret documents held by the RAF and USAAF admitted that contemporary radar technology could not recognize or track a "small number" of hostile aircraft: "When there is moderate or heavy density of friendly activity near the coast . . . when a stream of operational bombers is passing over an area, this is particularly true when the bombers are returning and losing height preparatory to landing . . . the fundamental limitation of the present system is that dense aerial activity in effect neutralizes the reporting system as a source of warning hostile activity . . . If the enemy increased his intruder activities from the present average level of one attack per 4.5 friendly bomber nights (and it is difficult to understand why he does not) the number of incidents might rise very considerably". The Gt Yarmouth area was one of those described as "very difficult from a tracking point of view because permanent echoes extend far out to sea . . . any hostile plotted into this area may be lost".

Why the Luftwaffe did not intrude more frequently has been directly attributed to Hitler, who saw no propaganda benefit in the destruction of bombers over England. Ignoring their increased vulnerability during take off or landing, he felt the German population would not have the morale-boosting evidence of success compared to bombers destroyed over the Fatherland. In October 1941, the units responsible for intruder operations were moved to other duties and, for a critical two years, the RAF was uninterrupted by this effective countermeasure. In mid 1943, the Germans re-examined the idea of intruder action but initial proposals became embroiled in Luftwaffe politics plus fears that the

Allies would capture an FuG220 Lichtenstein SN-2 night fighter radar. This was the only one effective against "window" and, again, because of Hitler's continuing opposition. One favourable factor was the introduction in May 1943 of the new Messerschmitt 410 Hornet. Based on an earlier, failed design, the Me410 was a fast, formidably armed fighter-bomber so it was not unnatural when one of the first bomber groups to re-equip, V/KG2, began experimenting with intruder action after bombing its objectives. During March 1944, V/KG2 provided the basis of II/KG51 and was allowed to resume intruder sorties from Soesterburg under Major Dietrich Puttfarken. In the three weeks prior to 22 April 1944, 11 aircraft were damaged or destroyed by KG51 including one 96BG Flying Fortress described in the author's best-selling book, *Eighth Air Force Bomber Stories* (also published by Patrick Stephens Limited).

The risk of intruder action was therefore known when Mission 311 was launched, and some groups were warned during briefing. As the 458BG's commander, Colonel James H Isbell recalls, "To the strategists at the Eighth Air Force Headquarters, every mission counted toward the success of the soon-to-be invasion. That is why we went, late as it was. It was a gamble, but in the overall scheme, worth the risk. Our group navigator took very little time in discovering that we'd be coming home after dark — we were to be 'tail-end-Charlie'. Sometimes we led the Eighth Air Force; sometimes we were last; sometimes we were in the middle of the steam, but always home before dark. Night was for the RAF. The ability of our pilots to fly at night was unquestionable, and their ability to fly night formation was not any great concern of mine. But suddenly I was concerned. My deputy, Lieutenant Colonel Jim Hogg, our Group Operations Officer, Lieutenant Colonel Bruno Fielding and I went into a huddle. As tail-end-Charlie, we'd be first to get it if the Luftwaffe followed us home. Further, Horsham St Faith was nearly the first base after the English coast (Rackheath being the first only by four or five miles to the east). We concluded that the entire group was vulnerable — not just those aircraft and crews in the air, but all 35 to 40 other Liberators which were parked on the ground. We devised a plan.

At mission briefing time that afternoon, we apprised the crews of the possibilities. All guns were to remain in place and loaded (it had become common practice to unload guns before crossing the English coast coming home). Pilots were to switch to tower frequency midway across the North Sea. Running lights were not to be used — save only the blue, low intensity formation lights and the forward pointing red passing lights. If 'bandits' were encountered, or if Group Flying Control should give the alert, the formation was to disperse and each aircraft was to follow an assigned heading and altitude to the north, away from the other USAAF bases in East Anglia. The outbound course was to be held for 20 minutes with radio silence. A listening watch was to be maintained in the event that there was to be an 'All Clear' sooner. (In

Colonel (later Brigadier General) James Isbell devised a plan to counter the threat of intruders. Pictured later in the war, Isbell cuts a mission-party cake with assistance from General Peck, left. (Martin Bowman)

our planning we calculated that 40 minutes would be enough to clear the area.) We briefed the crews that all fuel tanks had been topped off with the extra 40 minutes of fuel if it should be needed".

Isbell's instructions would indeed be needed. The Fortresses of the Third and First Air Divisions landed safely but, with the slaying of *Cee Gee II*, the wolves were in the flock and there was little else the shepherds could do.

Funnelling into East Anglia, some 270 Liberators were at risk. Fortunately, KG51 had sent only a small force of four Me410s, but the

The sleek lines of an Me410 similar to those used by KG51. This specimen was captured and evaluated by the RAF. (Philip Jarrett)

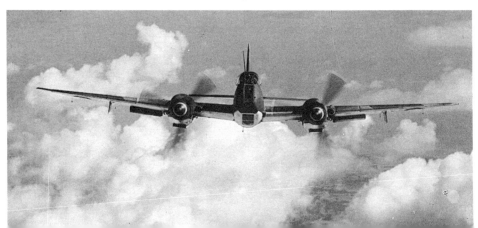

mayhem they created gave rise to reports of over 20 aircraft including Me109s, Me110s, Ju88s and the Me410s themselves. Keeping low, the Me410s hid in the lower darkness using residual, upper light for silhouetting their victims plus, in numerous cases, the bomber's own lights. Air raid alerts rippled through the region, RAF Mosquito night-fighters of 25 Squadron scrambled from Coltishall as AA defences sprang to readiness. Unable to track the enemy by radar meant following their movements through the Royal Observer Corps who now began reporting a series of attacks and plots of aircraft crashing — so many that some became confused. The carnage created during the next 20 minutes was witnessed by many East Anglians and events became legendary as "the night Jerry followed the Yanks home".

A few miles along the coast from Southwold lies the village of Kessingland. There, schoolboy Henry Bennett lived with his parents in a house on the seafront. Henry recalls, "On this particular evening the sound of returning aircraft was not heard until approximately 9.00 pm and 10.00 pm and it was at that time my father and I went out to view events. The bombers could not be seen in the darkness but the sound indicated large numbers coming in from the sea. Above the particular sound of these one could detect a higher speed aircraft and, whilst watching, the sound of gunfire was heard together with the visible signs of tracer bullets being fired. After only a few seconds one of the incoming bombers was lit with flames at the wing root — the fire rapidly spreading until all details of the aircraft were clearly visible. The plane began to turn and roll on its side in a dive at which point the entire wing with engines on the starboard side broke away and began to fall. All of this was happening in very close proximity to where we were standing, and in fact some small sections of the aircraft actually fell within our garden, whilst the main fuselage, wing etc were eventually strewn over quite a wide area of marshland some quarter mile inland". Henry had witnessed the loss of a Seething-based ship named *Repulser* by its pilot, Second Lieutenant Eugene V Pulcipher and crew. There were no survivors — and the intruders would inflict more grief on the 448BG during the next few minutes.

On board their *Vadie Raye*, Staff Sergeant Eugene Gaskins had vacated his nose turret after watching the first ship from the section ahead bank left into its final approach towards Seething's twinkling lines of friendly lights. It was not permissible to man the nose turret during touch down so Gene now joined the waist gunners, Staff Sergeants Francis X Sheehan and Ray K Lee for their own landing. Relaxing, they had casually discarded their flak jackets, dropping them along the fuselage floor. Doing likewise, Gene plugged his throat mike into a socket near the right waist window before resting his elbows on the window ledge to enjoy the beauty of a night landing. Sinking steadily from the last vestiges of daylight into the empurpled, darkening landmass, *Vadie Raye* led a section of three Liberators patiently waiting their turn to land. Captain Alvin D Skaggs now eased coastwards in

Killed in Kessingland, the crew of the 448BG ship Repulser *pictured before coming overseas. They survived only a month.*

accordance with the group's night landing procedure. This took them towards the port of Great Yarmouth where they would cross the coast, make a "u" turn over the sea and continue their descent into Seething's traffic pattern. With recognition lights and IFF (Identification Friend or Foe) sets on, they also took the precaution of firing flares giving the colours of the day. Douglas Skaggs could see light anti-aircraft fire over the coast and wanted to ensure his formation was not fired on in error.

Crew 64, the original crew for Vadie Raye. *Standing L-R Andrew Hall; Elbert Lozes; Douglas Skaggs; Don Todt; B F Baer. Kneeling, George Glevanik; Ray Lee; Francis Sheehan; Stanley Filipowicz; Gene Gaskins; Bill Jackson.* (Francis Sheehan)

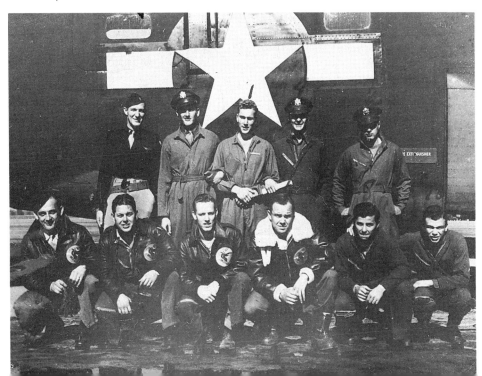

Enemy aircraft had been seen taking off as they left Europe but Skaggs thought they had returned to their bases. Unaware of intruders nearby, he assumed the coastal defences had become jittery. Crossing the town, they were just over the sea when Gene saw a harsh, unbroken rod of light — tracers — spurt from below straight into the belly of the B-24 alongside their right wing. To Gene, the 20 or 30 rounds fired clearly came from British gunners below. Later, they claimed to have fired at an intruder stalking the bombers. Gene had recognized the Liberator flown by First Lieutenant Cherry C Pitts and crew because his best friend Technical Sergeant Arthur E Angelo was the radio operator. In an instant, his friend's aircraft fireballed, plunged into the sea and vanished leaving a long, blazing smear on the water's surface marking the erasure of 10 lives.

A valediction of one man on board was recorded on 24 April by the 715BS diarist: "Maybe the people back in the States who loved him and whose death took away with him a part of themselves will hear some day of the courage of Technical Sergeant Ernest W Robinson Jr. It wasn't the kind of action that is likely to make a great stir, for it didn't involve killing a lot of Nazis or saving the lives of some of his comrades. His act of courage was something that went on inside of him and did not directly contribute to the success of an operation against the enemy. Yet maybe there was as much heroism in his conduct as there is in other types of courageous deeds, which, the results being evident, bring universal acclaim. On 19 April, Sergeant Robinson flew on the mission to Raphael, France, as a member of Lieutenant Roy W Davis's crew. The ship was hit by flak and on the way back over the channel it blew up. Of nine members of the crew, nothing is known. Sergeant Robinson miraculously came down safely and was picked up by the Air-Sea Rescue Service. Sergeant Robinson, with that experience behind him, was returned to this station on 20 April. His first request was to be allowed to fly the next mission. Sergeant Robinson was afraid if he didn't fly again right away, he would never have the nerve to fly again. How much courage did it take for him to ask for another mission a day after his plane blew up and he was the only member of the crew to come back? Quite a bit. He flew with Lieutenant Pitts on the 22nd. Today his body was found on the coast near Great Yarmouth".

The B-24 on *Vadie Raye's* left wing was also hit and peeled away on fire. But Skaggs suddenly had his own problems when a crimson glow flared inside the cowling of their number two engine. Banking steeply, *Vadie Raye* headed for Seething with flames daubing her position in the darkness. Below were three more pyres marking the demise of other aircraft, but still *Vadie Raye's* crew attributed the losses to error by British anti-aircraft gunners. Hurrying aft, the engineer, Technical Sergeant George Glevanik, assessed the damage before advising Skaggs to close the cowling flaps and open throttle, hoping to blow the fire out. This failed so they feathered the engine and continued descending, anxious but under control. Selecting gear down, Skaggs was relieved by the appearance of green lights on his instrument panel. Glevanik, peering with a flashlight from each waist window, could see that both yellow-painted down latches were visible, confirming their undercarriage had locked.

About five minutes had elapsed since they were hit, and *Vadie Raye*, now in the circuit, began banking into the down-wind leg of their approach. The nonchalance of sight-seeing had gone as Gene and the waist gunners checked their parachutes. Glevanik had left his on the flight deck and, in any case, they were almost too low to bale out. Wishing good luck to the gunners, Glevanik had just stepped into the bomb-bay when Gaskins glimpsed through the lower, after inspection windows, the flash of tracers streaking towards *Vadie Raye*. In an instant, the scene was dramatically lit by a series of harsh, blinding flashes orchestrated with a cacophony of cannon-shells lacerating their lower fuselage. Death was prevented only by their carelessly strewn flak jackets, which convulsed as they absorbed most of the blows. Gene still felt the blast on his legs, and, instantly recalling the horrifically sudden loss of Pitts' crew, his reactions were instinctive. He threw himself headlong from the waist window. Rolling out into the night sky, he glanced back to ensure he had missed the tail then tugged his ripcord. The jerk of his parachute opening slowed him but not his shoes, which whipped off into the darkness leaving Gene swinging like a demented pendulum. As his gyrations eased *Vadie Raye* had vanished but below him was the reflective sheen from another parachute and Gene shouted a greeting. Back came the familiar voice of Francis Sheehan asking Gene if he was OK. Other than blast or a piece of spent shrapnel hitting his legs Gene was unscathed, but Sheehan had been more seriously wounded and was losing blood.

Sitting on a bulkhead Sheehan, too, saw the double row of tracers flashing towards *Vadie Raye* from below. Before he could react, he felt a numbing blow in the calf of his left leg and sensed the sticky, wet spread of blood into his boot. Amid the chaos, he glimpsed Gene's departing form "hanging in mid-air" and, grasping the window's edge Sheehan followed suit, hoisting himself bodily out of the window. He must have delayed seconds longer opening his parachute and overtaken Gene in the fall.

For a few peaceful moments the two parachutists conversed, Gene asked Sheehan if he had his whistle in case they landed too far apart. Then Gene spotted electricity power lines looming up from the nightscape and frantically attempted to side slip — but, before achieving anything, he smacked into the ground on his back and lay breathless. Sitting up, he was surprised to see Sheehan's ghostly-grey form begin sitting up only 20 feet away. Detaching his parachute, Gene stumbled to his friend, his feet hurting on stones and ridges of hard soil. Sheehan's pale blue "Bugs Bunny" flying suit gave him a wraith-like appearance in darkness broken only by stars and the distant glow of aircraft wreckage burning in the direction of Seething, presumably the remains of *Vadie Raye*.

Gene knelt by his friend and they unzipped the leg of Sheehan's flying suit. It was too dark to see so the best they could manage was to wrap Gene's scarf around the wound, twist the trouser leg tightly and re-zip it to stem the loss of blood. Helping Sheehan stand, Gene provided support as he staggered painfully towards the outline of some farm buildings about half a mile distant. After about 20 yards, it became evident that movement increased the bleeding so Gene then carried the larger man on his back. Several times, the roar of low flying aircraft sent them diving into a ditch where they would crawl before resuming their piggy-back progress. Soon, both decided it would make more sense if Gene continued alone to fetch help. Settling Sheehan into the ditch for protection, Gene made better progress, clambered over one gate and picked his way like a paddler on pebbles across the next field to a gate into the farmyard. Judging in which direction the house lay, he ran alongside the barn, rounded a corner and almost crashed into a GI and his girlfriend canoodling against the barn wall. Quite who got the greater shock was unclear, but the couple's ardour cooled rapidly with the dishevelled airman's abrupt arrival. Explaining his predicament, Gene smelt the reek of whisky but the GI was not too drunk to help and quickly fetched another GI and his girl from inside the barn. Both girls were part of a Women's Land Army contingent working the farm. They hastened to get their superior, a lady Gene would always remember as one of the least attractive females he ever met but, ugly or not, she was authoritatively efficient and soon mustered a small party following Gene to collect Sheehan. Organizing the two GIs into linking hands she created a seat between them and soon had Sheehan on his way to the house. There Gene bathed his wound. Cutting away the lower leg of Sheehan's long-johns, Gene saw that a piece of shrapnel had gone through his left calf, but at least the wound was clean and had stopped bleeding. Swabbing it with hot water, Gene applied a bandage while the WLA leader fetched her car, a small saloon, into which Sheehan was assisted. Scuttling in darkness through a series of back lanes, they soon reached Seething where Gene's explanation to the guard gained access near the control tower.

Turning on to the perimeter track, they discovered their route to the dispensary was blocked by at least nine Liberators, all with engines running and themselves unable to proceed because of an obstruction elsewhere. Near the middle of the airfield, the blazing remains of a B-24 sent shadows flickering in dancing contortions on each bomber as they passed. Atop every fuselage sat gunners like mahouts directing an elephant procession as they shouted instructions to pilots inside. Reaching the tower, the airmen disembarked and Gene thanked their chauffeur before boarding the ambulance with Sheehan. After the "meat wagon" moved off, Gene remembered he should report the tragic loss of their crew. Too low to bale out, they must have gone down somewhere near the base. Telling the driver to stop, Gene leapt from the ambulance, ankle-deep into a muddy puddle. Somehow, this seemed the final indignity as he slopped into Interrogation, grabbed the cup of whisky thrust into his hand and downed it without realizing he usually never touched the stuff. Turning towards aircrew clustered around the interrogation tables, Gene needed that drink. There, like spectres, were his crew! Seeing him, their jaws also dropped. They were reporting the gunners missing, presumed dead, because they had departed at such a low altitude. Sadness transformed into a joyful reunion amid the first, excited exchanges that ultimately became stories repeatedly regaled in the years to come. Gene was amazed by their accounts, especially that from George Glevanik.

Taking no more than a pace along the bomb-bay catwalk George was caught in a crescendo of explosions, flashes and wind like a banshee as cannon shells tore away the bomb doors leaving him unscathed but precariously balanced over an open, black void. This onslaught stoked their already-burning number two engine and cut fuel lines feeding the other three. Skaggs sensed power ebbing away but could do nothing as *Vadie Raye* began to fall. Just then, George felt gasoline spraying into his face and, near the forward bulkhead, he saw several fierce bursts of flame. These were created by two severed, flexible fuel lines, frenzied by pressure from the pump into rampant dragons, hosing snorts of neat fuel into flames from the port inner engine. They were whipping wildly as George lunged after them from the catwalk. If he could catch and reconnect the fuel supply, *Vadie Raye* just might have a chance. As he balanced over the abyss, snatching at the flailing lines, he saw the radio operator, Technical Sergeant Stanley C Filipowicz donning his parachute intending to leap from the bomb-bay. Yelling at Filipowicz to stop, George hollered that they were already too low, fuel had drenched them both and one spark as his parachute opened would ignite it faster than tumbleweed in a bush fire. Over the roar of flames and the backfiring, fuel-starved engines, George shouted for Filipowicz to tell Skaggs he was trying to reconnect the broken lines. Bracing one foot on the fuselage wall, the other on the bulkhead, George straddled the chasm, almost losing his balance as he caught one, then another of the writhing pipelines. Reconnection to the smashed fuel transfer valve was impossible. His only hope was to bridge the two ends with his hands.

From the cockpit, Skaggs flashed on the landing lights, praying for flat terrain so some of them might survive a crash-landing. *Vadie Raye* was sinking, fast.

Clutching both lines, George wrapped his gloves around them gripping as tightly as the slithery, hard rubber allowed. Spurting from this imperfect joint, fuel sprayed into his eyes, nose and mouth but, choking, he hung on.

Almost into the trees, Skaggs sensed some power returning and opened wide the three good throttles. *Vadie Raye* stopped falling. Although unable to climb, their descent was arrested, but the power surge was uneven causing the ship to slew away from runway alignment. Shouting for support from his co-pilot, Captain William G Blum, Skaggs shoved hard on the right rudder but it took them both to hold *Vadie Raye*'s approach.

In the bomb-bay, George clung on despite burns to his arms and heat so intense that his flying suit, underneath his leather A2 jacket, became scorched to the point of disintegration. Any second, his gasoline-soaked clothing could ignite and turn him into a human torch.

Thundering across the runway's threshold, Skaggs set *Vadie Raye* down and she was still rolling at some 90 mph when the crew began evacuating from the top hatch. Filipowicz clambered out so close to one of the propellers that it clipped a slice from the heel of his shoe as he squirmed across the mainplane and slid off the trailing edge. Following closely, First Lieutenant Donald C Todt skittered along the runway trailing showers of sparks from the buckles of his parachute harness. Then came Technical Sergeant Ray K Lee, the left waist gunner. Earlier, Lee had seen Gaskins and Sheehan leap out followed by the tail-gunner, Staff Sergeant William E Jackson who had just stepped out of his turret when the attack occurred. When Lee hesitated, Jackson climbed into the window. Pausing, his back to Lee, feet dangling outside, Jackson turned to ask if they were too low. Before Lee answered, Jackson inadvertently pulled his ripcord, the parachute spilled into the slipstream, whisking him into the darkness. At interrogation, the tail gunner was the only one still unaccounted for. Lee attempted to follow but, climbing out backwards, he intended lowering himself to avoid the tail before releasing his grip. During this process, Lee slipped, his parachute pack caught inside the window leaving him still fastened to it but outside the rapidly descending bomber. No one could see his predicament and, when he managed to haul himself inboard again it was too late to jump and he braced himself for the landing.

The first George Glevanik knew of the touchdown was a jolt which flung him from the aircraft. Unfortunately, complete separation from *Vadie Raye* was prevented by the cord of his electrically-heated suit snagging a bomb rack and dragging him helplessly, face down along the concrete. Skaggs, unaware of this, knew the ship would burn out where it stopped and, to avoid blocking the runway, he eased her on to the grass alongside. Making matters worse, the intruder had shot the nosewheel tyre to pieces so, as Skaggs lowered the nose, they juddered violently along on the rim, gouging a deep furrow before lurching to a halt. Pulled into this rut, poor Glevanik was still attached until, just before *Vadie Raye* shuddered to a standstill, the cord snapped and he was thrown beneath the catwalk as the bomber settled back, pinning him to the ground. Able to move only his hands, George thought his back was broken and scrabbled frantically at the earth like a man buried alive, but the weight and pressure were too great. Flames seared his back. He was being simultaneously crushed and incinerated.

It seemed an eternity of terror. Then, inside the fuselage, oxygen bottles exploded and the blast lifted *Vadie Raye*. It was barely enough for him to scramble free, past a burning engine, to sit a moment, hardly believing he was still alive, then he ran like a startled hare. Somewhere in his mind, a voice screamed at him to get down but George, fleeing the twin horrors of being buried and burnt, had no intention of stopping. As he raced across the runway, he was suddenly tackled from behind and crashed on to the concrete, his curses drowned in the blast of cannon shells and roaring engines as an intruder raked the runway where he would have been.

In the confusion, George never discovered who saved him and, amazingly, none of his crew were seriously injured. The bombardier, First Lieutenant Elbert F Lozes, left from the nose hatch while Skaggs, following Blum from the top hatch, ran from the blazing wreck just before it erupted into a display of pyrotechnics and exploding ammunition which sent survivors and spectators scurrying for cover as the intruder maliciously increased the mayhem. Luckily, its attack caused no casualties or damage. Following interrogation, *Vadie Raye*'s crew were jubilant when Jackson appeared escorted by two Military Policemen who

Below left *Next morning the crew of* Vadie Raye *sifted through the remains of their B-24. Captain Doug Skaggs holds up the remains of his seat, only too pleased not to have been in it.* (Gene Gaskins)

Below right *Technical Sergeant George Glevanik ponders over the remains of his gun turret — his escape was amazing.* (Gene Gaskins)

Above left *Staff Sergeant Gene Gaskins examines the burnt-out nose turret of* Vadie Raye. (Gene Gaskins)

Above right *First Lieutenant Don Todt with his toddler's shoes — that night they acted as a talisman for his well-being.* (Gene Gaskins)

Below *Staff Sergeant Ray K Lee reflects on the mission's misadventures — an interesting comparison with the picture taken prior to take off.* (Gene Gaskins)

had at first thought he was a German parachutist. His departure had been so late and so low, his parachute hardly deployed before he hit the ground, somehow entangled so his contact with terra-firma was headfirst. This scraped not only the top off his leather flying helmet but also skinned a strip from his scalp leaving him incoherent and dazed when discovered by the MPs. Suspicious about his integrity, they took time establishing his identity and allowing his return to Seething.

Also suspicious, but for different reasons, was another 448BG flier who, around the same time, was crouching beneath a bush near the Suffolk town of Beccles. Tail Gunner, Staff Sergeant Raymond G Chartier had parachuted, convinced he was in France. Even when located by his co-pilot, First Lieutenant Richard H Watters, Chartier remained apprehensive, relaxing only when the occupants of the first house they found spoke English. The B-24 from which they descended, 42-94744, *Peggy Jo*, was most probably the one seen by Skaggs peeling away on fire. Flying his first mission on that aircraft was Second Lieutenant William E Edwards who later recalled, "During the return to home base it had become dark and as the squadron approached the base the field lights were turned on. We turned on our landing lights, then as we approached the traffic pattern were waved off. At this time, the instructor-navigator, nose turret gunner and I were en route from the nose to the flight deck. The plane proceeded to make a 180° turn to come back into the traffic pattern. This brought us out over the North Sea. By now, the three of us had returned to the nose and we were unaware that we were being pursued by German night fighters. Suddenly all hell broke loose. Our number three engine exploded and the entire right side of the plane was on fire. The plane went into a violent dive, then righted itself. After it went into the second dive, I yelled at the instructor-navigator, 'Let's get out of here!' I released the nose wheel and doors and helped the navigator get out, then assisted the nose gunner into his 'chute. I went out and the gunner followed".

When the ship failed to respond to the controls, Dick Watters rang the bale out alarm, opened the bomb bay doors and, glancing at the altimeter as he left the flight deck, noted their height as 2,500 feet. Jumping from the bomb bay, his parachute opened in time for a *very* close look at their attacker. Snarling by, Watters saw the sleek form of an Me410 seeking further victims.

Watching events from a safe vantage point near The Three Horseshoes pub, Special Police Constable Bert Wilson had been chatting to Police Constable Mann. Their idle, evening conversation had been disturbed by the increasing throb of bombers and both men broke off to watch the circling aircraft, lights on and firing red-green flares. Then came a second, much nastier chatter, that of German machines guns. Within seconds, several bombers were seen falling in flames. One turned, slowly descending towards Beccles as its crew baled out, the white of their parachutes clearly reflected in flames from the aircraft until it fell behind some trees. A flash lit the sky followed by a dull thud. The policemen judged the impact to be on Worlingham marshes, dangerously near the railway line. Bert's regular occupation was as a marshman so his familiarity with the fields, dykes and their many interconnecting planks or "leggers" would be invaluable for finding the crash and, hopefully, locating survivors. Proceeding down Marsh Lane, Bert saw wreckage on the Beccles to Lowestoft railway line near the gatekeeper's cottage.

Inside, Mrs Pye had already retired for the night. "I remember quite well now, I went to bed early that night as batteries in the wireless had run out and my two sons were asleep. I laid there and listened to the drone of the planes coming home when all of a sudden there was a mighty crash. A Liberator had crashed about 150 yards from my house across the line and dyke. By the grace of God my house was spared but lit up by the flames. I would have laid there in bed if it hadn't been for Bertie Wilson as he came and banged on my window and shouted to me to get up and look outside. What a shock it was too, as you could smell the petrol. A little while after, I think it was the pilot of that plane came walking through the gates and spoke to me and said 'Are you all right, Mom?' I was a bit shaky." Bert had discovered the airman, presumably First Lieutenant Melvin L Alspaugh, on the marshes, still entangled in his parachute, "white and ghost-like" but cursing profusely the British gunners who he blamed for shooting him down. It is possible they did, but Watters' close encounter with the Me410 indicates they fell victim to

Below left *Wreckage surrounds the crater created by First Lieutenant Melvin Alspaugh's aircraft on marshland near Beccles.* (R Watters)

Below right *Alspaugh with the largest piece he could find the following day — a crumpled section of rudder, with the 448BG identification code, Circle "I".* (R Watters)

Above left *Bill Edwards, Melvin Alspaugh and Dick Watters contemplate their contribution to disrupting British rail traffic as well as German, all on the same day!* (R Watters)

Above right *A pile of Liberator wreckage alongside the swiftly-repaired LNER track at Worlingham.* (R Watters)

an intruder. When Bert reached the wreckage, the soggy conditions had suffocated any flames. The railway track had been lifted however, and one wing was draped brokenly across it while the other was submerged with remains of the foreward fuselage in an adjoining dyke. Other parts were strewn into a nearby copse and across adjacent meadows. Hanging heavily in the atmosphere was the powerful stench of high-octane aviation fuel. Between them, Alspaugh and Watters soon accounted for the crew. They were unharmed except for Staff Sergeant Charles J Adams who had fractured his left ankle on landing.

Confusion and uncertainty relating to incidents affecting the 448BG that night can be found in official records, contemporary accounts and subsequent recollections of those involved. In a report to Eighth Air Force HQ, the group stated, "from 2215 to 2230 on the 22.4.44 when the crews from this station were in the flight pattern of this field awaiting landing instructions, they were attacked by two and possibly three enemy aircraft intruders. One intruder, an Me410, was shot down by one of our crews and two of our aircraft are lost from what is believed to be combined attack by enemy aircraft intruders and flak from friendly forces. The crew of the other aircraft all baled out safely, one gunner being wounded and the aircraft crashed alone. One aircraft landed with fire in number two engine from enemy aircraft action and fire immediately spread over the entire ship but all crew members successfully escaped. One gunner being wounded. Two other aircraft suffered major damage in landing. There was no direct attack by enemy aircraft made on this field and ground personnel and installations did not suffer damage".

A somewhat different perspective is offered by George DuPont of the 712BS.

I was a sergeant aircraft mechanic and propeller specialist 'employed' by the Air Force at $96.00 per month including overseas pay. Affectionately referred to as a 'ground pounder' (although I did fly as engineer on test hops, whisky runs to Prestwick etc) by air combat crews. On the day in question I had just turned 26 as it was my birthday and I believe Herman Goering, being unable to attend my birthday festival, felt some small token of German grace appropriate. At best I recall it was about 10.00 pm, the sky golden, blue, orange, purple unclouded. It was dusk. The mission had taken off close to noon (as late a departure as I can recall) due to fog in the morning. I had been up like the others since before dawn standing by for departure. Now it was twilight and the base was beginning to stir with the usual anxiety of awaiting our aircraft to return. Men gathering in small groups about the hardstands and fidgeting, wondering what our luck would be this time. How many losses? Whose crew? Who would be wounded, killed, missing? Subconsciously, your mind like a computer would flash names and faces before you of your buddies, comrades in this great struggle risking their lives this day on the tortuous trail towards victory. You'd sort of feel you were playing God, hoping you could wish them all back but, if not, at least God bring my 'adopted' crew home. We knew some better than others and mentally we 'adopted' them, sweating them out each mission and counting them off one by one. I would ask one of my buddies to take my Mars candy bar along so that when he returned from altitude it would be frozen. Also I knew he would have to return to give it back to me. I never lost a Mars bar.

At the control tower one or two figures appeared on the porch searching towards the east. Ambulances were lined up and firemen were donning their asbestos suits. They would soon be needed.

Another mechanic and I were seated on top of the roof of one of many shacks made from 1,000-2,000 lb bomb crates. We were near the perimeter road (taxiway) at the entrance to the cluster of hardstands west of the control tower. Softly, you could hear the dull drone of many aircraft engines. Searching now you could find the black dots silhouetted against this beautiful twilight sky still aglow in colour. I made a remark, 'wouldn't this be a time for the Jerries to come over?' My friend, obviously more mature and learned than I, blustered 'They wouldn't dare!' Our aircraft appeared to be over the coast at about 10,000 feet and suddenly I thought I saw a horizontal streak of lightning followed by an orange 'flare', I thought it seemed to be slowing, settling (descending). As we pondered this unusual phenomena a second streak of lightening and a second 'flare' appeared. As we watched a third we suddenly realized the lightning was tracer shells and the flares B-24s burning. Now the aircraft were getting much closer and it was getting dark. The first aircraft were landing in great haste and suddenly the sky was full of aircraft.

We jumped from our shack and ran to the nearest shelter which was a slit trench suddenly filled with people. It was behind the control tower and embraced some features indicating 'German architecture' (Jerry built). It was only five feet high, therefore all I could lose was my head since I was six feet tall even then. God, how I wished I'd been born a midget. It had another classic feature, lined with brick not sandbags or logs where shells and shrapnel could penetrate, but brick, where even one shell would clean out the whole trench as it ricocheted, leaving only the empty uniforms.

By this time the sky was black and filled with the noise of roaring engines passing overhead in helter-skelter pattern (mostly left hand as best I recall). Altitude seemed as low as 50 feet and, as they hurtled by in the now very dark, above the crescendo of engine roar could be heard the punctuation marks of machine guns and small arms fire. Tracers across the sky from aircraft to aircraft and sometimes ground to aircraft. A vision crossed my mind and I said, 'Let's get the hell out of here!' I had no helmet or weapon and, being fabricated of non-alloyed material, from the dim recesses of my mind I recall somewhere (on page 48 I believe) in the soldier's handbook it says an open field is the safest place. My buddy and I left the others in the trench (without properly bidding them adieu) and crawling on our bellies with our elbows (like John Wayne in "The Sands of Iwo Jima") worked our way to the centre of the field. We were somewhere near the main runway. Further to our left one aircraft had taxied off the runway on to the inactive runway and stopped prematurely to remove wounded. Suddenly a second B-24 taxied into him killing the left waist gunner at his window with the right wing tip. (I've a photo taken at the waist gun next day.)

As if this were not enough another aircraft stopped on the active runway I believe (no lights-dark) and promptly another aircraft ran into him, both aircraft exploding into a ball of fire. The sky was still full of noise, shadows and clatter. I decided the old soldier's handbook left much to be desired and wormed my way back towards our hardstand area.

A Lieutenant Parker had landed successfully and taxied back to his hardstand. After shutting down engines he bounded out of his ship and went into a rage, demanding bombs and fuel so he could get him a couple of ack-ack gunners on the coast. Seems as though the radar picked up the Jerries amidst our flock and someone gave the order to fire. His wing man was promptly blown out of the sky while Lieutenant Parker watched in horror and disbelief.

Now into this chaotic opera a new ingredient was added. At random overhead a staccato of light flashes would emanate from an aircraft and, searching, would suddenly illuminate the silvery form of a B-24 and, surprisingly, no tracers would follow. We were told later the RAF had sent up nightfighters.

By this time I had decided on a new technique of my own. 'Put something substantial between you and the on-coming aircraft and shells!' Each time I heard one coming my way (and, for a while, I thought they were all coming my way) I would duck behind a tree on the edge of our hardstand site or dive into a ditch. By now, I had improved on my original technique and decided that distance lends enchantment and now I was near the base officers' quarters. Suddenly an officer appeared and asked what day it was! The 22nd I told him. He went back but in a moment returned and said he thought it was the 21st. 'No' I told him, 'it is the 22nd.' He asked how I could be so sure so I told him it was my birthday and, anyway, what possible difference could it make? 'I'm writing a letter,' he replied. Just then another aircraft roared by skimming the barracks. We both dived into the ground. 'Happy Birthday,' he said.

During this whole affair, Colonel Mason told the Red Cross ladies to get back off the base. I found them later, chatting in a truck, the driver hiding under the chassis.

A contemporary account is given by Staff Sergeant Julius Rebeles of the 714BS who kept a diary of his missions. Hamm was his tenth. "This mission turned out to be a nightmare. We took off late in the afternoon to bomb the marshalling yard at Hamm. Only the Liberator groups went out as the Fortresses had gone to occupied France in the am. The target was well hit even with a well-directed barrage of anti-aircraft fire sent up at us. Soon after, as we headed south to skirt the Ruhr, a force of about 50 Me109s and FW190s hit us. We were well protected this time as our fighter escort of P-38s drove them off. I saw only one Liberator go down, and that was from the 93rd behind us. Upon skirting the Ruhr and heading north we ran into stiff headwinds that slowed us down so much that by the time we reached the coast between Calais and Ostend it was beginning to turn dark. We saw our fighter planes go down and strafe gun positions and airfields in this sector. We were given orders to stay at our gun positions until we landed, for German twin-engined intruders had been seen taking off from their bases in Belgium. When we reached the English coast it was dark (about 11 o'clock) and our running lights were turned on, our radio generator and others in the group began shooting the colours of the day with flare guns. This was for identification purposes only.

"We spotted our field and got into the traffic pattern to land; as we were approaching to land, the Liberator that we were supposed to be following burst into flames. A Ju88 had sneaked into the traffic pattern ahead of us and set the Liberator on fire. The Liberator landed and rolled off the runway to clear it for others to land, for everyone's fuel was low. About this time all hell broke loose over this section of England. The British anti-aircraft gunners were shooting at anything that was flying, and the Jerry intruders were having a picnic by shooting up the airfields at which the Liberators were landing. Most of the fields were lit up like Christmas trees and presented wonderful targets. Our pilot circled the field once and by switching on our landing lights we set down on our darkened field; the runway lights were out but the burning Liberator lit the field with an eerie glow. We also saw other planes burning on the ground in the near vicinity. One of these we found out the next day was an Me410 shot down by the tail gunner of Lieutenant Alspaugh's crew (whose plane was also shot down by this same German, all parachuted to safety). The pilot took a chance by coming in like that but it was better than running out of fuel and having to leave a good plane go down. After we landed and pulled off the runway we watched the show go on in the skies. Several aircraft were seen to go down in flames but we couldn't distinguish if it was friend or foe; we had our doubts though.

"In the morning we saw what had happened. There were three of our

The scene at Seething on Sunday 23 April 1944. Ice Cold Katie (41-28595), lies between 41-28240 and 41-29575, The Ruth E K Allah Hassid. (F X Sheehan)

The port side of Ice Cold Katie — *she was salvaged as a result of the mishap.* (F X Sheehan)

Liberators piled into one another as they taxied down the ramp to get away from the intruders . . . the crews got out of them and they smashed into each other . . . JUNK. A completely burned up Liberator and other planes were scattered around the field off the runways. We lost three other Liberators and one crew that night. Eighteen Liberators were destroyed by the intruders and British anti-aircraft guns. A number of neighbouring fields had a thorough raking over by machine gun and cannon fire. One group had only five serviceable aircraft on hand, at another an Me410 strafed a group of men around the control tower killing and wounding over 50 men".

A final account from Seething is given by Technical Sergeant James A Pegher, an engineer in the 713BS flying with Captain Tom Apple's crew. "I'm sure there have been many stories of this mission, a 'milk run' that turned into tragedy on our field. It got dark before we left the coast of France, we could see the tracer bullets arcing below us, again no damage. When we got in sight of our field there was a fire, when we got close enough we could see a plane burning on the landing end of our runway, then all the lights went out all over the area. The pilot told us on the intercom to take our positions and load the guns again as the enemy had followed us in and were shooting the planes down as they tried to land.

"Well, it was so dark that we couldn't see our own planes, except the wing light, then I saw a red running light coming head on in front of us. I was so damn scared, I pushed the mike button but couldn't speak. That instant, the navigator, Winter, yelled into the intercom to pull her up. The pilot, Apple, acted instantly and that old lady leapt over that on-coming '24, I saw that red light pass about 10 feet below us. With that, Apple said, 'I'm taking her in'. There were no lights, not even the tower could help, no fault of their own. I was now down with the pilots. Apple used the burning plane as a marker and lined up with the runway. He had to stay high enough to clear the flames and set her down about halfway down the runway. He flicked the landing lights on for a few seconds and, to our horror, there were two B-24s sitting in the grass at the end of the runway. He guided our plane between those two, knocking our wingtips off and stopped. I jumped down and opened the bomb bay doors and looked back towards the burning plane. Another plane was on the runway. I yelled as loud as I could for everyone to get out, there's another one coming. I started running across the grass and looked again towards the burning plane, the other plane was trying to stop, his brakes were screaming. I'm still running and I see the shadow of another man passing me. I started to laugh when I thought, 'Man, that guy could run if he didn't have that big parachute holding him back!' Later I found out that it was my best buddy, Powell. He must have hit the rip cord when he jumped the waist window.

"The other plane slid into ours, no visible injuries to the crew, four B-24s in a heap. Another laugh! The MPs showed up in their jeep with the cats eyes. They yelled 'Take cover, don't you know there's an air raid on?' Powell hollered back, 'Hell, it's safe down here, you should be up there!' "

Seething suffered more aircraft lost than any other group, and the seeds of historical inaccuracy were sown. This was not deliberate distortion, but rumours flourished because security prevented revelation of the facts, especially those inviting recurrence of the intruders' actions. DuPont's description of "both" aircraft exploding was *Vadie Raye*, and Rebeles' reference to "50" casualties caused by strafing relates to events on the 467BG base at Rackheath, five miles northeast of Norwich.

Returning to England with the 466BG, First Lieutenant Stalie C Reid's crew left their adopted group at the English coast and began their approach to Rackheath, pleased by the near-completion of their third mission. As the main wheels whirred down and locked, the gunners vacated their turrets in preparation for landing. The probing white beam of their starboard landing light sought reassuring contact with the familiar, friendly farmland on final approach. Chattering into Reid's headphones came anxious voices of other pilots pressing for permission to land, so many that they jammed the tower's attempts to transmit an intruders alert. Reid continued his descent oblivious of the sinister shapes stealing upon him from the darkness astern. At 1,000 feet, his B-24 was struck by cannon shells from one, possibly two, intruders who closed to 60 yards, setting numbers three and four engines ablaze and

First Lieutenant Stalie C Reid's crew, 467BG. Shot down near Barsham. Rear L-R: Sylvio L Dery, Engineer; John H Biggs, Gunner; George S Hamilton, Gunner; Sergeant Vielbig (not on Mission 311); Mervin M Shank, Gunner; Walter W Kovalenko, Radio. Front L-R: Louis A Alier, Bombardier; James G Ferguson, Navigator; Warren W Mason, Co-Pilot; Stalie C Reid, Pilot. (M Shank)

causing oxygen bottles in the fuselage to explode. As the ship fell swiftly into a spin, only four gunners escaped, but Sergeant Edward W Hoke tore loose from his parachute harness and plummeted to his death near the village of Ringsfield. Reid and his remaining five crew died when the bomber blew up on fields in Barsham, close to the schoolhouse. Sergeants Mervin M Shank, John H Biggs and George S Hamilton all suffered facial burns. They appreciated the kindness of a local woman who bathed their wounds in cold tea before they were taken to hospital.

Trailing Reid into land was his friend, First Lieutenant James K Newhouse in *Wallowing Wilbert* which had kept with the main 467BG formation, letting down steeply to avoid a layer of cloud over the North

Wallowing Wilbert's pilot, First Lieutenant James K Newhouse, cursed Reid before realizing his friend was under attack. (M Bailey)

Sea. About half way across, the group broke into elements of three aircraft, each intending to reach Rackheath via Splasher 5 at Mundesley before overflying the airfield for landing instructions. Newhouse took additional guidance from a more basic navigational aid and followed the "iron beam" — railway lines leading into the Rackheath circuit. He recalls, "The railroad tracks functioned well that night but we had the most horrible sensation of knowing there were many planes milling around, many of them lost from their home fields. We were never properly alerted as to the danger that we had 'bandits' in the area. I suppose the only similar picture I could equate with, so you could understand how scared we were, would be to compare being in a small, darkened area, with little or no light, and knowing that several maniacs were in the room with you and were swinging baseball bats. You see, we were all going at least 150-200 mph and a B-24, even emptied, is not what I would call a manoeuvrable airplane in confined quarters. Anyway, I managed to get lined up on my proper airstrip, ie Rackheath, and was on my approach leg — had my gear and flaps down and was throttling back — when this other ship, which later proved to be that of Lieutenant Reid, cut me out of the pattern by flying under me. He received a resounding cursing from me as I pulled up and staggered on round. But my crew reported there was a Messerschmitt on his tail and we realized we were all under attack. I managed to go round and was grateful to go through unscathed although the field was a shambles and the attack was still going on".

En route to Rackheath Second Lieutenant Deutsch kept *The Snooper* on course by taking GEE fixes, but he noted in his log at 2211 that, "Too many airplanes going to SPL.5". Making their first pass across the airfield, his crew found it under attack and *The Snooper* slipped furtively away into the darkness, returning to land unhindered at 2238 hours.

Second Lieutenant James A Roden and crew were less fortunate. Mr W Hammond of Withersdale Street saw a vic of three Liberators approaching the village with their lights on and wheels down when an intruder pounced, pouring several bursts into the middle aircraft. Slanting in from 10 o'clock, the shells sliced off the bomber's tail unit which crashed on to the Weybread road, terrifying a British motorist. Plunging inverted, Roden's ship fell from 500 feet on to a hill top near Bluebell Wood, Withersdale. Flaring into a funeral pyre for its crew, the blazing wreckage illuminated the darkness like a grotesque beacon, visible for miles across the countryside. There were no survivors from its crew of ten.

Not content with this, several intruders swooped on Rackheath itself. Walt Mitchell on board *Lil Peach* later recorded, "As for the 22 April Hamm mission, we were one of the first crews back. We were in the pattern right behind Stalie Reid when Reid's plane was hit, burst into flames and went down. We landed and had completed our roll and were at the end of the runway when a German aircraft (Ju88) came right over us and dropped a bomb which exploded 50 to 100 feet in front of us, just to the left of the runway. Our navigator, Howard Stubbs of Ottumwa, was in the upper hatch and caught a piece of shrapnel in his thumb. After that we taxied to our hardstand, went in to briefing and then to the mess. I know we were the first crew back because we were the only crew in the mess and the Mess Sergeant at first tried to refuse us service because he had orders to serve only the returning crews. We had to convince him that we had just returned".

The bomb which fell near *Lil Peach* also wounded three crewmen on Lieutenant Redick's crew and was the first of five dropped on Rackheath. Coincidentally, an exercise in airfield protection was under way. Aircraft mechanic Allan J Welters had earlier returned to the 789 Squadron engineering hut after working late only to find the hut empty, the weapons racks unlocked and a note on his carbine ordering him to join other base personnel behind the bomb dump to hunt for "saboteurs". It was his birthday but plans to meet his friends Al Gerards and Daniel Miney had to be abandoned. Carrying his carbine, he was soon trooping reluctantly along the east side of the bomb dump in thickening darkness. Accustomed to Pratt & Whitney engines, Welters quickly detected a "strange sounding" drone approaching from the northeast, the same direction as the returning bombers. "It was just above the tree tops, coming at an angle somewhat to my right and toward me. I got a creepish feeling up my spine and back of the head. It felt like a bad situation was about to take place." Raising his weapon, Welters aimed at the stranger but hesitated in case it was an RAF machine. If it were German, surely the airfield's guns would be firing? It was too dark to see any insignia as the aircraft roared past and Welters had just lowered his gun, resuming his journey, when the first bomb detonated.

Welters' friend, Private Daniel E Miney from the 1229th Quartermaster Service Company, was tragically caught in the open and torn apart by the blast, while Sergeant Michael P Mahoney was fortunate to escape only slightly wounded. Having crept in with its lights on, deceiving the defences, the intruder surged away before swinging into another pass. Four more 50 kg bombs whistled from the darkness. Two fell in Rackheath village, destroying a bungalow and damaging 20 other dwellings, the others exploded near the end of the runway and Lieutenant Dickinson's *Osage Express* was damaged when it taxied into a crater.

Still airborne, Lieutenant Wood's aircraft was attacked from astern at 500 feet as he passed over Wroxham. With his number four engine burning and vibrating badly, Wood scraped *Slugger Jr* safely into land. Vivid memories of the scene are recalled by First Lieutenant Charles W Grace whose lead crew had not been scheduled to fly. "Because it was the first operational mission to return after dark I, along with all the rest of the group, were vitally interested in the success of such a mission. I had walked to the flight line, and was beside a brick wall when the first bomb struck nearby. A piece of shrapnel, the size of a peach pip, missed

Slugger Jr. *was attacked in the traffic pattern over Wroxham and struggled into Rackheath with number four engine on fire.* (M Bailey)

Piloted by Lieutenant Reed, the 467BG's famous Witchcraft *sustained some flak damage but landed safely at Rackheath. Tended by caring groundcrew,* Witchcraft *flew many more missions, 65 when pictured in September 1944.* (M Bailey)

The Thunder Mug *landed at Rackheath after six hours 23 minutes flying time. Lieutenant Kleinshrots and crew had used 1,850 gallons of fuel.* (M Bailey)

my right ear by approximately six inches (which I later dug out of the wall and kept for a souvenir). I ran for cover but did witness the entire episode from a shelter and was totally amazed at all I saw. In the twilight, I was able to make out the silhouettes of twin engined enemy bombers as they made several strafing runs and dropped their bombs. As our own bombers would start a final approach for landing and turn on their landing lights, the enemy aircraft would fire on them. I witnessed one of the B-24s abort his landing upon realizing something was amiss and gain several thousand feet over Norwich where he was shot down by the British AA guns. It seemed that in the mass of confusion everyone was shooting at each other."

Furious at the assault on their airbase, many personnel retaliated with small-arms fire. But, strangely, a record of ammunition expended by guns officially defending Rackheath shows they used only 60 rounds of .50 calibre. Once again, a farrago of misfortunes created contradiction and the 467BG files relate how the "Group airfield was attacked. Some observers claim runway buzzed by Ju88 at 2210 hours. Others say this aircraft a B-24. Aircraft number 357, 458BG, attempted landing at Rackheath. This may be aircraft in question. Times do not jibe. Shortly after 2210 hours Ju88 dropped one approx 50 kg HE bomb off end of runway then in use, lights on, from about 150 feet . . ." Elsewhere, the 467BG recorded "one Ju88, one Me109 and one Me210 or 110 joined the landing traffic pattern and, from minimum altitude, bombed and strafed from 6 o'clock planes as they landed". Muddling events even more was the claim by a British gunner that the intruder was a Mosquito which failed to identify itself and might even be "enemy operated". No evidence can be found to support this and any Mosquito seen was undoubtedly hunting for Me410s of KG51. Nor can the sighting of an Me109 be taken seriously because it lacked the operational range.

Some of the confusion was exacerbated by indiscreet comments which then became part of local folklore, as recounted by Mr C T Dungar of Rackheath village.

I was a messenger with the Home Guard. Me and my mate had to keep in contact with Home Guard, ARP, observer Post and the Newfoundland Ack Ack Regiment, stationed in part of Rackheath Hall, and the Ops Room of the 467BG Liberator base at Rackheath, which covered most of the Estate and parts of Salhouse. I remember the local people talking later in the afternoon. They were worried because the only planes to return to base out of 26 were two which had to abort the mission with engine and generator troubles. Many people looked on them as part of the village, knowing most of them by their names or motifs and knew where they stood on the airfield. Later on that evening, I had to take a report from Beech House about an exercise in which the Home Guard was supposed to try and capture the airfield. I had to give this to Master Sergeant Hogan who worked on the radio telephone intelligence in the Ops room. As I stopped at the picket post, my Pass and ID card were checked by a tall, blonde Swedish-American named Hutchinson who we knew as Hutch, a hard, tough guy from Galveston, Texas. He told me the guys were very worried about the ships as they had run into very bad weather over the target area, had strayed and got lost, some groups being so far off course had mistaken the Bristol Channel for the (English) Channel, eventually trying to find RAF Valley. Some were lucky, others ran out of gas, crashing in parts of the Welsh mountains after more than 11 hours in the air.

I had supper with them, a normal thing two or three times a week, and enjoyed a packet of Camel or Chesterfields helped down by tomato juice. Then about 8.15 pm, the sky suddenly became full of aircraft from all directions, some with navigation lights on, some with the very bright landing lights in the wings, others with one under the nose turret, desperately trying to spot the airfield. The poor sods had never flown at night before, and some with only six weeks training in the States. After what seemed about 10 minutes, the main runway 145 East to West was lit up and about four Liberators got down. As the next one came in and was about half way along the runway, all hell suddenly let loose as a Messerschmitt 110 opened up with machine gun and cannon fire. The gunner in the upper turret of the B-24 returned the fire as it slewed off the runway, its nose wheel collapsed and finished up with its nose section, engine cowling and props badly damaged. One man who was working on another Liberator at dispersal was hit with cannon fire and cut completely in half and you could drive a jeep through a hole in the plane's fuselage. From then on it was complete panic, men were rushing about shouting, 'The Krauts are raiding the field' and letting sub rifles and revolvers off everywhere. After that it was complete chaos with planes trying to land at will . . . some even landed downwind on the short runway as they got desperately low on gas.

Then, as everyone thought another one was trying to get in, it turned out to be a Junkers 88 and it tried to bomb the main runway. One fell on the edge of the perimeter track, another failed to explode, but the last fell on the third bungalow past the 'Sole and Heel' public house, killing a woman and her son. As the skirmish went on, with everyone firing at anything in the air in total panic, a Mosquito which had taken off from Swannington on its way to Berlin was shot down crashing at Ludham killing both of its crew. After that dreadful night of panic, the local Liberator bases lost 17 aircraft, either shooting themselves down, or shot down by the enemy or just crashing out of gas. It was very lucky the wind wasn't in the other direction that night or those bombs would have fell in the middle of the bomb dump and it would have been goodnight Rackheath and Wroxham.

The civilian casualties mentioned by Mr Dungar cannot be verified and his account has other apocryphal aspects blended with some authenticity. Nonetheless, his recollections clearly illustrate the care and concern shown by local communities for their aeronautical neighbours. Schoolboys found the advent of so many airbases in the region particularly exciting. And, such is the species, they were not squeamish when it came to collecting souvenirs from mishaps which grimly attached themselves to an airfield's operational statistics. The drama of 22 April 1944 was no exception. Malcolm Martin of Beccles offers a typical account.

As a boy of 15 I witnessed this disaster accompanied by my father, standing outside our home at 40 Ravensmeer, Beccles. It was dark at the time and at first we did not realize what was happening, apart from the obvious activity and sounds of battle in the sky. We thought it could be enemy bombers intercepted by our fighters but realized that — at that stage of the war — it was unlikely. The wing lights of some aircraft also puzzled us. It was something we had not seen in wartime. It soon became clear what was happening; I saw the unmistakable outline of a Liberator bomber lit up by fire, heading towards the ground. I was extremely interested in aircraft spotting during the war. I still have my copies of the "Aeroplane Spotter" of that period. I think that my father and I then realized that the Americans had, for the first time, returned after dark, and either our fighters had erroneously intercepted them or, as it transpired, enemy fighters had followed them home.

American Liberators and Fortresses circling the town were a familiar sight most mornings as they gained height and formation to set out over the coast. Later in the day, but before dark, we would see them return, often straggling and with damaged tailplanes or wings. But never after dark.

That evening must have been a considerable victory for the German Air Force as the sky over Beccles seemed to glow with crashing, incandescent aeroplanes. I was so fascinated that I cannot recall being frightened as one was in an air-raid. Rumours at the time had it that 17 aircraft were brought down, that the American gunners had been given the 'standdown' as they crossed the coast and that they were stripping and cleaning their guns when they were attacked.

One plane crashed on the Beccles to Lowestoft railway line at Worlingham, and another on to fields at Barsham near Beccles. I visited this wreckage on the following Sunday morning. The tailplane was in a field to the east of the Beccles and Bungay road and the remains of the main aircraft were close to the road in a field to the west. Two roadside trees had been damaged by the fire. The wreckage was still burning and several gruesome relics were scattered around. There was no guard, probably so many crashes had extended the available troops. You will appreciate that boys of the war years were ardent souvenir hunters, crashed aircraft (Allied and German) being fair game. We had been hardened by numerous crashes in the area since 1940 and, although we often discussed the terrible sights we saw, I think we became a little detached from it all. Our 'currency' was machine gun ammunition, self-sealing rubber from petrol tanks and perspex from windscreens which could be shaped into all sorts of novelties. Few outhouses or garden sheds were without relics of some sort. I am pretty sure my friend retrieved a belt of ¹/₂" machine gun ammunition from the Barsham crash. He had it laid out on a bench in his 'den' when a Special Constable, a friend of the family, looked in and saw it. He was advised to lose it quickly. Another youth took a trade bicycle to the Barsham plane and removed a complete ¹/₂" machine gun, carefully placed this in a sack and took it back to Beccles . . .

After being hit by flak, First Lieutenant Kenneth L Driscoll maintained formation on three engines until detaching himself from the 467BG after crossing the enemy coast. The crew faced a more protracted journey but felt it worthwhile for easing the strain on their good engines during the sea-crossing. Lieutenant Harold Pantis bent to his charts and calculated a course and estimated time of arrival over the airfield but, when it elapsed, they found themselves above darkened countryside with no recognition from Rackheath which *had* to be below. Six times Driscoll overflew the position Pantis gave and was wary of other aircraft meandering like lost sheep. Fearing a collision, he chose a straight, northeasterly heading for five minutes, allowing Pantis to verify his navigation before retracing their route. Once more, the navigator insisted the airfield lay beneath them but it stayed invisible and stubbornly silent as the crew's anxiety intensified. Then, after at least three orbits, the runway lights came on. Landing swiftly, Driscoll learnt the reason for Rackheath's reluctance and the crew's faith in Pantis was restored. Now accounted for by the 467BG, they felt their earlier misfortune may have proved providential.

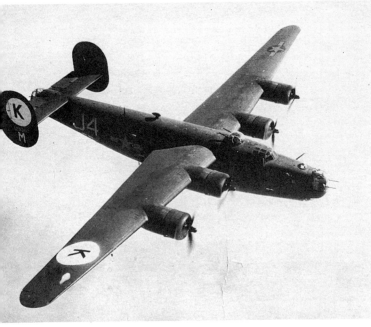

Among the 458BG Liberators inbound to Horsham St Faith was 41-29300 Lorelie *flown by First Lieutenant F DeNeffe and crew. Alerted by Colonel Isbell, they landed safely at Attlebridge. Others were less fortunate.* (A North)

Establishing lists of killed and missing airmen proved impossible immediately after the attack because many ships landed away from base, either deliberately or in desperation. Having warned his 458BG about the likelihood of intruders, Colonel Isbell now anxiously awaited his group's arrival at Horsham St Faith. "After dinner that evening, Colonel

Pictured a few days before the Mission to Hamm, Meat Around The Corner *is seen with L-R: Lieutenant Ruhl, William Etheridge, unknown and Lieutenant Richard L Moses. Moses died on 22 April when flying as navigator with the Harris crew.* (A North)

Right Meat Around
The Corner *was flown
on Mission 311 by
Second Lieutenant R W
Davis and crew. Pictured
earlier in the war, her
nose-art was changed to
avoid her crew being ill-
treated if captured with
this version as opposed to
the skunk.* (A North)

Below *Flown by First
Lieutenant Andrew,*
Rhapsody In Junk
*received flak damage
during the mission but
avoided the intruders
when warned by Horsham
St Faith's control tower.*

House and I went for a drive around the aerodrome. At dusk we
stopped at Flying Control to wait for the mission's return. Standing on
the balcony, we watched other elements of the USAAF bombers as they
descended towards their home base. We recognized the 458th still a
good 20 miles to the east — no lights showing but the forward passing

lights. They were further recognized for the excellent and close formation they flew (I had a fetish about their returning from a mission in a prideful way because I saw so many other outfits with stragglers and that looked like they had taken a licking). As we watched, the fireworks began, 20 mm cannon! I knew what it was. I ran inside, took the mike and gave the alert. Runway lights, approach lights, everything visible was put out. Then we watched two aircraft go down."

Co-piloting one of those aircraft was Second Lieutenant Robert T Couch Jr. "Jake" Couch had originally been assigned as co-pilot to First Lieutenant Teague G Harris Jr before being given a crew of his own. Finding them not scheduled for Mission 311, Jake volunteered for a vacant co-pilot's slot with his old crew. Like many Americans, Jake had been "adopted" by a local family, Les and Vi Murton, and spent many hours relaxing in their Norwich home. Les had flown in the First World War and knew domestic normalities could alleviate combat stress. In the few weeks since Jake arrived, the Murtons' fondness for the young flier had grown and a bond developed between his family and theirs which spanned several decades. Jake had married shortly before coming overseas but the pace of training had given him only three weeks with his bride, and now he was cramming missions in to complete his tour early and rejoin Judy. The Murtons understood this but worried about

The Harris crew. Rear L-R: Teague Harris, Pilot; Jake Couch, Co-Pilot; Robert Ahrens, Bombardier; Richard L Moses, Navigator. Front L-R: Francis X McKenna, Radio; Clifford L Oder, Top-Turret; Howard E Found, Right Waist Gunner; M W Kahl (not on Hamm mission); Eldridge L Carpenter, Left Waist Gunner.

the number of operations he was flying and Vi became increasingly apprehensive whenever the bombers trembled the window panes of her home near the airfield. Jake, imbued with youthful exuberance, continued taunting fate.

Ten miles southeast of Norwich at 6,000 feet, two intruders swept from the darkness raking with cannon and machine-gun fire the aircraft captained by Harris and Second Lieutenant Charles W "Red" Stilson. Within seconds, both bombers were ablaze, their pilots fighting for control. Harris saw Stilson's ship ignite as cannon shells pulverized his own port wing, destroying his controls. Simultaneously, he was convinced he saw a barrage of anti-aircraft fire surrounding them. He and Jake stood no chance of keeping airborne as flames surged on to the flight deck and, seconds later, Harris felt the ship falling rapidly despite their efforts. In an agony of fire, he struggled from his seat through the conflagration, groping for the bomb-bay. His next recollection was of lying in the wreckage, hands gently lifting him. Was it God? Then he passed into unconsciousness.

Stilson and his co-pilot, Second Lieutenant J E Worton rang the bale out alarm and four crewmen parachuted into the darkness as their B-24 lost altitude with both starboard engines burning. Preparing to leave, Worton hesitated, waiting for Stilson but the pilot, convinced there were men still on board, continued struggling for control and ordered Worton to jump. Suddenly, the ship was struck again from below. Muffled cries over the intercom confirmed some of his men, perhaps wounded, had been unable to escape. By now, the B-24 was a shambles, the propeller had vanished from number three engine, number four smeared flames across the wing, and number two engine was screeching wildly out of control. With only one effective engine, Stilson skilfully kept airborne until Horsham's runway was almost in his grasp, but he realized it was just too far. Barely over the rooftops, Stilson saw a clearing and slipped the bomber down for a crash-landing.

Les and Vi Murton had been with friends to "The Bull" for a drink when the sirens began their plaintive wail, then came the crash alarm for raiders overhead. Bundling outside, they heard a tremendous roar and dived for cover as an aircraft scraped over bungalows nearby. Flames streaming from faltering engines, it strived for the runway at Horsham but then crunched to earth only yards from "The Bull". Slithering some distance, it shed pieces in a torment of torn metal before its nose gouged in, the fuselage broke apart and the hulk finally stopped. Ignoring the risk of exploding ammunition, Les and his friend, Harry Hall, leapt over the hedge and ran to the wreckage. Clambering into the torn flight deck, Les extricated Stilson, stunned but still alive and protected by the cocoon of his new-style armoured seat. The right waist gunner, Staff Sergeant A Silverman and the radio operator, Technical Sergeant W R Pearce were dead and Second Lieutenant M C Marshall, the bombardier, died later in hospital.

On the southwestern side of Norwich, near the Tuckswood Inn, other

Wreckage of Second Lieutenant Charles "Red" Stilson's aircraft near The Bull public house. Note how flames and smoke have smeared the lower right rudder. Engineers are dismantling the bomber for salvage. (Brig Gen J H Isbell)

Right *Adopted by the Murton family of Norwich, Jake Couch died when his aircraft crashed near the Tuckswood Inn. His Purple Heart is now displayed in the Second Air Division Memorial Library.* (Les & Vi Murton)

Below *Local people watch from the roadway as the broken tail section from Harris's ship is cleared from a meadow, now part of the Hewitt School playing field.* (C Gotts)

rescuers found a badly-burned pilot amid the debris of his bomber. His back was broken but Harris would recover after months of hospitalization. Jake, his co-pilot, had been almost cut in half during the crash and died instantly, along with five other airmen. By strange coincidence, their bomber had fallen on land belonging to Vi Murton's father and now part of a school playing field. The following day, the news was broken to the Murtons, along with a request that they say nothing to Jake's family for 30 days. Letters expressing their love and

sharing hopes for his future sat unanswered until the grim bureaucracy of war caught up. Les and Vi Murton never forgot the young American whose life they briefly shared and always cherished.

Other East Anglians would always remember witnessing the events that cost Jake and many others their lives. Mr H L Pittam, then resident in Poringland, saw a Liberator attacked.

I was on leave that night from the RAF and, as there were no air raid sirens in the district, the only warning was the alarm bell of the light AA units guarding the radar station at Stoke Holy Cross. I went outside on hearing the bell and could see some searchlights and scattered AA fire over Gt Yarmouth. My next door neighbour, an air raid warden, said the Yanks had gone out that day and weren't back yet, but I didn't link the two. I could hear the bombers coming in sounding very heavy and I knew from past experience that the Americans weren't trained to night operations in the air.

It was a sort of half lit sky and a Liberator flew over going north towards Norwich. He was at about 500 feet and I knew he was in the landing pattern for perhaps Seething. Suddenly the tail gunner opened fire, just as a fighter flew over behind him. It was twin-engined and I thought it was an Me110. They were now firing at each other with tracers and cannon hitting each aircraft. Then the tail gunner stopped firing and I supposed he had been hit.

A small red glow appeared under the port inner engine and slowly got brighter as the Liberator flew steadily on towards Norwich. Meanwhile, as the fighter turned to starboard, the mid-upper gunner fired and the .5s tore in to the under fuselage of the fighter which turned away, still to starboard and flew slowly northeast towards Framham Pigot with engines banging and surging. He was, or appeared to be, losing height when I lost sight of him heading away.

The Liberator meanwhile flew on but now all the port wing was ablaze and he seemed to slip behind the trees on the hill. I wondered then if he would drop on Norwich. Overhead, I could see the shapes of bombers literally flying in all directions and suddenly the sky was lit up with tracers again as aircraft fired at each other. I could not detect any fighters in the melee but as I watched, I could see that the tracers were from bombers and I realized that the Liberators were firing at each other! As the noise decreased and the bombers diverted to other airfields, I counted 12 big fires in the area around me for a distance of some miles, with the faint popping as ammunition exploded in crashed aircraft. There was no all-clear from the AA site and the silence was very deafening.

Whether Mr Pittam saw the Harris ship attacked is inconclusive because both the tail and top turret gunners perished and no claims were made. However, Sergeant Lewis Brumble, left waist gunner on the aptly named, *Last Card Louie*, flown by First Lieutenant H W Wells, was given credit for the destruction of an Me410 from 6,000 feet at 2230 hours. The Combat Form completed during interrogation reads, "As aircraft was returning to base after mission, enemy intruders attacked around 2215 in darkness. One Me410 made a pass from 2 o'clock high, circled and attacked again. Aircraft was not in any set formation and gunners were all on alert for return of enemy aircraft. When southeast of Rackheath aerodrome, Me410 came in again from 2 o'clock low and passed below aircraft 441. Left waist gunner fired at least 100 rounds, tracer hitting behind pilots' compartment as enemy aircraft passed beyond (our) aircraft. Enemy aircraft fell on right wing and dove straight into the ground on fire. Large explosion when he hit ground".

As will be seen, a 389BG Liberator also claimed the destruction of an Me410 in the same area but of two Me410s lost that night, only one was confirmed. Ron Cain of Bergh Apton had been indoors listening to the radio when the drone of many aero-engines drew him outside to observe the spectacle of Liberators landing at night. Watching, he saw a twin-engined aircraft closing in on a B-24 and tracers flashed like an assassin's dagger. Simultaneously, one of the bomber's waist guns struck back hitting the intruder which burst into flames. Engines screaming, it dived steeply to oblivion and exploded in a field at Ashby St Mary.

Visiting the scene very early next morning, Ron saw a large crater surrounded for some distance by scattered unrecognizable debris, but one of the pieces he picked up was marked "Me410". The nose and engines were buried and young Ron saw a parachute pack amid wreckage in the hole and, hoping for a prize his chums would envy, he clambered down over lumps of disgorged earth. Reaching his intended trophy, Ron was disappointed to find it so scorched that it disintegrated at the slightest touch, and he scrambled clear in search of other mementoes. Meanwhile, his father, Walter Cain, on duty with another Home Guardsman, had the grisly chore of collecting human remains mingled amidst pieces of aircraft. It was a task not for the squeamish. The two men wandered the field using their bayonets like park-keepers, transferring what they found into sacks. During this sombre process, Walter Cain found a wallet containing quite an amount of Dutch currency and handed it to the authorities. Ron was a little less forthcoming with his next find. An unusual feature of the Me410 was its two remotely-operated, rearward-firing 13 mm MG131 machine guns in barbettes on either side of the aft fuselage. Near the edge of the field, Ron found one of these, bent but a superb souvenir, so he surreptitiously dragged it into the undergrowth for later retrieval. Unfortunately, when the time came, it had vanished, apparently found by the RAF recovery team who arrived later that morning. They also recovered the cockpit canopy which had fallen with a flying helmet some distance from the main site, suggesting the crew had attempted to bale out. At first, only the pilot, Oberleutnant Klaus Krüger could be identified, presumably because of the wallet. His radio operator, Feldwebel Michael Reichardt was not traced until later. Their aircraft, coded 9K+HP, werke number 420458, yielded "no new information" to

Major Dietrich Puttfarken disappeared during the "Night of the Intruders". A holder of the Knight's Cross, he commanded the long-range night fighter staffel of KG51.
(Wolfgang Dierich)

British Intelligence, nor were the Allies aware that II/KG51 had lost a second aircraft in action over England. Uncertainty surrounds the disappearance of 9K+MN, werke number 420314, because no trace of it has ever been found. Whether it vanished unseen into one of the region's many broads or, more likely, disappeared limping homewards over the North Sea after sustaining damage is unlikely ever to be known. Its loss was significant because its pilot was the staffel commander, Major Dietrich Puttfarken, along with Oberfeldwebel Willi Lux as his radio operator.

Adding to the confusion, a contemporary 458BG public relations press release credited Stilson's gunners with destroying their attacker. More credence can be given to the Silver Star subsequently presented to Stilson for his courage. Years later, another 458BG flier, Glenn R Matson, confessed to his own comparative lack of heroism that night. Writing in the Second Air Division Newsletter, Glenn recalled, "22 April 1944 was a stand down day for our crew so we did not have to fly . . . I sat around all day. Went to Dome trainer for a while and got bored. I decided to get a pass and go to Norwich. It was refused. I said to hell with them and went AWOL. I got dressed and went out the Burma Road. As usual I got all drunked up. Some English sailor sold me a bottle of some very bad booze, bathtub type. At about 10.30 at night, I am staggering along a ditch at the end of the runway when I heard the darned awfullest noise. Couldn't believe what I was hearing. It was anti-aircraft guns going off all around me. Out of the dark came this B-24 roaring down the runway and over the top of me. Pursued by a Ju88 or a Me110. Jumping for the ditch, I lay there for awhile until it quieted down. I took off for the debriefing hut with my bottle of booze. I got there as the crews were coming in. These guys looked like ghosts, pallid and drawn and scared from their dreadful experience. One guy came in carrying his popped parachute. He looked like he could use a drink, so I offered him one from my bottle. That was the last time I saw that bottle . . ."

A more sober view of events is offered by 458BG pilot, Captain John L Weber. "We were on a long final approach to Horsham, gear and flaps down, when tracers starting coming from behind us, passing on below and going on ahead. I yelled over the intercom to Callahan, the tail gunner, 'Do you see a fighter back there?' He came right back with, 'Yeah, I see him'. I hollered, 'Why aren't you firing'? He came back with, 'I'm waiting for him to get in range'. With that, the entire crew came on the intercom laughing and yelling for Ray to start firing. About this time the runway lights went out and the tower advised everyone to disperse and try to shake off the fighters. We went up the Wash and circled until things quietened down, then came back to land.

"My next recollection is of standing at the bar in the Combat Crew Mess when 'The A-rab', who if my memory is correct was Lieutenant Stilson's co-pilot, Lieutenant Worton, came in the door dragging his open parachute behind him. As I remember, we had a difficult time getting him to leave the bar and report in to his squadron. He had baled out at low altitude and it had taken him quite a long time to find his way home in the dark".

To sooth nerves still jangling, a late night movie, *Going My Way*, was organized and numbers of combat crewmen soon found themselves absorbed in the story of Bing Crosby as a crooning Irish Priest overcoming gentler adversities in his New York parish. As his Group settled, Colonel Isbell took stock. "We stood to lose 26 aircraft that night, each with at least 10 members aboard. We lost only two aircraft and nine men. It was a miracle that we lost only nine of the 20 on board these aircraft".

Another Group Commander concerned for his airmen was Colonel Robert B Miller who was joined at Hethel by Generals Hodges and Timberlake. Miller's men had little night flying experience, and the presence of two senior officers sharing the control tower balcony only increased Miller's anxiety. Eager to observe the 389BG's return, the two Generals got more than they bargained for. Homeward bound with their lights on, the 389BG formation was infiltrated near Gt Yarmouth by an intruder who audaciously switched on his own lights to appear less sinister if noticed by nearby American bombers. Sidling along the edge of the Liberator formation, it crept unnoticed towards the leading

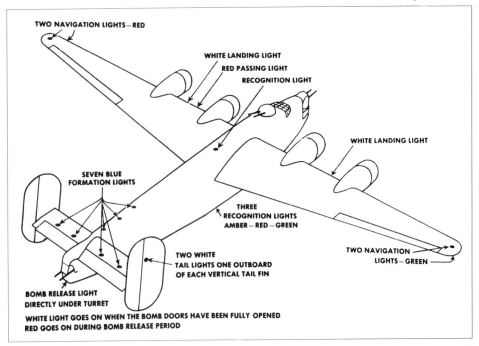

TWO NAVIGATION LIGHTS – RED

WHITE LANDING LIGHT
RED PASSING LIGHT
RECOGNITION LIGHT

WHITE LANDING LIGHT

SEVEN BLUE
FORMATION LIGHTS

THREE
RECOGNITION LIGHTS
AMBER – RED – GREEN

TWO WHITE
TAIL LIGHTS ONE OUTBOARD
OF EACH VERTICAL TAIL FIN

TWO NAVIGATION
LIGHTS – GREEN

BOMB RELEASE LIGHT
DIRECTLY UNDER TURRET

WHITE LIGHT GOES ON WHEN THE BOMB DOORS HAVE BEEN FULLY OPENED
RED GOES ON DURING BOMB RELEASE PERIOD

"Homeward bound with their lights on" — this diagram shows the purpose and arrangement for a Liberator's lights.

sections and then infiltrated alongside the B-24 flown by First Lieutenant P T Wilkerson and crew. Droning over the wide, flat Norfolk marshlands, the spectacle of so many bombers drew residents into doorways and gardens of the area's small communities and isolated dwellings.

"Peter recognized it instantly as an Me210 or 410 series, their silhouettes were almost identical". The Me210 shown here failed to meet expectations but provided the basis for the Me410. (Deutsche Aerospace)

Wilkerson's aircraft disintegrated over Cantley. The broken off port rudder rests on a meadow near the village. (H H Christensen)

In Cantley, 11 year old Peter Morrish was enthralled by the show. But then, chillingly, he spotted the intruder's minatory manoeuvres as it slid furtively into the bomber formation on the starboard side of a B-24. An avid aviation enthusiast, Peter recognized it instantly as an Me210 or 410 series, their silhouettes were almost identical. Like a ravenous but cunning wolf, it stalked a prey still oblivious to the threat. Peter stood, powerless to intervene, transfixed by the drama unfolding overhead as the Me410 eased in front of its victim. Perhaps out of ammunition for its forward-firing armament, the German fighter was sneaking into an advantageous position for its barbette guns, ahead of and slightly below a B-24. The rasp of twin machine guns rattled sharply above the sound of engines as it sprayed Wilkerson's aircraft.

From the Liberator's nose turret, Staff Sergeant J R Murray responded instantly as did the right waist gunner, Staff Sergeant M B Cabtle. The 389BG records claim they destroyed the Me410. Local eyewitnesses say it broke away, racing seawards as the B-24, its engines and fuel tanks riddled, caught fire and spiralled out of formation from about 3,000 feet. Its descent appeared deceptively lazy as it circled Cantley, burning fiercely. Inside, the crew struggled desperately to don parachutes and escape. Some figures emerged, then a section of wing sheered off and the bomber tore apart, spilling itself in flaming debris over the countryside. Airmen whose parachutes failed to open in time were later discovered embedded in the boggy terrain, another was impaled on the branches of an oak tree in the Morrishes' garden. Ammunition and pieces of aircraft clattered on to the rooftops of Cantley but civilian casualties were spared when heavier sections smashed on to the railway embankment and marshland adjoining the Norwich to Gt Yarmouth line.

Local residents, reacting swiftly, were soon out searching for survivors. Billy Gladden had been strolling home across the marshes when he paused, perching himself on the railway crossing gates to view the returning bombers. Seconds later the attack occurred. A Liberator burst into flames and began curving earthwards in a starboard turn towards the river Yare before swinging round and heading for Cantley itself. To Billy, it seemed as if the pilot sensed this because it veered away from the village, and a parachute emerged just as the bomber exploded. Recovering from the fear of being hit by debris, Billy then heard cries for help coming from the darkness dotted with small fires and the popple of ammunition cooking off in the heat. Searching the marshes, Billy found two airmen, one with a broken leg. Hurrying off for help, Billy met a US Army motor cyclist and together they called an ambulance.

The Morrish home was the local First Aid Post and had a Chevrolet ambulance donated by the American people earlier in the war. Driven by Peter's father, it required considerable skill to negotiate narrow,

The account given by young Peter Morrish of an aircraft firing backwards was initially treated with disbelief until his recognition skills were tested. Then an officer, shown here, had the chance to examine the wreckage and confirm the trajectory of bullets which brought down the bomber. (H H Christensen)

marshland tracks in the dark but he eventually reached the first airman still entangled in his parachute and suffering from shock plus a compound fracture of one leg. The second airman had already been collected so Mr Morrish returned home to find several Americans receiving first aid with the hapless Lieutenant Wilkerson sitting agitatedly on the edge of an armchair, convinced a "Spitfire" had shot them down. Young Peter's input was initially disregarded but, after he had proved his aircraft recognition skills to some American Intelligence Officers, his account was taken seriously. Other eyewitnesses not only verified his story but had seen other intruders amidst the American formation. Ralph Spooner, standing in the garden of his bungalow in Church Road did not see the first fighter until it machine gunned Wilkerson's aircraft, but he then noticed two or three others. After Wilkerson's aircraft crashed, Ralph put his wife and young daughter into the air raid shelter before joining a neighbour, Arthur Thompson, searching for airmen seen baling out. Hurrying along the railway line, they noticed the stench of aviation fuel strengthening as they neared sections of wreckage not on fire but gurgling gasoline into pools on the meadow. Arthur still had a cigarette. Ralph snapped at his companion to extinguish it before they blew themselves up. Finding no survivors amid the debris, they widened their search and two bodies were discovered floating in nearby dykes. By 0200, all 11 aircrew had been accounted for, with six dead, three injured and two unscathed.

News of Wilkerson's loss heightened tension at Hethel as base personnel "sweated in" their comrades. Two aircraft landed safely but the nosewheel of First Lieutenant E M Rubich's ship collapsed after a heavy touchdown, sending the Liberator scraping along the runway in a shower of sparks. A small fire in the nose was speedily doused using extinguishers, but the main runway was now blocked. With over 20 ships still airborne and intruders amok, the 389BG faced a catastrophe. But Hodges and Timberlake saw at first hand an efficient reaction by Flying Control personnel who rapidly shifted their caravan from runway 240 to runway 17. With so much "top brass" present, MPs had been posted to prevent unauthorized personnel accessing the tower. There was also a dance on the base so support staff and airmen not flying that day, some with visiting lady friends, had taken vantage points to observe the unusual spectacle of a group night landing. Rubich's spectacular arrival had been without any casualties. However, such luck was not destined to last. Approaching Hethel from the northeast at 1,500 feet on the downwind leg, Second Lieutenant Edward W Foley's ship was hit by an intruder making a single, swooping pass from 3 o'clock high before speeding away into the lower darkness. Cannon shells set Foley's number two engine alight and lacerated the hydraulic system rendering his brakes useless. Damage sustained by the throttle control linkage also jammed his engines into high rpm. Less than a minute later, Foley's crew were convinced two British AA guns on the outskirts of Norwich opened fire when tracers curved up and into their starboard wing. This

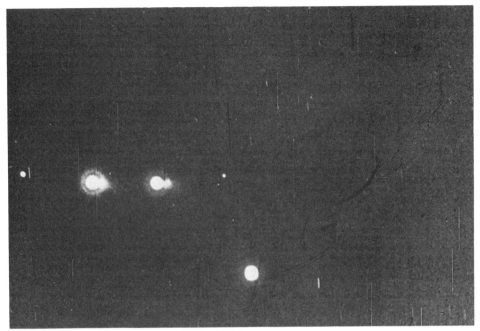

"Those on the tower saw the flash of cannon and stood, horrified, as lights from the in-coming Liberator sank towards trees skirting the airfield." Foley's Liberator was guided in by a flare; its lights are left of centre as it struggles in to land. (USAF Official)

fire could have been from the same or a second intruder. But, "friendly" or otherwise, Foley and his co-pilot, Second Lieutenant L F Muir were fighting for control and facing a high-speed landing with no brakes.

Those on the tower saw the flash of cannon. They stood, horrified, as lights from the in-coming Liberator sank towards trees skirting the airfield. Others, seeing the aircraft slew and wobble, thought it was an intruder searching for a line of fire into the control tower. Only when it crossed the boundary could they see the reflections from four propellers shimmering in the runway lights. With rubber squealing, the bomber touched down, then Foley found his left tyre was flat. Running some 500 feet, he and Muir kept a steady course. But the yaw overwhelmed their efforts and pulled the bomber from the runway, straight towards the tower. Engines howling, some 25 tons of aircraft bore down on the building like the charge of an enraged bull elephant. As spectators on the field scattered there was growing consternation among the tower's occupants and distinguished guests. Hurtling across the signals square, the runaway bomber tore up the big code letters "HJ", narrowly missed the tower, smashed headlong into the radar technicians' workshop and erupted in flames. An enormous fireball surged skywards wrapped in smoke so thick it shadowed even in the night sky.

As Gunnery Officer, Captain John Driscoll had been showing a friend and his young lady over the gunners' training apparatus when the air-

A member of the 2032nd Engineer Aviation Fire Fighting Platoon plays his hose into the conflagration created by Foley's B-24 at Hethel. (USAF Official)

raid alert went. Then aircraft appeared overhead, some firing flares. From a distance, John saw a B-24 land and slew off the runway, crashing into buildings near the tower. Whoever it was, John knew one thing — there would be friends of his on board. Jumping into the gunnery-training flatbed truck, John sped towards the blaze. Nearing the scene, he estimated there were over 100 people encircling the burning aircraft, at a safe distance but like celebrants around a bonfire. Closer in he saw the strangely shaped silhouettes of firefighters from the 2032nd Engineer Aviation Fire Fighting Platoon garbed in their cumbersome asbestos suits and already spraying foam over the wreck. Braking hard, John leapt from his truck almost before it stopped and demanded to know from on-lookers if all the crew were out. No-one seemed certain, nor were the medics and MP. So, shielding his face against the glare and heat, John dashed towards the aircraft's smashed nose, not yet swallowed by spreading flames. Peering through torn aluminium and shattered perspex, he saw what looked like the fabric of a jacket reflected in the flames. John, pushing his way in, saw several figures prone amidst the debris and quickly grabbed the nearest, hauling the man backwards from the wreckage as firefighters doused them both in foam. Surging from ruptured tanks, gasoline continued feeding the conflagration and it was clear to John that the bomber and its remaining crew would soon be consumed. Flares and ammunition were exploding and one bullet, ricocheting off a piece of wreckage, struck him. Fortunately, it lacked velocity and only stung as he ducked back into the fuselage. Grasping

Fire illuminates the shattered radar shack as Z-Bar *blazes a beacon across the airfield and countryside — a tempting target for further intruder action.* (USAF Official)

Flames surge skywards as Captain John Driscoll rushes to aid airmen still trapped in the wreckage. (USAF Official)

On 23 April, John Driscoll's courage was recognized when General Doolittle presented him with the Airman's Medal standing in front of the burnt out bomber. (J J Driscoll)

How narrowly Z-Bar *missed Hethel's control tower can clearly be seen in tracks left by the careening bomber.* (USAF Official)

The wreckage of Z-Bar *and the building it gutted costing the lives of two men inside.* (USAF Official)

another body, John hoisted the man clear, then returned for a third airman whose removal exposed a fourth. This time, someone else assisted and together they dragged the victim clear as flames made further access impossible.

It was soon established that all 10 aircrew were alive, but two technicians in the radar shop had perished. As the doors of the last ambulance slammed shut, John knew that there was nothing further he

Engines lie in the building's broken framework. The top-turret's twin machine guns indicate how little was left of the fuselage. (USAF Official)

could do. Being covered in foam had protected him from serious burns but his hair and eyebrows were singed and his best uniform looked considerably upset by its treatment. Smartening himself as best he could, John returned to the dance-hall — only to be refused admission because of his appearance! However, General Timberlake had witnessed events and contacted Lieutenant General James H Doolittle. Next day, the famous commander of the Eighth Air Force flew his P-38 into Hethel and, as well as being apprised about events, Doolittle personally presented Driscoll with the Airman's Medal, symbolically standing in front of the burnt out B-24.

A few miles from Hethel an intruder tried to wreak similar havoc, attacking aircraft of the 93BG landing at Hardwick. Living at Darrow Farm, Denton, beneath Hardwick's approach path, Ruth Johnson had gone into the farmyard with her parents to wonder at the giant, brightly lit aircraft descending from the darkness. Their farm was so close to the airfield that Ruth remembers "landing light poles all over the place". In daylight, crews waved, but now sharp white beams lanced brilliantly downwards. In a world of wartime blackouts, such brightness was exciting and, as they were about to learn, dangerous. Suddenly, there came a series of vivid flashes and loud bangs close overhead. Frightened, she and her mother did not know what they were but, cursing the Germans, her father yelled at them to take cover and the family dived to the floor in a nearby toolshed.

Someone else failing to realize what was happening was the Liberator pilot just about to land. Second Lieutenant Albert B Cool had touched down no more than 10 seconds when his ship *Annie's Cousin Fanny* was attacked. Feeling the B-24 lurch, he thought a tyre had accidently blown, not knowing the puncture came from bullets ricocheting off the runway behind them. Dumbfounded by a clatter like gravel thrown at the fuselage, other crewmen thought Cool had dragged their tail as they landed. In the waist, Sergeant Wallace B Schwantes understood what was happening when he looked down through the hatch to see tracers streaming beneath the fuselage. Apparently the intruder had missed, but his approach angle was so shallow that bullets and shells were bouncing off the runway in pursuit of *Fanny*. Airfield defences opened fire but ceased for fear of hitting the B-24. Perhaps the airfield's gunners deterred the intruder or he simply missed, but *Fanny* rolled to a halt without further damage.

Following Cool into land was Second Lieutenant Hugh I Malley with First Lieutenant Thomas B Parry, flying his first mission as a co-pilot with an experienced crew before taking his own into action. Tom recorded in his diary, "We took off at 1700 and bombed the railroad yards at Hamm, Germany. Heavy flak was encountered in the target area and Me109s made one pass at our formation. At dusk we crossed the Channel and let down for a night landing at 2200. Just before touchdown, I noticed what appeared to be sparks on the runway ahead. Someone shouted 'Bandits' on the radio and I realized that the sparks were bullets ricocheting off the runway from a German fighter on my tail. The runway lights went off as we touched down and all hell broke loose. Everyone on the ground and in the air seemed to be firing and tracers streaked the sky. We finally got the aircraft stopped on a concrete hardstand used for single aircraft parking. I jumped out and began to crawl across that concrete in the dark as the German fighters strafed the field. I had the distinct impression that all of northern England must have been concrete before I finally reached the edge and dived into a hole that may or may not have been there prior to my arrival. Most of our aircraft, and those from neighbouring fields were forced to fly around without lights and I suspect that more were lost from collisions than to German fire. It was a wild introduction to combat".

Apart from damage to *Annie's Cousin Fanny*, and bullets ricocheting into barracks, Hardwick suffered no further damage. Nor were any aircraft lost in collisions as Tom Parry feared.

The 453BG lost another B-24 when Lieutenant Sanders' right undercarriage leg collapsed on landing at Tibenham, fortunately without causing any casualties. Another 453BG scared its crew and onlookers at Old Buckenham when bombs which had stubbornly refused to release over the target and since, fell out on landing and went bowling down the runway without detonating. Meanwhile, as the 735BS diarist recorded, ". . . a mad house was in full swing. British anti-aircraft were firing at everything they saw. Jerry night fighters were following the bombers all around the pattern, right down to the final approach. It was not uncommon to hear somebody say 'turn your lights on' followed by a hail of tracers and 20 mm cannon fire. British manned defence guns helped by firing at everything that crossed the field — bomber or fighter. Our luck held through that mess. A few planes were badly shot up, but no-one was hurt. Of the 24 ships the Group sent to Hamm, only Munsey failed to return".

Other airfields experienced minor intruder activity or none at all. Near Shipdham, First Lieutenant Charles E Arnold and crew were shot at in the traffic pattern but landed safely with other 44BG aircrew who, during interrogation expressed disillusionment with night flying. The 392BG at Wendling watched events over neighbouring bases but were untroubled themselves. Similarly, spectators from Tibenham saw several aircraft destroyed without loss themselves but 445BG historians noted, "This bold stroke by the German Air Force won it new respect".

At Flixton, a dance in the Officers' Club was interrupted by events as Mrs Joyce Carey, nee Page, recalls. "I was 18 years old and regularly on a Saturday night I went to USAAF officers' dances at the various bases in Norfolk. Transport was provided from Norwich (usually outside City Hall). On the night of 22 April 1944 I went to Flixton base, near Bungay, arriving in the early evening. I met my date, a navigator who was off duty that night having been flying the previous day. I had hardly got my strawberry shortcake and icecream when the 'alert' went and we all went outside the mess hall. In the dusk the sky was lit up by (as we thought) flares as the returning planes came in to land. After standing outside about 10 minutes, we heard the sound of explosions and were told to go into the air raid shelter. The next thing was all the men were called on immediate duty, and we girls were left standing outside the shelter — still eating my icecream. Then we could see that the Germans were in amongst the Liberators shooting them down — noise and confusion and lights in the sky all around. Due to the emergency we were more or less forgotten about, and could do nothing but stand and watch helplessly. I know that on that night I did not arrive home until 3.00 am as the truck drivers were all employed on the emergency. Usual time of arrival back in Norwich was 1.00 am."

Not far from Joyce Page enjoying her icecream, Mabel Brooks also worried about friends she knew were on the mission. "During the war I lived with my husband and daughter of 10 years right on the edge of one side of Flixton aerodrome. Only about six yards from our gate was the first sentry box of the American air base. My neighbours and my family had to carry a pass card to get to the village, the men to get to their work on the farm and my daughter and the girls next door carried one to get to school. We met several of the men and were kept busy

Crew 70. 706BS 446BG. Rear L-R: Julian Dixon, Radio Operator; Clarence Lien, Tail Gunner; John Peterson, Waist Gunner; Ray Walker, Engineer; Warren McMillan, Ball Turret; Scott Hilliard, Gunner. Front L-R: "Pappy" Henderson, Pilot; Robert Tannahill, Navigator; "Mac" McCarty, Bombardier; E Dale Howard, Co-Pilot. (V A McCarty)

doing their laundry and sewing jobs. I worked for many of the flying men and adopted one aircrew who flew in a Liberator named *Dinky Duck*. This particular Saturday we knew the planes were going out and it was a habit of the boys to look out of the top and give us a wave. We watched them go and I must confess we hoped and prayed that all would be well. Then when it got dark we heard the drone in the distance and knew some were returning. I think we were all a bit excited so we stood out at the front of the house to watch the planes come in. It was a magnificent sight. The huge lights lit up the place. After a while we got the white warning and in only a few seconds came the red warning that meant we had to go indoors as we had a table shelter indoors. In less than five minutes I crept upstairs and all was quiet on our airfield, not a light to be seen or a sound of any plane — enemy or ours. There was no firing over Flixton, no guns fired and we had no planes down on the airfield, everywhere was in darkness. My husband and I then ventured outside and what a sight! We didn't see any parachutes but the planes just fell from the skies like flies. There were huge fires at Hardwick and Seething, we just stood watching and were nearly numb as each plane fell. Our thoughts were of the men in the planes, wondering if we would ever see our friends again . . ."

First Lieutenant Vere A McCarty, bombardier on *Dinky Duck* takes up the story.

It was dusk as we returned across the channel and it was early darkness as we made our let-down. I had come out of the nose in preparation to land and as was customary for me, I was standing between the pilot and co-pilot counting off the airspeed as we landed. As I recall, all our guns were secured. I did not have earphones, so I do not know who first reported 'bandits' but there was an airplane on our tail only seconds before we were to have sat down on the runway. Pappy (pilot, First Lieutenant O W Henderson) put on full power and, as the intruder tried to get below our tail, Pappy took to the tree tops. I could see houses and trees zip past off our wingtips as we hedgehopped inland.

By now it was quite dark. Pappy could get no response to requests for landing instructions. He feared to set down on a lighted field, not knowing whether it may be a dummy decoy. He headed north. In the distance we saw lights, very dimly, coming on for a bit then going out. As we got closer the lights were broken by what appeared to be aircraft taking off. Pappy timed an approach with a take-off and slipped in behind and landed as the other lifted off. As he taxied in we were introduced to British security as armed vehicles immediately became our escort.

As we deplaned, my head struck a projection in the dark and began bleeding profusely. In attempting to stop the flow, I missed some of the first exchange between Pappy and our somewhat shaken hosts. We were escorted before a senior officer where we were first severely reprimanded for interrupting their night mission take-off. Then we were taken to the dining area where there was first a whisky, then a warm meal. We soon learned that we had landed at a Lancaster aerodrome near King's Lynn. We were not permitted to call our base because the communications blackout was to continue while their planes were out. We met a number of RAF flyers. We exchanged our experiences and discussed pros and cons relating to daylight versus nightime bombing. Neither side wanted the other's job. Pappy lifted the Dinky Duck *off before breakfast the next morning. When we parked at the hardstand we were met by a not-too-sober ground crew. They had stayed up all night holding a wake for the crew of the* Dinky Duck.

At another RAF Station also near King's Lynn, the pilot of British 279 Air-Sea Rescue Squadron Hudson AE213 was also delighted to meet terra-firma in one piece. Flight Lieutenant H C F Goff and his crew were returning from RAF station Detling in Kent to their base at Bircham Newton in Norfolk. Flying at 1,500 feet, they stayed seaward to avoid the notoriously trigger-happy gunners around Felixstowe, and crossed the coast of Suffolk near Aldeburgh. Frank Goff knew something was wrong when he saw the evil glow from numerous orbs of flame that had seemingly erupted on the earth's crust from hell itself. He knew what they meant and saw another aircraft burning on one of the Liberator bases near Norwich. Elsewhere, the powerful landing light beams from other B-24s cut into the darkness as they sought sanctuary. Frank guessed intruders had been active. This was startlingly confirmed only seconds later when a shape surfaced from the gloom less than 200 feet from his port wing and Frank found himself staring at the sinister outline of an Me410. It was so close, he scarcely dared breathe, and clearly saw its crew peering at his own twin-engined, twin-finned

Flight Lieutenant Frank Goff blundered into the action and was more than a little disconcerted to see an Me410 alongside his Hudson. (H C F Goff)

Wandering into the battle, a Hudson was no match for the Me410. (Flight)

silhouette, seeking to identify it. With skies full of Liberators, the Me410 possibly assumed they were a Luftwaffe compatriot, perhaps a Dornier. Frank had no intention of allowing them more time for recognition training let alone target practice. Sheering steeply away, he dived, weaving downwards into the night's now friendly embrace, his heart racing from fear of cannons closing in. He knew his ponderous Hudson was no match for the viciously armed intruder and stood no chance of out running it. Fortunately, the Me410 seemed startled by his abrupt departure and apparently made no attempt to follow. Keeping a wary eye, the Hudson scuttled back to Bircham Newton feeling much as a rabbit does knowing the fox is abroad.

Hunting the fox proved frustrating for the 25 Squadron Mosquito nightfighters scrambled from Coltishall. Pilot Officer K V Panter and Warrant Officer A W Mogg took off first at 2215 hours but the intruders eluded them amid the many Liberators still airborne. Five minutes later, Flying Officers J S Henderson and R A Nicholls raced off into the darkness, soon closing in on a bogey which also emerged as a B-24. Their second bogey was a different disappointment, an outward bound Lancaster. Flight Sergeants J E C Tait (RAAF) and E P Letchford were vectored on to a bogey but their air interception radar malfunctioned and contact was lost. A second, fast moving contact transformed into another Mosquito, as did a third. Despite maintaining an all-night vigil, 25 Squadron's fortunes failed to improve. Four further plots into Suffolk and Lincolnshire also evaded the defences and the only conquest confirmed over England that night was Krüger's Me410. At least four gunners across three groups either claimed or were accredited with its destruction. The true victor may never be established along with other facts relating to incidents that night. At least one public relations office

A wolf in sheep's clothing. Former adversaries, a captured Me410 leads an RAF Mosquito during comparative trials. (Philip Jarrett)

press release re-allocated the victory, and other contemporary press accounts understandably censored or edited events.

Wishing to learn the full impact of the intruder action, Lieutenant General Spaatz issued a directive ordering all Second Air Division groups to provide details. The anxiety caused by Luftwaffe tacticians is reflected by the closing paragraph of the telex. "The importance and need for accuracy, clarity and completeness of this information can not be over emphasized. Requires immediate action and use of personnel best qualified. Must be in form for consolidation and forwarding to Lieutenant General Spaatz and Doolittle". Summarizing the mayhem several days later, reporting officers said 15 enemy aircraft had been sighted and 20 Liberators attacked by 12 of the 15. Ten B-24s were damaged by intruders before they landed, two were damaged on the ground and eight crashed or crash landed. Personnel casualties, "attributable to enemy intruder action" were:

1. In air: Seven killed; 17 wounded; and one missing.
2. On ground: One killed and five injured.
3. Crash or crash landed: 29 killed and one injured.

It seems they omitted from these figures those unfortunate souls who fell to "friendly" fire or whose loss could not be directly linked to intruder action. The reality is that casualties caused by the presence of intruders were much higher and bring the death toll to nearly 60. It is clear the chaos created merited the concern demonstrated by USAAF commanders. At a 2 CBW mission critique held on 23 April, General Timberlake discussed with his senior officers methods of overcoming the night landing difficulties and commented, "Our problem is different from

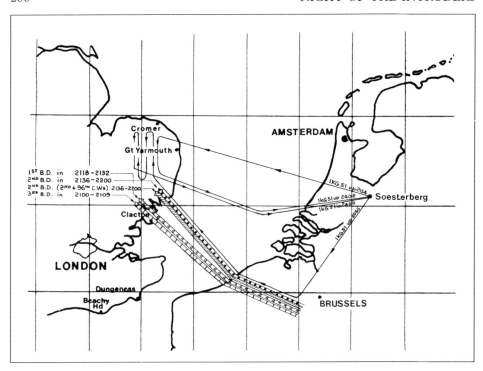

Based on an RAF Wireless Intelligence Service report, this diagram plots intruder movements from signals picked up by eavesdropping on German transmissions and from Royal Observer Corps reports. (I. Loades)

the British. They come back singly, we come back in a big group and it's not a question of 24 aircraft, it's a question of 700 aircraft. Let's think about it." They did. And the conclusion became apparent when no further USAAF missions of such magnitude were launched where they risked another "Night of the Intruders".

•CHAPTER TEN•

Last Casualties

AS AMERICAN AIRCREW slept, celebrated survival or received medical attention, "the Night of the Intruders" slipped into Saint George's Day and, before dawn, events would claim three of England's sons.

At RAF station Ashbourne in Derbyshire, 42 Operational Training Unit provided the final stages of training for multi-engined aircrew prior to operational postings. Sergeant Kenneth Rusby had begun training as a pilot in Rhodesia nearly two years earlier but "washed out" because of difficulties learning to land. Given longer, he would have overcome the

Sergeant Ken Rusby's navigational skills were recognized after he failed pilot training. (K Rusby)

Intended as a medium bomber, the Albemarle proved unsuitable and was relegated to roles in training, transport and towing gliders. An example pictured following D-Day. (Mrs M Brackenborough)

problem but hard-pressed instructors had no time for concentrated, individual tuition taking longer than an acceptable average. However, they had noticed Ken's aptitude for navigation and he was encouraged into this new role, returning to England in July 1943. Joining 42 OTU, he was soon guiding their ungainly Armstrong Whitworth Albemarles around the countryside. Intended as a medium bomber, the Albemarle had proved unsuitable and was relegated to roles in training, transport and towing gliders.

During the early hours of 23 April, Ken and his crew clambered into Albemarle V1610 intent on a routine, low-level, cross country exercise. All sergeants, the crew blended well and banter soon subsided in the seriousness of pre-flight checks and taxi-ing into their slot as second aircraft to take off. John E Hutchinson lifted the Albemarle away at 0243 hours, heading for Sleaford. Tony Whittome, the bomb aimer, looked forward to the latter part of their planned route because it neared the thatched cottage at Castor in Northamptonshire which he and his wife had converted from an old barn. Freda was a telephonist in the ARP Centre at Peterborough and, droning south, he could be forgiven for thinking of home and family, so near yet so far. The radio operator, Johnny Davis, concentrated on tuning his receiver for transmissions affecting their plans, while the bomber's defence rested with their air-gunner, Ron Thurgood. After an hour and 20 minutes, the Albemarle was cruising steadily across the Lincolnshire leg of its journey, on course for completing the exercise as planned. Then, near Kirton, the sudden

Airmen from 42OTU share a lighter moment. Top to bottom: Jimmy Metcalf, Harold Armstrong, Fred Eliason, Ken Rusby, Ron "Joe" Thurgood, Johnny Davis, John Hutchinson. Fate played a cruel hand for those on board Albermarle V1610. (K Rusby)

crash of cannon fire blasted their port wing, flicking the Albermarle into a vicious, starboard bank. Thrown from his seat, Davis landed heavily on the floor and was some seconds reconnecting to the intercom. Pulling himself up, he could see the port wing burning and, as he pushed home his r/t jackplug, he heard Hutchinson give the order to bale out. Tossing aside his helmet, Davis clipped his parachute on and grasped the emergency release for the hatch overhead. Terrifyingly, nothing happened. Panic surged as he struggled to release it. Suddenly, the hatch vanished and he scrambled out, being pulled off the starboard wing by the violent slipstream.

In Taylor's Farm, Kirton Fen, 12 year old Betty Wilson had been sound asleep when the roar of gunfire and a terrible explosion overhead frightened her awake. Startled, she sat up as her parents dashed into the room urging her and her younger sister to get up as the roar of aero-engines terminated in a blast close to the house. Fully awake, Betty saw that the room was alive with angry shadows and, staring in amazement through the window, she clearly saw flames reflecting orange-white off a parachute descending almost on top of the wreckage. Hastening downstairs, her mother lit the oil lamp while her father donned his coat and left for the nearest telephone in Leonard Hall's house, about one mile distant. Mounting his bicycle, he urged his wife to lock the doors because it must be a German plane. Hardly had he departed when Betty and her family were scared by an urgent knocking. Guarding her

The funeral of John E Hutchinson at Stockport Crematorium. Ron Thurgood, second on right, helps carry his pilot's coffin. (K Rusby)

children, Mrs Wilson did not move at first, but then they heard a voice pleading, "Please let me in, I'm Sergeant Davis from Derby Airport". Betty heard the relief in her mother's voice as she made for the door. "He's not a German, I think he's a Welshman" she reassured her children as she unlocked the house to admit armfuls of white parachute and a very distraught airman. Obviously still in shock, Davis kept talking about the explosion, how he could not escape, the jammed hatch — and, with anxiety haunting his face, he worried about the others. When he explained which side of the house he had landed, Mrs Wilson could give some reassurance because the parachute they saw was not his. Comforted, Davis gratefully accepted some tea and waited until Mr Wilson returned with news of another airman at the Castle Inn. Cheered by this, Johnny Davis set off to meet his friend and discovered Ron Thurgood, shaken but uninjured.

As dawn turned the glowing embers of Albemarle V1610 into sad wisps of grey smoke and shattered aluminium, hopes for Ken Rusby, John Hutchinson and Tony Whittome faded. Later, the grim process of recovering their bodies began, and telegrams were sent, tarnishing further lives with the stains of war. Once again, the cruelty of truth was understandably withheld. Four days after being shot down, Davis and Thurgood attended a Court of Inquiry into the "accident involving Albermarle V1610". It seems, once again, that more lives had been lost in a case of mistaken identity undoubtedly encouraged by intruder activities earlier that night.

CHAPTER ELEVEN

Aftermath

IN 1947, THE year I was born, the remains of Munsey and Crall were recovered from the wreckage of *Cee Gee II*. Such were the circumstances, it was impossible to individually identify the two heroes and today they share a common grave in Jefferson Barracks National Cemetery, Saint Louis, Missouri.

For many years the aircraft lay undisturbed. I grew up with an avid interest in aviation, developing ultimately into research and aviation archaeology as described in my book, *Final Flights* (also published by Patrick Stephens Limited). Inevitably, accounts describing the loss of *Cee Gee II* stirred my imagination and I first visited the site in 1964. Local inhabitants recalled the bomber's fiery passage over the coast near Southwold and its dreadful denouement on marshland in the Blyth estuary. Sadly, who the men were was unknown, nor were the circumstances of their loss understood. Hand-digging on the site my

Two pilots who made a courageous run for the English coast in Cee Gee II *now share a common grave in their native soil.* (Don Olds)

The undercarriage leg from Cee Gee II, *unearthed in 1968 during drainage operations on Reydon marshes.* (M D Baker)

friends and I found a maker's plate confirming the type as a B-24, the remains of a radio receiver, perspex fragments and numerous pieces of aluminium surrounding a central boggy crater too deep to work in and effectively protected by a swan presiding on her nest. Knowledge of the incident was acquired like the wreckage itself — fragments of information, stories of other victims. "The night Jerry followed the Yanks home" was frequently mentioned and often embellished.

Soon I understood there had been a significant air-battle over East Anglia on 22 April 1944, and the Reydon B-24 was only one of many lost that night. Inexperienced and unable to make further headway with research or recovery, I turned my attention elsewhere until, in August 1968, the local media reported, "US plane wreckage found at Reydon". Television pictures showed the massive undercarriage leg from a Liberator while announcing how the "Flying Fortress" had sunk without trace in a wartime crash only now being "discovered" during drainage work by the East Suffolk and Norfolk River Authority. Worried about bodies and bombs, Charles Roberts, the Area Engineer, called the USAF at Bentwaters and the story was out. Once it was realized the site was known locally and there was little likelihood of ordnance or the need to recover lost crewmen the story diminished, but attention had been drawn to the site and persistent souvenir hunters incensed local landowners when crops were damaged and cattle allowed to stray. This handicapped efforts by those genuinely interested in recovering the landing gear for a museum display. Since 1968, legislation has made it illegal to recover and remove aircraft without a licence. In those days, however, it was a case of allowing matters to calm down and then

Deep in it. The author on the site of Cee Gee II, *1970.*

gaining the landowner's consent to retrieve the undercarriage and conduct additional, limited excavations.

In the summer of 1970, we revisited the site and, while the more technically competent set about dismantling the undercarriage, Paul Crickmore and I searched for smaller pieces worthy of display. The previously inaccessible crater had vanished putting the crash at the intersection of two dykes. Cutting deeply into the marsh, the River Authorities had unwittingly planned their new dyke right through the remains of *Cee Gee II*. Even so, the publicity added little to the information available, but two finds that day triggered important progress. Detaching squares of turf to be replaced later, we scrutinized the roots for smaller finds possibly entangled. This procedure paid dividends when Paul found a watch which had stopped at exactly 2147 hours and four seconds. Deeply moving was the thought that the life of its wearer had almost certainly terminated in the violence of that instant in time. Hoping the case would be engraved, we cleaned our find carefully but the only inscriptions were those relating to its type and manufacturing specifications. The next discovery left no doubts. Lifting one square of turf, it fractured and there, glinting in the crack, I recognized the undeniable rectangular shape of an airman's dog-tag. Other than brushing off the soil, no cleaning was necessary to reveal the details: "J S Munsey 0-686583. T42-43. 0. Mrs Mary G Munsey, West Main Road, Norman, Oklahoma. P". The 0 prefixed number was Munsey's service number, T42-43 confirmed his anti-tetanus injections, '0' was his blood group and 'P' denoted the Protestant religion. Returning this to the United States Army Mortuary System in Europe prompted an investigation and release of information vital for my research.

By 1981, the story was largely complete and others had added to it by

Aluminium glinting in the sunlight, a pannier crammed full of ammunition is pulled from the marsh in 1981.

recovering additional wreckage including a machine gun and sections of armour plating. The belief persisted that larger pieces still existed deep alongside or below the dyke bed. In March that year a mechanical excavator capable of reaching over 20 feet probed into the marsh. Although this was mounted on a raft of railway sleepers, there still existed the fear of it sliding into the boggy terrain and its manoeuvrability was restricted. Even so, several large sections of wing were found as well as a pannier of ammunition, the remains of the ball

The author provides scale for a machine gun from Cee Gee II.

Not unlike the scene nearly three decades earlier, a self-sealing fuel tank is exposed by our activities at Worlingham in 1968.

turret, its guns and gunsight. Honouring the courage shown by those who flew *Cee Gee II*, some of the more notable finds now reside in East Anglian aviation museums such as the 390BG Memorial Air Museum at Parham and the 100BG Museum at Thorpe Abbotts.

Ingenious in theory, poor in practice. Don (left) and Ron tried making a cage to work in drier conditions around one of the bomber's engines but it snagged other debris and could not be pressed in enough to surround its target.

Brutal but effective, the drag-line makes work easier and cleaner.

Also displayed are items from Lieutenant Alspaugh's *Peggy Jo*, but some wreckage still lies beneath the Lowestoft to Beccles railway, despite major excavations in 1968. That year, two brothers, Ron and Don Buxton, fascinated by events witnessed as children, followed up rumours of a B-24 buried alongside the railway embankment near Beccles. Given

Maps found in the wreckage of Peggy Jo *clearly illustrated the route taken and contradicted at least one account of the mission published in the 1960s. Pencilled over the coast at Egmond, the route in.*

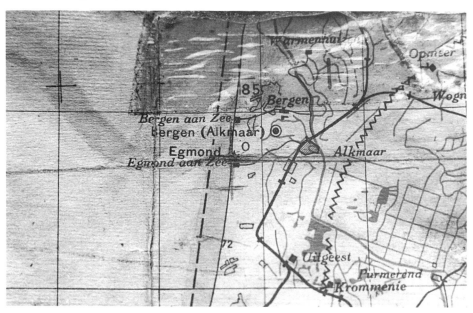

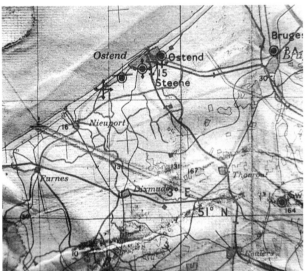

Above *The approach to Hamm, marked with a "T" for target.*

Left *Route out near Nieuport.*

Below *Navigational computer found in the wreckage.*

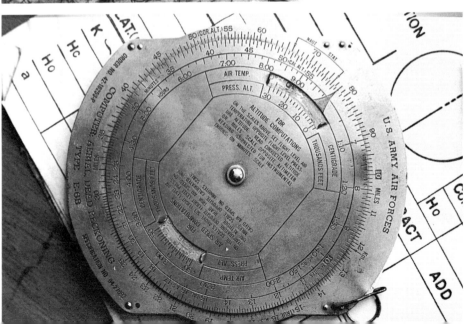

the landowner's permission, they located the site and began several strenuous weekends of spade and winch-work resulting in the removal of a main undercarriage leg, but attempts to retrieve an engine were thwarted. I had by this time been recruited to the team. Working waist deep in the mire, we found movement difficult — and our proximity to a nearby sewerage farm seemed only too real given the mud's texture, colour and fragrance. Deciding little else could be achieved without machinery, the Buxtons demonstrated their genius with matters mechanical and restored a derelict JCB in return for its use.

Their efforts were rewarded as masses of material emerged from the rapidly expanding crater — until someone noticed a crack encircling the machine and enlarging every second. The bank was subsiding! A rush to rescue the JCB ensued and was narrowly won. But we had reached its maximum stretch and depth, which left us despondent about pieces still submerged. Sympathizing with our predicament, the landowner lent us an almost new Priestman Junior dragline which trundled across the marsh one Sunday morning, with us as slaves shifting sleepers from rear to front enabling its stately progress to continue. Its longer jib extended the reach and enlarged the excavations into a crater over 30 feet in diameter and some 20 feet deep. From this were removed three Pratt & Whitney engines, propellers and innumerable smaller artifacts including Carlson's briefcase containing route maps to Hamm and a notebook giving information about Mission 311 and earlier raids. Found also was a paperback novel, *The Bangkok Murder Case*, still readable if somewhat crass in content. Once again, recovery work was confounded by conditions when we saw cracks appear in the railway embankment and an observing British Railways employee disappeared, sliding neatly into the dyke. One wit noted that this was probably the fastest he had moved in years! Our work concluded amid debris from the bomber's forward fuselage, including the pilots' emergency bomb release, remains of the bombsight, even a leather A2 jacket endorsed with its owner's nickname "Westy" on the back, and chewing gum in one of the pockets. Reluctantly, we ceased work awaiting closure of the railway line.

Another group not unhappy with the idea of a reduced rail service was the Norfolk and Suffolk Aviation Museum whose members had been working on Wilkerson's ship at Cantley. Member Alan M Hague witnessed events that night and saw Harris's ship attacked. Exchanging stories at school on the Monday, Alan heard of the Cantley crash from his friend John Guymer and visited the scene the following Saturday. Although the site was guarded, the two boys saw pieces strewn over a wide area and Alan reckoned that recovery personnel would not find everything. Years later he returned to search for wreckage still extant and worthy of display in the museum's collection at Flixton. In 1975, to the delight of the museum team, hours spent patiently probing the marsh with metal rods were rewarded by a solid "thunk" beneath the turf. Surprisingly close to the surface they retrieved an undercarriage leg and tyre.

An even greater coup was achieved by the N and SAM when they completed recovery work on Krüger's Me410. Earlier efforts in 1971 — led by local enthusiasts Val Grimble and Ray Allard with assistance from Ron Cain — had established the existence of substantial remains. Val recalls, "Unloading the gear we spread out and walked carefully all over the central area as Ron Cain indicated that the spot as he remembered it was fairly 'middle-ish'! There was a small stable standing in the field so we decided to fan out to try and find any surface particles to give us a clue as to the crash area. The field was completely normal . . . absolutely nothing to indicate anything had ever happened, let alone an

Above *The tyre and undercarriage leg from Wilkerson's aircraft, retrieved in 1975 for the Norfolk and Suffolk Aviation Museum.* (B Lain)

Left *October 1971. Aviation excavators at the crash site of Krüger's Me410. Peter Woods (left) and Gordon Knights are in the trench, Ray Allard leans on his shovel — all concerned are pleased with their efforts.* (V Grimble)

aircraft crashing there with great violence. We weren't getting very far after an hour or so, then I picked up a small piece of alloy followed by a piece of tyre rubber. Someone else picked up another object which turned out to be a cannon shell base, another was found followed by more metal pieces." Of a later visit that autumn Val writes, "We pegged some stakes out around the area in which the detector readings were strongest and we increased the penetration of these readings by digging holes and lowering the detectors in — signals even stronger. We started digging and in no time were striking alloy pieces at a mere foot or so down — some were quite large and took a while to get out . . ."

Above *Engine from Me410 9K+HP now displayed in the Norfolk and Suffolk Aviation Museum, Flixton, Suffolk.*

Right *Detail from a painting depicting the destruction of Krüger's Me410.* (J. Reeve)

Circumstances prevented further work that year and over a decade elapsed before significant excavations were permitted. These culminated when the Norfolk and Suffolk Aviation Museum removed a buckled 13 mm MG131 machine gun barrel from one of the barbettes, a 20 mm MG151 cannon and one of the Daimler Benz DB603 A2 engines, now restored and exhibited at Flixton.

Other finds, while less spectacular, demonstrate determination and hours of patiently plodding the windswept farmland. Henry Bennett never forgot the awesome spectacle of Pulcipher's B-24 plunging in flames near his home. Walking across the marshes the following morning, he and his father found fields littered with evidence of the tragedy. One wing lay on the surface minus engines, both torn off and embedded; a solitary flying boot standing in a meadow; a sealed canvas pouch marked "Secret and Confidential", which Henry took to the Police Station. Elsewhere, a bright yellow dinghy had fallen free and inflated to sit incongruously on waves made by the plough. Easily seen, this was removed, but other items lay hidden in reedbeds, woodland foliage or simply penetrated the area's many marsh-meadows. As an adult, Henry now finds these when he returns to the countryside, evoking many childhood memories including those of a bomber taking 10 young airmen to extinction on land now gentle with cattle and crops. Having visited the scene myself and peered upwards at trees in the spinney where Young and Durant hung dead in their parachutes, I could feel the forlorn spirits sigh, making the leaves whisper like lost voices. Perhaps imagination, but I sensed an eeriness pervading this site that

Even after many years abroad Henry Bennett was haunted by the sight of Second Lieutenant Pulcipher's B-24 plunging to earth near his wartime home. Now living near Reading, he pays an annual pilgrimage to the lonely Suffolk marsh, searching for reminders of the tragedy. Like others, he feels the loss of so many young airmen should not be forgotten.
(H G Bennett)

was unfelt elsewhere. One local woman spoke of figures seen wandering the marsh, calling in the darkness. Our activities added a small assortment of pieces to the collection now displayed in Seething's former control tower. Meanwhile, Henry perseveres and one day hopes an engine reputedly buried will emerge to become the centre-piece for a memorial to the crew.

Cleaned, restored and documented, smaller artefacts can serve a similar purpose. Searching the harvest stubble cresting a hill near Bluebell Wood, Withersdale, I soon realized that, although little remained where Roden's bomber torched its grim beacon nearly 50 years earlier, the fire's ferocity was traceable in a layer of charred soil and globules of molten aluminium solidified amid an ash of ammunition, exploded cases and countless bullets.

Care must be exercised with ancient ordnance. The point was emphasized when I joined members of the Anglian Aeronautical Preservation Society, searching for remains of Roy Osborn's P-38. Because of the aircraft's armament, caution was advised by AAPS Chairman Dan Engle, and 20 mm cannon shells with .50 calibre ammunition were gently set aside for proper disposal. Not identified at first were several rusting tubes, each less than a foot long and a couple of inches in diameter. Then, as I was working amid the roots of a tree,

Members of the Anglian Aeronautical Preservation Society work on the woodland site where Colonel Roy Osborn's P-38 plummeted to destruction. L-R: David Dodge, the author, Derek Brown, Stephen Brown, Mark Brown, other unknown. (Eastern Daily Press)

Roy Osborn's seat harness unearthed 40 years after he abandoned his troublesome fighter.

my spade cut through the extremity of another one and revealed a most unwelcome clue to its origin — the fin of a mortar bomb! It transpired the army had used this land on Lord Ivaugh's estate for training and, not expecting mortars on a P-38, we failed to recognize them until the fin appeared. Continuing with additional care, we were pleased to find a propeller boss, parts from an engine, and Osborn's seat harness unclipped when he left the troublesome twin to her fate and added his own adventure to events on 22 April 1944.

The misadventures of the AAPS were surpassed by the Lincolnshire Aircraft Recovery Group during work on Albemarle V1610, as related by member David Stubley:

Almost from the time the group first formed, there had been rumours that an Albemarle had crashed during the war, in the vicinity of Kirton Fen, between Boston and Coningsby. However, it was not until 1986 that the site was located on land farmed by brothers Barry and Gerald Hall. Although too young to remember the crash, both brothers had found small pieces from the aircraft over the years, and following metal detector searches, which confirmed substantial remains close to the surface, gave their permission to recover the aircraft as soon as the crops were cleared. The group now set about obtaining what would prove to be the most difficult ingredient of a successful dig, permission from the Ministry of Defence.

Obviously, during the search for the site, the group had picked up various rumours concerning the identity and circumstances of the crash: "The aircraft had been shot down by RAF Coningsby ground defences." "It had crashed attempting to land at Coningsby." "It had been shot down by a Beaufighter." The recovery crew had said it was a three engined prototype and dates varied from 1940 to 1945. Most identified the aircraft as an Albemarle, however one or two insisted it was a Blenheim. The fate of the crew also varied from all killed to all baled out. The specific identification as an Albemarle was unusual as the type could be considered a rare bird in the country's wartime sky. Initial research soon proved that of 602 aircraft built, 502 were prefix 'P' or 'V' serials, and were included in the books of RAF aircraft serials published by Air Britain.

An initial check of these showed some listing as crashing in Lincolnshire, however, this still left 100 aircraft built under serials LV482 to LV623. The next step was to check the aircraft accident record cards, but again no mention of an aircraft crashing in the area concerned could be found. Consideration was given to P1605, listed as crashing on approach to Cottesmore. However, at over 30 miles distant from the site, this was ruled out as a very remote possibility. Other aircraft shown as missing or lost were also ruled out as the location of the crash was clearly known at the time. Still without the aircraft's identity, and with the harvest approaching, the group tried a speculative application to the MOD quoting the aircraft type, however, this was refused due to inadequate information, as expected. Small fragments recovered from the surface at the site provided no further clues and although sympathetic, the MOD also refused permission to recover part of the more substantial wreckage already located with metal detectors in the hope of finding some proof of identity as any land disturbance strictly falls under the protection of the Military Remains Act 1986, and to do so without permission could be considered an offence.

It was at this time that a chance conversation indicated that Albemarles had been stationed in Lincolnshire at RAF Elsham Wolds shortly after the war. Examination of records proved that 21 HGCU had indeed operated the type there between December 1945 and November 1946. A return was made to the records, but further checks yielded no new information. The harvest, delayed by poor weather, came and went, and with the farmers wishing to re-crop the land the group had to pass over the chance of a dig in 1987.

One other item of interest was noted when Simon Parry's excellent "Intruders over Britain" was published and quoted Albemarle V1610 as being shot down on 22 April 1944. With rumours that our aircraft had been shot down, this invited careful consideration. However, the location given was near Gt Yarmouth, over 100 miles away, and this was discounted.

Having exhausted all leads on Albemarles crashed, the group's thoughts turned to other types of aircraft, and soon Blenheim L6744, listed as abandoned three miles southwest of Tattershall, was under consideration. Although not exact, this location had possibilities. With some of the identifications being as a Blenheim, and information indicating that the aircraft was coming from the Tattershall direction when it crashed, this was thought to be a very likely candidate, and an application was made to the MOD stating the aircraft to be recovered was "believed to be" the Blenheim. Permission was duly received.

August 1988 came with a spell of fine weather, and it was just prior to the third weekend that a call from the farmers confirmed the crops were cleared, and the group would have three or four weeks to do the job. Having arranged for a digger for the following week, the group decided to carry out a preliminary hand dig to remove the wreckage previously located by a metal detector near the surface, in order to avoid delay when the digger arrived. The first find was a propeller blade descending into the ground at an angle of 45°. It was disappointing to find that this ended in a corroded stub instead of the hoped for engine. Attention then moved to an area where Jim Brown was working, round a tangle of pipes, cables and wreckage, at a depth of two feet. Gradually as this was cleared an ominous cylinder was revealed lying across wreckage at Jim's feet. At first it was thought that this might be the top of an undercarriage leg. However, treating anything of a cylindrical nature with suspicion, it was carefully moved to the surface. The item proved to be some 30" long and 8" in diameter, appearing to be of rough casting and suffering heavy corrosion at both ends, which appeared to be flat. There also appeared to be no visible pipes or attachments. It was now clear that the item was not readily identifiable, and whilst fairly satisfied that it was not a bomb in the full sense of the term, the group were mindful of photoflashes etc, which could be equally lethal, and the decision was made to call for the EOD to examine the item. Following the obligatory police inspection, it was confirmed that the EOD would attend within 24 hours, and the site was cleared. Being only 40 miles from the RAF EOD unit at Wittering, the group were surprised when a REME unit under Captain Moody arrived from Chatham. Also being unable to identify it, he decided that a controlled explosion to open the object was in order. Being in a bone dry former cornfield, the attendance of the Fire Brigade was requested, and amidst many flashing blue lights the item was opened for further inspection at 11.00 in the evening. The following examination found

Dave Stubley watches as a propeller boss from Albemarle V1610 is hoisted to the surface. (D Stubley)

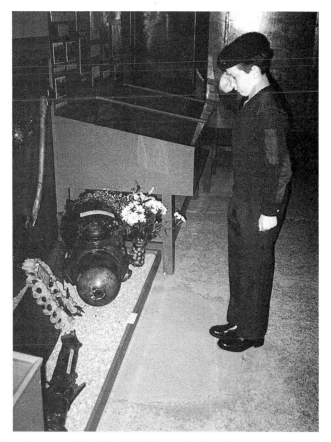

Standing proudly in front of relics from the lost Albemarle, James Rusby salutes the grandfather he never knew. (K Rusby)

that the cylinder contained an unidentified fluid, and the site was declared safe.

The following weekend brought less pleasant weather, and the attendance of the JCB. Following the excitement of the previous week, the full excavation of the site proved to be an anticlimax, the hoped for engines not being found. Items recovered showed extensive signs of fire damage, and included several shattered engine cylinders and parts, but no positive proof of identity. The only major item recovered in good condition was a propeller boss at a depth of seven feet. Although nothing was found in the wreckage to indicate the aircraft's identity, during the excavation the site was visited by local resident Bernard Mastin, who again repeated that the aircraft was an Albemarle, recalled that a member of the crew was called Tom Whittome, and that the aircraft was from Derby airfield. This tied in with a name listed in "Intruders over Britain" as the crew of V1610 from 42 OTU operating from Ashborne near Derby.

This now left the group with the problem of having recovered the wrong aircraft, and contact was made with the MOD to explain the situation. Much understanding was shown and the problem was soon cleared by the submission of a revised application to recover, and the eventual granting of a licence.

Although the material results of the site were somewhat disappointing, the group learned many lessons from its recovery, not least that however much research and paperwork is done, nothing can substitute for the vital item of local knowledge at the right time.

Following their recovery of parts, I was pleased to assist in tracing the son of Ken Rusby, named after his father, who had separately researched his RAF career. Linking LARG efforts with mine, those of Simon Parry and Ken inspired the dedication in 1992 of a memorial in the Lincolnshire Aviation Heritage Centre at East Kirkby. This was attended by family, LARG members and other guests. A plaque was unveiled by Ken and his mother, while a touching tribute was paid by the late airman's grandson, 13 year old James Rusby, in laying a wreath with his sister, Janet. Proud of his Air Training Corps uniform, James had inherited a love of aviation and, in a moving gesture, saluted the grandfather he never knew but whose readiness to defend James's inheritance of freedom typified the spirit of a special generation prepared to stand against tyranny.

That mistakes were made during Mission 311 and its aftermath is now clear, but no-one can deny the dedication and courage of those involved.

CHAPTER TWELVE

Loose Ends

WHILE SOME INCIDENTS during Mission 311 unravelled readily during my research, others doggedly defied exposure. No work describing events so complex and confusing can claim it has everything right. Official records are flawed, memories fallible.

During preparation of this book, it emerged that one of the aircraft lost over Europe fell on a house in the Belgian village of Edegem. The Vercannem family — father, mother and four children aged nine, six, two, and just seven months old — all perished, along with Irene Von Brems-Van Steen and her one year old granddaughter.

Eight people perished when a Liberator crashed on this house in Edegem in Belgium. Where the aircraft came from is still a mystery. (A F Rely)

Apparently the empty bomber made "an almost perfect landing until it hit a pole, slid into three houses and exploded". Initial leads indicated one of the two 303BG B-17s lost, but investigations by the noted Belgian researcher Achille Francois Rely indicated a B-24. He wrote, "According to several eyewitnesses, the damaged aircraft tried to land at the aerodrome of Deurne/Antwerp but the flak kept firing at it. Most people say it was a B-17 but, for many of them, every American four-engined bomber looked like a Flying Fortress. One witness, with seemingly more knowledge of American aircraft of World War II, is convinced it was a B-24 because he remembers the two vertical rudders. Some of the crew members parachuted into the nearby village of Boechout and one was injured falling through the roof of a woodmill. According to the now retired burgomaster ". . . they were made POW by Germans of a nearby garrison". Unfortunately, the aircraft has so far eluded efforts to identify it, but the episode deserves mention out of respect for those who died owing to a misfortune of war.

Of the civilian casualties allegedly occurring when the intruders' bombs fell on Rackheath, the prominent East Anglian aviation historian, Robert J Collis, could find no official verification of the incident. Nor has anyone been able to identify the two airmen who perished in the radar shack at Hethel. Some unit diarists went into great detail, others recorded only the briefest of accounts or entirely omitted events of historical significance. With German archives, research was handicapped because records of KG51's intruder activities are scant and their horrendous casualties later on meant I could trace no surviving participants in the attack. Both sides were enmeshed in a bitter combat for air supremacy.

Brigadier General James H Isbell had a point when he responded to one query, "The fact that you found no explanation in the archives is indicative of the faint importance we attached to historians and history. Hell! We had a war to win!" However, he later conceded, "I wish we had done a better job of recording the facts".

Appendix

FOR RESEARCHERS AND historians the following appendix provides additional information about aircraft lost during Mission 311.

KEY:
- POW = Prisoner of War
- KIA = Killed in Action
- RTD = Returned to Duty
- S = Survived
- MIA = Missing in Action
- E = Evadee
- ⋆ = With Resistance
- (W) = Wounded
- (I) = Injured
- (D) = Ditched
- (C) = Crashed on take-off
- (B) = Baled out over England

THIRD AIR DIVISION

390BG 570BS B-17G 42-38130

Pilot	Reich Harold E	1st Lt	KIA
Co-Pilot	Bergemann Lester W	2nd Lt	POW
Navigator	Frey John W	2nd Lt	POW
Bombardier	O'Connell Francis G	Staff Sgt	POW
Radio Op	Marsini Carl E	Tech Sgt	POW
Top Turret	Huron Horace	Tech Sgt	POW
Ball Turret	Filippone Peter M	Staff Sgt	POW
Tail Gunner	Zediak John M	Staff Sgt	KIA
Right Waist	Rocchio George F	Staff Sgt	POW
Left Waist	Link Frank Jr	Staff Sgt	POW

100BG 349BS B-17G 42-37783 Dobie

Pilot	Harte Frank W	1st Lt	KIA
Co-Pilot	Coppinger John J	2nd Lt	POW
Navigator	Conley Carl F	2nd Lt	KIA
Bombardier	Meyer Wallace J	Tech Sgt	POW
Radio Op	Rodkey Weston H	Tech Sgt	POW
Engineer	Carlson Paul V	Tech Sgt	POW
Ball Turret	McIntosh Felix W	Staff Sgt	POW
Right Waist	McDonald Thomas C	Staff Sgt	KIA
Left Waist	Celey Edward T	Staff Sgt	POW
Tail Gunner	McMullin George W	Staff Sgt	POW

385BG 551BS B-17G 42-38200

Pilot	Cornwell Cleatis	1st Lt	POW
Co-Pilot	Cook Harlan L	2nd Lt	POW
Navigator	Hitzel Ray F	2nd Lt	POW
Togglier	Dimig Delbert R	Staff Sgt	POW
Top Turret	Kennedy John A	Tech Sgt	POW
Radio Op	Urban Wheeler V	Tech Sgt	POW
Ball Turret	Diemer Francis S	Sgt	POW
Left Waist	Janzen Irving M	Staff Sgt	POW
Right Waist	Bartell George J	Staff Sgt	POW
Tail Gunner	Peel Robert G	Staff Sgt	POW

385BG 548BS B-17G 42-39773 War Cry

Pilot	McDevitt John C	2nd Lt	POW
Co-Pilot	Claflin Howard B	2nd Lt	POW
Navigator	Nickless Charles A	2nd Lt	POW
Bombardier	Wickter Lawrence D	2nd Lt	POW
Top Turret	Lane Edward F	Staff Sgt	POW
Radio Op	Foss Lawrence A Jr	Sgt	POW
Ball Turret	Walker Marvin K	Sgt	POW
Tail Gunner	Moss George S	Sgt	POW
Right Waist	Gregory Philip T	Sgt	POW
Left Waist	Montagna Dominic	Sgt	POW

447BG 708BS B-17G 42-31724

Pilot	Gilleran Thomas W	1st Lt	POW
Co-Pilot	Mamlock Henry E	2nd Lt	POW
Navigator	Lazarus Richard L	2nd Lt	POW
Bombardier	Wigdorwitz Louis T	2nd Lt	POW
Radio Op	Tuck Harliy H	Tech Sgt	POW
Top Turret	McHugh Charles H	Tech Sgt	POW
Ball Turret	Harris M D	Staff Sgt	POW
Tail Gunner	Worley Donald A	Staff Sgt	POW
Left Waist	Hawley Fred T	Staff Sgt	POW
Right Waist	Kealer Eugene A	Staff Sgt	POW

FIRST AIR DIVISION

303BG 385BS B-17G 42-39785 VK-H Thru Hel'en Hiwater

Pilot	Larson Roy A	2nd Lt	KIA
Co-Pilot	Duncan Ronald H	2nd Lt	POW
Navigator	Levy Herbert F	2nd Lt	POW
Bombardier	Feinman Milton	2nd Lt	KIA
Top Turret	Campbell Thomas J	Staff Sgt	KIA
Radio Op	Culp Everett E	Staff Sgt	POW

Ball Turret	Brim Lee R	Sgt	POW
Right Waist	Thayer Duane P	Sgt	POW
Left Waist	Schinker Arthur W	Sgt	POW
Tail Gunner	Hodge Herman L	Sgt	POW

303BG 359BS B-17G 42-39807
BN-K Nero

Pilot	Seddon John R	2nd Lt	POW
Co-Pilot	Burks Charles D	2nd Lt	POW
Navigator	Fitzpatrick George M	2nd Lt	POW
Bombardier	Meldrich Walter A	2nd Lt	POW
Top Turret	Rogers Edward F	Staff Sgt	POW
Radio Op	Hess John C	Staff Sgt	POW
Ball Turret	Maloney Donald F	Sgt	POW
Right Waist	Holcomb I E	Sgt	POW
Left Waist	Newchick John	Sgt	POW
Tail Gunner	Mummery William T	Sgt	POW

91BG 324BS B-17G 42-40000
Just Nothing

Pilot	Hesse Harvey G	Capt	KIA
Co-Pilot	Lee Charles D	Major	POW
Navigator	Suldan Jay H	1st Lt	POW
Navigator	Ryan John W	1st Lt	POW
Bombardier	Marshall Provost	Capt	POW
Top Turret	Williams Charles E	Tech Sgt	KIA
Radio Op	Snavely Fred A	Tech Sgt	POW
Ball Turret	Bunn Harlan D Jr	Staff Sgt	POW
Tail Gunner	Krahling Francis C	2nd Lt	POW
Right Waist	Sterle Leonard J	Staff Sgt	POW
Left Waist	Guy John E	Staff Sgt	POW

SECOND AIR DIVISION

445BG 703BS B-24H 42-50325

Pilot	Sadlon Edward W	1st Lt	POW
Co-Pilot	Karopczyc Joseph	2nd Lt	POW
Navigator	Kulp Marlin F	2nd Lt	KIA
Bombardier	Carle Erwin J	1st Lt	POW
Top Turret	Connolly Robert C	Tech Sgt	POW
Radio Op	Yost Charles J	Tech Sgt	POW
Waist Gunner	Johnson Earl B	Staff Sgt	POW
Ball Turret	Dory Peter A	Staff Sgt	POW
Waist Gunner	Florio Thomas	Staff Sgt	POW
Tail Gunner	Clemente James V	Staff Sgt	POW

445BG 700BS B-24H 41-29306

Pilot	Sneed Francis C	1st Lt	POW
Co-Pilot	Riddle Charles L	2nd Lt	POW
Navigator	Hargis Ray O	2nd Lt	POW
Bombardier	Bryant John W	2nd Lt	POW
Radio Op	Varty Robert	Staff Sgt	KIA
Top Turret	Kilinski Harry A	Sgt	POW
Ball Turret	White Harold E	Sgt	POW
Waist Gunner	Mahoney John F	Staff Sgt	KIA*
Waist Gunner	Coffman Charles B	Sgt	POW
Tail Gunner	Cockriel James R	Sgt	E

453BG 735BS B-24H 42-64490 H6-U
Cee Gee II

Pilot	Munsey James S	1st Lt	KIA
Co-Pilot	Crall Robert O	2nd Lt	KIA
Navigator	Helfand Leon	2nd Lt	S

Bombardier	Orlowski Arthur	2nd Lt	S
Radio Op	Grady William C	Tech Sgt	KIA
Tail Gunner	McClure Ralph W	Staff Sgt	S
Ball Turret	Brown Norman W	Sgt	S
Top Turret	Conway Grover G	Tech Sgt	KIA
Right Waist	Laux Kenneth G	Staff Sgt	S
Left Waist	McKinney John F	Tech Sgt	KIA

389BG 567BS B-24D 42-63963 X

Pilot	Stotter Willard P	Capt	RTD
Comm Pilot	Burton Paul T	Lt Col	RTD
Co-Pilot	Baber George J Jr	1st Lt	RTD
Navigator	Powell John E	1st Lt	POW
Bombardier	Gins Myron	1st Lt	RTD
Radio Op	Arndt Albert A	Tech Sgt	POW
Top Turret	Bagwell Lewis E	Tech Sgt	POW
Observer	Saniuk Michael S	Staff Sgt	POW
Right Waist	Parker Lee T	Tech Sgt	POW
Left Waist	Burr Dudley A	Staff Sgt	POW
Tail Gunner	Belcher Harvey T	Staff Sgt	POW

389BG 565BS B-24J 42-109915 -Z

Pilot	Wilkerson F T	1st Lt	S
Co-Pilot	Senell C S Jr	1st Lt	KIA
Navigator	Campbell L A	1st Lt	S(W)
Bombardier	Sullivan R F	1st Lt	S(W)
Radio Op	Terlesky F	Tech Sgt	KIA
Top Turret	Dotter R L	Staff Sgt	KIA
Ball Turret	Gray G C	Tech Sgt	KIA
Right Waist	Cabtle M B	Staff Sgt	S
Left Waist	Reed N S	Staff Sgt	KIA
Tail Gunner	Bunting H S	Staff Sgt	S(W)
Nose Turret	Murray J R	Staff Sgt	KIA

389BG 565BS B-24J 44-40085 Z-

Pilot	Foley Edward W	2nd Lt	S
Co-Pilot	Muir L F	2nd Lt	S
Navigator	Kinnard R	1st Lt	S
Bombardier	Adee J	1st Lt	S
Radio Op	Smith J E	Sgt	S
Top Turret	Garrigus E V	Staff Sgt	S
Ball Turret	Hamilton R L	Staff Sgt	S
Right Waist	Behee C E	Staff Sgt	S
Left Waist	Brown G E	Staff Sgt	S
Tail Gunner	Jacobs G W	Staff Sgt	S

392BG 579BS B-24H 42-52605 J

Pilot	Everhart Wyeth C	Capt	POW
Co-Pilot	Hammond Gordon L	1st Lt	POW
Navigator	Kornman Harold C	1st Lt	POW
Bombardier	Sands John E	2nd Lt	POW
Radio Op	Beard James W	Tech Sgt	POW
Right Waist	Andrews William E	Tech Sgt	POW
Top Turret	Rinks Alfred P	Tech Sgt	POW
Ball Turret	Ross Jack R	Tech Sgt	POW
Left Waist	Fowler Robert G	Staff Sgt	POW
Tail Gunner	Beseda John F	Staff Sgt	POW
Observer	Cox Robert L	Major	POW
Nose Gunner	Weber Fred J	2nd Lt	POW

448BG 715BS B-24H 41-28843
Repulser

Pilot	Pulcipher Eugene V	2nd Lt	KIA

Co-Pilot	Meier Elmer P	2nd Lt	KIA
Bombardier	Carcelli William	2nd Lt	KIA
Left Waist	Durant William H	Sgt	KIA
Nose Turret	Davis William S	Sgt	KIA
Top Turret	Hardin James R	Staff Sgt	KIA
Gunner	Young Maynard H	Sgt	KIA
Radio Op	Romanosky Chester J	Staff Sgt	KIA
Navigator	Fahr George S	2nd Lt	KIA
Tail Turret	Spellman Carl E	Sgt	KIA

448BG 715BS B-24H 42-52608

Pilot	Pitts Cherry C	1st Lt	KIA
Co-Pilot	Merkling John L	2nd Lt	KIA
Navigator	Wilder Charles W Jr	2nd Lt	KIA
Bombardier	Schrom Clifford R	2nd Lt	KIA
Radio Op	Angelo Arthur	Tech Sgt	KIA
Top Turret	Harwood Thomas H	Staff Sgt	KIA
Right Waist	Robinson Ernest W Jr	Tech Sgt	KIA
Ball Turret	Vetter Harry F	Staff Sgt	KIA
Left Waist	Werner Samuel	Tech Sgt	KIA
Tail Gunner	Wilson Stanley L	Staff Sgt	KIA

448BG 715BS B-24H 42-94744
Peggy Jo

Pilot	Alspaugh Melvin L	1st Lt	S
Co-Pilot	Watters Richard H	1st Lt	S
Navigator	Carlson William A	1st Lt	S
Bombardier	Edwards William E	2nd Lt	S
Radio Op	Holter Donald L	Tech Sgt	S
Tail Gunner	Chartier Raymond G	Staff Sgt	S
Top Turret	Adams Charles J	Staff Sgt	S(I)
Gunner	Barney Harold V	Staff Sgt	S
Gunner	Anderson Jack E	Tech Sgt	S
Gunner	Worsman Owen W	Staff Sgt	S

448BG 715BS B-24J 42-73497
Vadie Raye

Pilot	Skaggs Alvin D	Capt	S
Co-Pilot	Blum William G	Capt	S
Navigator	Todt Donald C	1st Lt	S
Bombardier	Lozes Elbert F	1st Lt	S
Nose Turret	Gaskins Eugene	Staff Sgt	S
Radio Op	Filipowicz Stanley C	Tech Sgt	S
Top Turret	Glevanik George	Tech Sgt	S
Waist Gunner	Lee Ray K	Staff Sgt	S
Waist Gunner	Sheehan Francis X	Staff Sgt	S(W)
Tail Gunner	Jackson William E	Staff Sgt	S(I)

458BG 753BS B-24H 41-29273
Flak Magnet

Pilot	Spaven George N Jr	1st Lt	KIA
Co-Pilot	Zedeker Robert L	2nd Lt	RTD
Navigator	Kowal Peter	2nd Lt	POW
Bombardier	Mortinson James F	2nd Lt	POW
Radio Op	Cole Cedric C	Staff Sgt	POW
Top Turret	Wedding James H	Tech Sgt	POW
Ball Turret	Scheiding Lawrence J	Staff Sgt	POW
Right Waist	Allin Robert Louis	Sgt	POW
Tail Gunner	Peacher Herman A	Staff Sgt	POW
Left Waist	Fittinger James L	Staff Sgt	POW

458BG 754BS B-24H 42-52353 J

Pilot	Harris Teague G Jr	1st Lt	S(I)

Co-Pilot	Couch Robert T	2nd Lt	KIA
Navigator	Moses Richard L	2nd Lt	KIA
Bombardier	Ahrens Robert E	2nd Lt	S
Radio Op	McKenna Francis X	Tech Sgt	KIA
Top Turret	Oder Clifford L	Sgt	KIA
Right Waist	Found Howard E	Staff Sgt	KIA
Left Waist	Carpenter Eldridge L	Staff Sgt	S(I)
Ball Turret	Carpenter Edwin B	Sgt	S(I)
Tail Gunner	Morin Fernard G	Staff Sgt	KIA

458BG 754BS B-24J 42-100357 D

Pilot	Stilson Charles W	2nd Lt	S(I)
Co-Pilot	Worton Joseph E	2nd Lt	S(I)
Navigator	Sawyer Raymond E	2nd Lt	S(I)
Bombardier	Marshall Melvin C	2nd Lt	KIA
Top Turret	Blake James E	Tech Sgt	S
Radio Op	Pearce William R	Tech Sgt	KIA
Right Waist	Silverman Arthur	Staff Sgt	KIA
Left Waist	Connelly Clarence C	Staff Sgt	S
Ball Turret	Johnson William L	Staff Sgt	S(I)
Tail Turret	Katten K	Staff Sgt	S(I)

467BG 788BS B-24H 42-52536 K

Pilot	Roden James A	2nd Lt	KIA
Co-Pilot	Maxey J H	2nd Lt	KIA
Navigator	Landis Wellington E	2nd Lt	KIA
Bombardier	Wilson Robert E	2nd Lt	KIA
Top Turret	Violette Louis J	Staff Sgt	KIA
Tail Gunner	Horak Richard E	Staff Sgt	KIA
Ball Turret	McGonigle Charles D	Staff Sgt	KIA
Radio Op	Carter George E	Staff Sgt	KIA
Waist Gunner	Howe James R	Staff Sgt	KIA
Waist Gunner	Orr Riley E	Staff Sgt	KIA

467BG 791BS B-24H 42-52445 D

Pilot	Reid Stalie C	1st Lt	KIA
Co-Pilot	Mason Warren W	2nd Lt	KIA
Navigator	Ferguson James G	2nd Lt	KIA
Bombardier	Alier Louis A	2nd Lt	KIA
Radio Op	Kovalenko Walter W	Staff Sgt	KIA
Top Turret	Dery Sylvio L	Staff Sgt	KIA
Gunner	Shank Mervin M	Sgt	S(W)
Gunner	Hoke Edward W	Sgt	KIA
Gunner	Biggs John H	Sgt	S(W)
Gunner	Hamilton George S	Sgt	S(W)

USAAF fighters

4FG 336FS P-51B 43-6802

Pilot	Nelson Robert F	1st Lt	POW

55FG 343FS P-38J 42-67966 CY-Q
Little Man

Pilot	Penners Clair A	1st Lt	POW

55FG Headquarters P38J 42-68048 CY-J

Pilot	Guthrie Bernie V	Capt	MIA

352FG 328FS P-51B 42-106624

Pilot	Long Marion V	1st Lt	POW

353FG 351FS P-47D 42-75114 YJ-M Boston Bulldog

| Pilot | Trudeau Paul J | 1st Lt | S(D) |

353FG 352FS P-47D 42-28390

| Pilot | Guertz Robert P | 1st Lt | S(C) |

359FG 370FS P-47D 42-75263

| Pilot | Thomas Earl W Jr | 2nd Lt | MIA |

361FG 374FS P-47D 42-75521

| Pilot | Norman James M Jr | 1st Lt | KIA |

362FG (406FG) 514FS P-47D 42-75596

| Pilot | Arth Gene L | Major | KIA |

363FG 380FS P-51B 43-6330 A9-G Beachcomber

| Pilot | Maxwell Paul R | 2nd Lt | POW |

363FG 380FS P-51

| Pilot | Sharrock John A Jr | 1st Lt | E |

363FG 381FS P-51B 43-6769

| Pilot | Miller Ward F | 1st Lt | POW |

363FG 381FS P-51B 43-6426 Pegasus

| Pilot | Doerr George R | Capt | POW |

364FG 383FS P-38J 42-104176

| Pilot | Osborn Roy W | Colonel | S(B) |

368FG 395FS P-47D 42-76575

| Pilot | Goodwin James W | Capt | MIA |

RAF

19 Squadron RAF Mustang FX990

| Pilot | Chisholm W A | P/O | MIA |

42 OTU Albemarle V1610

Pilot	Hutchinson John E	Sgt	KIA
Navigator	Rusby Kenneth	Sgt	KIA
Air Bomber	Whittome Anthony A	Sgt	KIA
Radio Op	Davis John	Sgt	S
Gunner	Thurgood Ronald	Sgt	S

LUFTWAFFE

1./JG1 FW190A-8 107101 White 3

| Pilot | Giers Arnold | Uffz | KIA |

2./JG1 FW190A-7 550893 Black 16

| Pilot | Neuner Herbert | Obfhr | S(W) |

3./JG1 FW190A-8 170097 Yellow 2

| Pilot | Eh Herbert-Konrad | Lt | S(W) |

4./JG1 FW190A-8 580142 White 8

| Pilot | Born Heinrich | Gefr | KIA |

4./JG1 FW190A-7 430483 White 5

| Pilot | Froschauer Johann | Uffz | S(W) |

3./JG1 Me-109G-5 110051 White 1

| Pilot | Schmude Hortari | Hptm | KIA |

7./JG1 Me-109G-6 440300 White 8

| Pilot | Ibing Kurt | Lt | S(W) |

7./JG1 Me-109G-5 110071 White 9

| Pilot | Reimitz Gerhard | Fw | S(W) |

7./JG1 Me-109G-5 110081 White 10

| Pilot | Peischl Johann | Ogfr | KIA |

8./JG1 Me-109G-6 163066 Yellow 11

| Pilot | Kluckmann Willi | Gfr | KIA |

8./JG1 Me-109G-6 441028 Yellow 9

| Pilot | Göhre Joachim | Lt | KIA |

9./JG1 Me-109G-6 163085 Yellow 19

| Pilot | Heck Franz-Wilhelm | Ofw | KIA |

9./JG1 Me-109G-6 163071 Yellow 22

| Pilot | Fricke Konrad | Obgefr | KIA |

9./JG1 Me-109G-6 441011 Yellow 17

| Pilot | Ziegenfuss Kurt | Uffz | KIA |

8./JG2 Me-109G-6 15916 Blue 4

| Pilot | Rätzer Helmut | Uffz | KIA |

7./JG2 Me-109G-6 162035 Yellow 11

| Pilot | Will Erwin | Uffz | KIA |

4./JG26 FW190A-6 530755 Blue 16

| Pilot | Neu Wolfgang | Oblt | KIA |

4./JG27 Me-109G-6 162696 Black 9

| Pilot | Mentnich Karl Josef | Ofw | S(W) |

1./JG3 Me-109-6 411682 White 8

| Pilot | Presbar Peter-Paul | Lt | KIA |

1./JG3 Me-109-5 110365 White 5

| Pilot | Schnitzler Karl | Uffz | S(W) |

3./JG3 Me109

| Pilot | Doering Heribert | | S |

5./JG1 FW190A-8 170106 Black 8

| Pilot | Weber Heinz | Uffz | S |

5./JG1 FW190A-8 170102 Black 10

| Pilot | Blech George | Flgr | S |

6./KG51 Me410A-1 420458 9K + HP

| Pilot | Krüger Klaus | Oblt | KIA |
| Radio/Gunner | Reichardt Michael | Fw | KIA |

5./KG51 Me410A-1 420314 9K + MN

| Pilot | Puttfarken Dietrich | Hptm | MIA |
| Radio/Gunner | Lux Willi | Ofw | MIA |

Index